D1405717

Perennials

for the

Backyard Gardener

Perennials

for the

Backyard Gardener

Patricia L. Turcotte

The Countryman Press
Woodstock, Vermont

Copyright © 1993 by Patricia L. Turcotte

First Edition, 1993

All rights reserved. No part of this book may be reproduced in any form or by any electronic or mechanical means including information storage and retrieval systems without permission in writing from the publisher, except by a reviewer who may quote brief passages.

Library of Congress Cataloging-in-Publication Data
Turcotte, Patricia.
Perennials for the backyard gardener/Patricia L. Turcotte.
p.   cm.
Includes bibliographical references (p.   ) and index.
ISBN 0-88150-281-2
1. Perennials.   2. Perennials—United States.   I. Title.
SB434.T87   1993
635.9'32'0973—dc20   93-26464
CIP

Cover and text design by Georganna Towne
Interior art by Karen Savary © The Countryman Press, Inc.
Photographs by Ronald W. Turcotte except as noted

Printed in the United States of America
Color sections printed in the Republic of Korea

Published by The Countryman Press, Inc.
P.O. Box 175, Woodstock, Vermont 05091

10 9 8 7 6 5 4 3 2 1

Dedication

A special thanks to my husband not only for his photographs,
but for just being there when I needed him for the past thirty-six years.
And love to Scott and Patty, Kelo and Debbie, and my wonderful grandchildren—
Kelo, Hunter, Jessica, Zoe, Nichole, Anna, and baby Jordon.

Contents

Dianthus caryophyllus Clove pink • *Doronicum cordatum* Leopard's-bane • *Gnaphalium (Helichrysum)* Fairy gold • *Hernaria glabra* Rupturewort • *Heuchera sanguinea* Coral bells • *Hosta (Funkia)* • *Iberis sempervirens* Candytuft • *Jasione laevis (perennis)* Sheeps bit • *Lamium* Deadnettles • *Leontopodium alpinum* Edelweiss • *Mentha pulegium* English pennyroyal • *Nepeta mussinii* Catnip mussinii • *Omphalodes verna* Navelwort, blue-eyed Mary • *Phlox subulata* Creeping phlox • *Primula vulgaris* Primrose • *Prunella grandiflora* Allheal • *Saponaria ocymoides* Soapwort • *Saxifraga* Saxifraga • *Sedum* Sedums • *Sempervivum* Hens and chickens • *Stachys byzantina (lanata)* Lamb's ear • *Thymus* Thyme • *Viola odorata* Violets

Achillea millefolium roseum Red yarrow • *Alchemilla vulgaris* Lady's mantle • *Anaphalis margaritacea* Pearly everlasting • *Aquilegia* Columbine • *Artemisia absinthium* Wormwood • *Astilbe* Spirea • *Campanula* Bellflower • *Catananche caerulea* Cupid's dart • *Centaurea dealbata* Pink cornflower • *Chrysanthemum coccineum* Painted daisy • *Chrysanthemum parthenium* Feverfew • *Chrysanthemum X maximum* Shasta daisy • *Coreopsis* Tickseed • *Dicentra* Bleeding hearts • *Dictamnus* Gasplant • *Erigeron* Fleabane • *Euphorbia epithymoides (E. polychroma)* Spurge • *Fern* Fern • *Geranium* Cranesbill geranium • *Gypsophila paniculata* Baby's breath • *Helenium autumnale* Helen's flower • *Hosta (Funkia)* • *Hyssopus officinalis* Hyssop • *Iris* Iris • *Lavendula* Lavender • *Liatris spicata* Gayfeather • *Linum perenne* Blue flax • *Lobelia siphilitica* Great blue lobelia • *Lupinus* Lupine • *Lychnis chalcedonica* Maltese cross • *Malva moschata* Muskmallow • *Mentha* Mints • *Mertensia virginica* Virginia blue bells • *Monarda didyma* Beebalm • *Oenothera fruticosa* Sundrops • *Ononis spinosa* Restharrow • *Platycodon grandiflorus* Balloon flower • *Polemonium caeruleum* Jacob's ladder • *Pulmonaria officinalis* Lungwort • *Ruta graveolens* Rue • *Santolina* Santolinas • *Scabiosifolia nagoya* Patrinia • *Sedum spectabile* Stonecrop • *Thermopsis* False lupine • *Tradescantia virginiana* Spiderwort • *Trollius* Globe flower • *Veronica* Speedwell

Achillea filipendulina Cloth-of-gold yarrow • *Achillea ptarmica* White pearl yarrow • *Aconitum napellus* Monkshood • *Agastache foeniculum* Anise-hyssop • *Anthemis tinctoria* Golden marguerite • *Artemisia abrotanum* Southernwood • *Artemisia ludoviciana* Silver king • *Aruncus dioicus* Goatsbeard • *Aster novae-angliae* Michaelmas daisy • *Baptisia* Baptisia • *Centaurea macrocephala* Yellow cornflower • *Cimicifuga racemosa* Snakeroot • *Clematis* Clematis • *Delphinium* Delphinium • *Echinacea purpurea* Purple coneflower • *Echinops* Globe thistle • *Eupatorium purpureum* Joe-Pye weed • *Ferns* (see Middle-Range Perennials) • *Hemerocallis* Lilies • *Lysimachia clethroides* Gooseneck loosestrife • *Lysimachia punctata* Yellow loosestrife • *Paeonia* Peonies • *Papaver* Poppy • *Phlox paniculata* Border phlox • *Physostegia virginiana* Obedient plant • *Polygonatum* Solomon's seal • *Rosa* Roses • *Rudbeckia* Black-eyed Susan, golden glow • *Tanacetum vulgare* Tansy • *Valeriana officinalis* Valerian • *Yucca filamentosa* Yucca

Acknowledgments

Although a writer gets all the credit for a book, there are so many wonderful people involved in making it a reality. I know I can't thank you all, but I do want to give a special thanks to some of you I enjoyed working with: my publishers Gordon Pine and Carl Taylor; Robin Dutcher-Bayer, with whom it has been a pleasure to work; Cornelia Wright; Michael Gray; Georganna Towne; and Scott Turcotte. For photographs: thanks to Ronald W. Turcotte (all photographs unless otherwise credited); Gordon C. Pine; Michael H. Dodge of White Flower Farm, Litchfield, Connecticut; and David Talbot of Talbots' Herb and Perennial Farm in Hartland, Vermont. Special thanks to Lynne Hall and David Brandau for providing photographs of their extensive gardens. They have been growing their own organic, hardy perennials for over 10 years at the Standing Stone Perennial Farm on Back River Road in Royalton, Vermont.

Part One

Designing and Planning
the Garden

Introduction

The first spring we lived on this farm, we discovered many interesting perennial plants that had been left by the former owners. Because the farmstead had been vacant for over a year, weeds were the biggest crop to meet the eye. But as we slowly mowed, weeded, and cleaned the area we discovered some wonderful treasures: fragrant lemon daylilies, narcissi, cranesbill geraniums, tall golden glows, huge peonies, and many beautiful old-fashioned species of roses. With the perennials I had brought from my previous home I had a good start on a perennial garden.

Now, gardening is a year-round activity for me at Wormwood Farm. As the melting snow provides moisture for the sleeping spring bulbs, I am potting up tiny seeds with anticipation of great flowers. Spring and summer months are filled with weeding, mowing, cleaning, and enjoying the beauty of the harvest. As fall slowly turns the leaves on the maples red and yellow, hoes and rakes are put away and evergreen boughs are cut to cover certain plants. We become almost thankful for the coming winter rest period.

Just before Christmas, the seed catalogs start coming and I'm tempted away from holiday decorations and shopping to study new species and relish the colorful photographs. After the holidays I study more magazines, catalogs, and books on gardening as I plan and replan my garden land spaces.

This book is the result of a lifetime spent gardening and studying. There are many reasons to garden: to make the land space attractive, to have plant material for arrangements and craft work, as a form of exercise or meditation, and just for the pure enjoyment of working with natural materials. I hope as you read this book that you, too, will find the enjoyment gardening has brought to me throughout my lifetime.

The information in *Perennials for the Backyard Gardener* is based on my experiences in zone 4 where we have cold snow-covered winters, wet springs, and frequent drought conditions in July and August. But most of this information should apply to those who garden in zones 3–7.

I have tried to answer the questions people asked me during the twelve years I sold perennials and herbs. Now, I garden only for my own pleasure and lecture on herbs and perennials. My gardens are smaller, and changes have been made so I can slow down and smell the roses instead of spending all my time weeding them.

This book is divided into two parts for easier reading and studying. The first part provides information on how to grow perennial plants and how to design and plan your own garden. It also gives good, old-fashioned practical garden advice on soil, light, and moisture requirements. The best advice anyone can give on gardening is: "Know your own land space and know the plant you are going to put there: its soil, light, and moisture needs, and any special requirements and habits it has."

The second part of this book consists of perennial profiles, so that you can quickly find the information you need on any perennial. I have listed them according to height groups because I often have someone say, "I need a perennial that grows not taller than two feet" or "I need a very low-growing perennial." I have added a chapter on perennial bulbs and also one on those seeming misfits, the biennial plants, because I feel they are necessary to the perennial garden scheme.

The appendix lists addresses for catalogs, Extension Services, and plant societies, and also has fun information about flower families, plant lore, and state flowers.

Throughout the book, a plant's common name appears first followed by its botanical name. This repetition will help you learn the botanical names. When you see only one name, like iris, bergenia, yucca, or baptisia, you will know that the common and botanical names are the same. Keep in mind the common names listed are those that are common in my New England area. There may be a different common name for the same plant in your area. Synonyms that are known to me are listed in the profiles.

The suggested pronunciation I give is for the way I have learned it, although many plant names have several different acceptable pronunciations. Plant pronunciation is not governed by any rules, and so there is considerable disagreement even among the experts on just which pronunciation to use. Botanical names are derived from Latin, Greek, and Anglo-Saxon words, which adds to the confusion with pronunciation. The stressed syllable is in boldface type to help: for example, the bleeding heart *Dicentra* is pronounced "die-**sen**-tra."

My wish is that you will enjoy this book and the wonderful world of gardening in your own backyard. I hope you find in your garden the pleasure and peacefulness that I find in mine.

If you have any questions that are not answered in this book, you can write me at RFD #1, Box 1800, Lisbon Falls, Maine 04252. Please enclose a self-addressed, stamped large envelope.

From my garden to yours,
Patricia L. Turcotte

CHAPTER ONE

A Look at Perennials

*Let the beds be planted as permanently and as well as possible
so that there will remain little to do for years.*
William Robinson (1838–1900)

In botanical terms, a perennial is a plant or root that lives in excess of two years. Trees, shrubs, many herbs and flowers, and a few vegetables fit into this category, but for the purposes of this book we are concerned with only herbaceous perennial flowers, plus a very few evergreens and woody perennial flowers. A herbaceous perennial is a plant that dies back to the ground in the winter, growing up again in the spring from its root to repeat its seasonal performance and share its seasonal beauty with the world.

No one factor guarantees successful perennial gardening. You need a combination of the right conditions: climate, soil pH, soil texture, moisture content, light, and how you care for the plant all contribute to your success.

Get to know your perennial and you will enjoy good gardening. For example, let us say you planted sea thrift (*Armeria*) in a well-drained soil in full sun. You would enjoy several years of pretty pink-and-white globelike flowers, springing from grassy tufts. But if you planted those same plants in a poorly drained, moist soil in partial shade, they would slowly rot away in the first growing season.

Now what if you have that moist area and want to plant sea thrift anyway? You could build raised beds, providing the plants with the necessary drainage, or you could plant them in large movable containers, setting them where you want color. The better you understand your plants' needs, the more you can accommodate them and have the garden of your dreams at the same time.

Why Grow Perennials?

After the initial planting, loyal perennial plants return faithfully every spring. This makes perennials time-effective in terms of yearly planting. But don't be fooled into thinking just because you have a perennial garden that it will be maintenance-free. You may see books on the so-called maintenance-free garden, but please believe me—there is no such thing if you have more than three plants in your garden. Gardening consists of planting, weeding, fertilizing, some watering, and occasionally dividing plants.

Perennials are also cost-effective. After the initial planting you can divide and take cuttings from your own plants to start new ones. This free garden material can be used to expand your gardens or given to your friends and relatives for their own. Or (and this happens to many a hobbyist) you can start your own garden business.

Of course, one main reason for perennial gardening is to add beauty to the landscape and value to your home. Perennials planted on banks and sloped areas will also aid in controlling soil erosion. And if those reasons do not convince you to grow perennials, think of all the beautiful fresh flower arrange-

Sempervivum is an evergreen perennial that does not die back to the ground each winter.

ments you can enjoy on your dining-room table. A pretty arrangement of flowers on my table all summer makes me feel rich. For winter arrangements I collect and dry botanical materials. Perennials that dry especially well include yarrows (*Achillea*), coral bells (*Heuchera sanguinea*), silver king (*Artemisia ludoviciana*), globe thistle (*Echinops*), and baby's breath (*Gypsophilia*). See the appendix for additional perennials for your winter dried crafting.

Many popular potpourri ingredients come from perennials. Lavender (*Lavendula*), anise-hyssop (*Agastache foeniculum*), and mints (*Mentha*) are only a few of the scented plants you can dry and use. Petals from just about any flower can be dried and added to the potpourri jar for color.

In recent years several perennials have become popular as edible plants. Clove pinks (*Dianthus*), roses (*Rosa*), chive blossoms (*Allium schoenoprasum*), and beebalm (*Monarda didyma*) are just a few.

Warning: Never eat any plant that you cannot *absolutely* correctly identify. There are many poisonous plants, some of which closely resemble edible plants.

Plant Hardiness

To further characterize the perennial plants in this book, I have divided them into two categories, tender perennials and hardy perennials. For the purposes of this book, the *tender* perennials are those that are not hardy in my own state of Maine, zone 4. However, plant hardiness varies in different parts of the country. Any plant not able to grow year-round in your particular area is considered a tender perennial.

Hardiness is generally defined as being able to endure the level of cold and frost in a given region. For example, the fragrant lemon verbena (*Aloysia triphylla*) needs to be brought indoors in the winter in Maine (zone 4) but can be left outside all winter in Georgia (zone 8). A very cold zone 8 winter may kill some of the leaves, but not the root. Another criterion of plant hardiness is how much heat and dryness a plant can tolerate—a Joe-Pye weed in Arizona would be considered a tender perennial and would require an artificial watering method. Zone maps (see appendix) provide general guidelines to what can be grown in a given area, and your local extension service can give you information about specific plant hardiness.

But what if you really want to plant a perennial that is not hardy in your zone? You can do one of three things.

1. Treat the plant as an annual, replanting a new one each spring.
2. Plant the perennial in the soil in spring after all danger of frost has passed. In the fall dig it up and keep it in a pot inside during the cold months.
3. Grow the plant in a container, moving it in and out as the seasons change.

Hardy perennials are winter hardy; some species actually need a cold dormant period to survive. Evergreens and woody perennials do not die back to the ground in the winter. They go through the cold season in a dormant state with their woody stems and foliage intact. They often look droopy and unappealing during this period. When spring returns they bounce back to life once again, repeating their summer drama. Among the evergreens are hens and chickens (*Sempervivum*), candytuft (*Iberis sempervirens*), sea thrift (*Armeria*), lavender (*Lavendula*), and certain dianthus species.

Garden books and catalogs list zone hardiness, but that does not mean you cannot grow some of the species listed for higher zones than your area. I like to encourage people to experiment with growing plants not common to their region. The secret is to provide the ideal conditions that a certain plant needs. Each area has its cold and warmer spots; even within the land space each of us has to garden in there are mini-climate pockets. For example, you may be able to grow something on the warmer south side of a building that would perish on the colder north side. When cultivating a plant that is usually grown in a higher zone, be sure to protect it during the winter. I have found that certain plants just need to find the right location to grow well. If I have a plant that is not producing as it should (and my soil pH and texture are correct) then I move it to another spot—this is often all it needs.

Annuals and Biennials

We might call perennials the anchors of the garden, with annuals and biennials as their companions. Let us look at the life cycle of the other plants we use for our flower gardens.

Annuals are plants that complete their life cycle in a one-year period—from seed to flower to seed pod. Examples are petunias, ageratums, and marigolds (*Tagetes*).

Biennials take two years to complete their life cycle. Year one produces foliage, many times just a rosette-shaped clump of foliage. The second year is the growth year, producing flowers and then seeds. Several of the biennials self-seed. Sweet William (*Dianthus barbatus*) drops its seeds early enough in

PHOTO BY MICHAEL H. DODGE, WHITE FLOWER FARM

Digitalis, *a biennial, self-seeds after flowering.*

the season to start new seedlings; then it flowers the following spring, making this biennial seem like a perennial to the novice. Other biennials that self-seed are foxglove (*Digitalis*) and Siberian wallflower (*Cheiranthus cheiri*).

How Long Will My Perennial Live?

This is a question I am often asked. With the right soil and light conditions, sufficient moisture, and proper care, a perennial's life span can equal ours.

When gardening we tend to forget that a plant is also a living organism like animals and humans—with a few minor differences. A plant is stationary; it cannot get up and walk around to seek out its own food. Nevertheless, a perennial is born from its seed, grows as it takes in water and food, responds to stimulation, and produces flowers or fruit as it matures. It reproduces its own kind and when the time comes, like other organisms, it dies.

Like a human's life span, a plant's life can be shortened by disease or accidents—like the early spring my neighbor's two very large gray work horses got loose and took a stroll through my backyard gardens, leaving behind big three-inch-deep hoofprints and broken plants.

The peony often outlives the gardener who planted it.

Perennials do not bloom continuously or possess eternal life. Much to our dismay, their purpose on this earth is not to please mankind, but in fact to reproduce their own species—and perhaps serve as a source of food for various animals and insects.

Each species of plant has its own particular life span. The peony, for example, is one of the longest-lived perennials, often outliving the gardener who planted it. The peony can often be found in old deserted farmyards along with two other long-lived plants, the sunshine-yellow golden glow (*Rudbeckia*) and the succulent, edible rhubarb (*Rheum officinale*), flourishing despite years of weeds and neglect.

Other perennials may be coined short-lived perennials, just barely making it past the two-year status of the biennial plants. Shasta daisy (*Chrysanthemum maximum*) and coral bells (*Heuchera sanguinea*) are two good examples of short-lived perennials. You can increase the life span of short-lived perennials by dividing them every other year and by starting new plants annually.

In the case of coral bells, the plants are short-lived because of their tendency to heave themselves out of the soil. You can add years to this plant's life by adding additional soil in spring and fall, spreading the soil over the center of the plant and around it. When the plant becomes too mounded, then divide the whole thing, lowering it in the soil and making more plants.

Winter warmth and thaws will heave up some plants if you do not have a good snow cover. In early spring when the soil is soft (and usually mucky in our area), gently push the plant back into place. In areas where there is no good snow cover, evergreen boughs as winter protection will help prevent heaving.

Winter Dormancy

Dormancy is the period when a plant rests for a certain length of time after it has flowered and produced its seed pods. This process usually happens during the wintertime. Exceptions are leopard's-bane (*Doronicum*), poppies (*Papaver*), and many spring bulbs that lose their foliage after spring flowering. They rest through the summer until the next year.

Plants that rest during the winter are woken in the spring by certain environmental cues that release a special inhibitor in the plant. These cues can be longer days or the increased warmth and intensity of the sun when it begins to travel higher in the sky. Without this inhibitor, a plant might start growing in every winter warm spell, causing undue stress and damage from subsequent frosts.

Certain plants need a cold dormancy period to survive. Every year I like to bring a dish of hens and chickens (*Sempervivum*) inside for some winter green. Since they need a cold dormancy period, I pot them up in the fall and put them on the front steps so I don't forget them, leaving them out for several hard frosts and snows. Right after the hustle and bustle of the Christmas holidays, I bring in the sad-looking pot of hens. Within a week or two they revive to make living centerpieces on the coffee table. If this period of dormancy is not provided, the little rosettes would become elongated and the plant would eventually die of exhaustion.

Botanical Names and Plant Families

I hesitate to add too much information on botanical names for fear that you might think I am going beyond the backyard-garden level. If you want to have just a few plants in your garden and care nothing for the botanical this and that, skip to the next chapter. But if you are interested in learning how to advance your knowledge of plants or want to have a little fun with the meaning of your plants' names, stay with me for a page or two.

Before I became interested in gardening as a serious study subject, I had little interest in learning all those difficult botanical names. Little did I realize I was already speaking Latin and Greek when I talked about tulips, chrysanthemums, irises, or delphiniums! As my interest in learning all I could about plants grew, I found it necessary to learn their correct names. It was sort of like knowing my friends only by their first names. How could I look up their phone numbers and addresses if I didn't know their full names?

Many good books are available on plant nomenclature, but many are written in such scientific language that we tend to shy away from them. My own plant knowledge came in bits and pieces over the past twelve years as my thirst for more information increased. Some of the books I found helpful are listed in the bibliography.

The more I learn the more I find there is to learn. The history and myths that abound in garden lore are fascinating. But beware—gardening can become addictive!

Carl Linnaeus established the system of binomial nomenclature in 1753.

PHOTO BY GORDON C. PINE

Heuchera sanguinea *are often short-lived because their shallow roots heave out of the soil.*

Under this system, the first word of a botanical name tells you the plant's *genus*, or family, and the second tells what the *species* is. If a third term appears in quotes, it signifies a specific variety of that genus and species. For example, for *Armeria maritima* "Dusseldorf pride," *Armeria* is the genus, *maritima* is the species, and "Dusseldorf pride" is a special variety of the plant.

There is, of course, a good reason for these botanical names. By putting plants of similar properties together, they help make sense of the plant kingdom. They also enable botanists, as well as serious gardeners, to communicate with other like-minded people around the world. Since common plant names change not only from country to country but from region to region, the botanical names help serious gardeners who are looking for a special species or variety of plant.

Knowing a plant's botanical name and what family it belongs to is useful in identifying some of its characteristics like place of origin, color, and habits. Take the perennial candytuft. Its botanical name, *Iberis sempervirens*, tells us the plant is a native of Spain, or Iberia (*Iberis*) and that it is an evergreen plant (*Sempervirens*). The shallow-rooted hens and chickens has a similar name, *Sempervivum*, or "always alive." This tells us that plants with the botanical name *sempervivens* or *-virens* are evergreen plants and do not die back to the ground in the wintertime. They may not look very attractive during the winter because they are in dormancy, but they will perk up quickly in the early spring.

There are many names that designate the color of the plant's foliage or flowers (usually flowers). Here are a few examples to whet your appetite:

RED: *ruber, sanguineus, rutilans*

WHITE: *albus, candidus, argenteus* (silvery white)

BLUE: *caeruleus, azureus*

YELLOW: *luteolus, aureus*

GREEN: *viridis, virens*

PURPLE: *purpureus*

Other words you will encounter indicate a plant's size, such as *nana*, which informs you the plant will be small or dwarf, or *giganteus*, which is just as it sounds, very large. *Vulgare* means common or ordinary. Plants used for medicines in the past have *officinalis* in their names. *Depressus*, or flattened, indicates the form of the plant or its flowers, as in the mat daisy (*Anacyclus depressus*), a daisy-type perennial that looks as if it has been flattened to the ground. *Phlox repens* tells us that this phlox is of the creeping variety.

The plant family names put plants of similar properties together to help make sense out of the plant kingdom. Taxonomists (people who name plants) still use Linnaeus's system. However, their job is not as simple as memorizing plant names. They not only name new plant discoveries, they also change old names and switch the plants around in different families. Usually as soon as you have it all straight, they change something! You will notice some of these changes in this book. If you are used to seeing artemisias and other daisy family members listed under *compositae*, you will now see it under its newer designation, *asteraceae*. The appendix lists family names of plants, both old and new, as well as the names we are using here.

Keep in mind that botanical changes take a long time to become established in the general population. If you are going to study botanical names, keep a record of both the old and the new, especially if you are reading older garden books.

One example of a change that is finally being used by most books and catalogs is the botanical name for the rock garden plant basket of gold. Formerly called *Alyssum saxatile*, it is now referred to as *Aurina saxatile*. The old name, *alyssum*, meant that it cured madness and rabies; the plant was once listed as an herb, but it is rarely seen in modern herb books. The new name *aurina* means "golden flowers," which the plant so abundantly provides in the spring. *Aurina* is from the Latin *aureus*, or yellow. *Saxatile* was not changed because it means "among the rocks," where this perennial prefers to grow. Now you know that the basket of gold is a yellow-flowered plant that likes dry rocky soil, so it will make a good rock garden plant.

The plant profiles in part 2 list the botanical names of each perennial along with its family. In addition, family names are listed in the appendix.

Now if at this point you are saying "I can't learn all that botanical jibber-jabber," you're wrong—if I can do it, you can, too. I used two steps to learn the names: first, I made a wooden garden marker for each plant, writing both the common and the botanical name on it. As I worked in the garden I saw the names over and over and learned them. The second way I learned the names is to make flash cards with the common name on one side and the botanical name on the reverse. I nearly drove my husband crazy asking for his help with this, but just maybe he learned a name or two.

CHAPTER TWO

Designing with Perennials

Then did I see a pleasant Paradize,
Full of sweete floures and daintiest delights,
Such as on earth man could no more devize,
With pleasures choyce to feed his cheerefull sprights.
—Edmund Spenser, "The Ruines of Time"

Sometimes, as we go on garden tours or enjoy the great botanical gardens, we become overwhelmed with all the plantings and work involved. We visualize those great gardens, where everything seems so perfect, in our own backyard. We picture ourselves strolling along paths, surrounded by beautiful plants that seem to have been mysteriously placed there.

As you gather your senses and return to reality you might ask yourself, "Could I possibly have anything so pretty on a small scale without all the help employed by the large gardens?" Yes, you can! If you want something badly enough you can do it. It will involve learning about your plants, planning your garden, and investing a good amount of physical work to accomplish your plans, but it will be worth it. Hopefully this book will provide you the necessary information and some inspiration for designing, planting, and caring for your own backyard garden.

First Thoughts

Plan your garden size for the time you can actually spend taking care of it. Don't forget to leave some time just to enjoy walking through your garden, or perhaps plan on adding a bench to sit on where you can enjoy it. A gardener's enthusiasm often outgrows the time and energy available for upkeep. This happened to me early in my gardening career. After I had planted several gardens, I planned and executed a 200-foot border across the back of my lawn. After the third year it became a jungle of weeds and matted plants. My time and, more honestly, my energy ran out, preventing proper care, so the border was dug up, tilled, and converted back to lawn. The moral of the story is, when planning, know how much time you can spend working in the garden, and who else may also be willing to work (and for how long!).

The second consideration is money. How much of your budget will you be able to devote to the garden? I am a very frugal person and like to work with low budgets. This can be done with a little hard work and some ingenuity. Gardening friends are more than willing to offer cuttings and divisions of plants. Seeds offer a good return on the investment. Natural "found" materials, such as rocks, can border the gardens. You can make compost to add nutrients to the soil, and if you live near a farming area you can get manures free or for a small fee. On the other hand, if you don't mind spending more money, there are all sorts of high-tech equipment and additives and expensive plants you can use in your garden that will give good results with less effort.

Where Will I Find the Information I Need?

This book will provide you with all the basic information you need to become a backyard gardener. But *please* do not stop here. Buy all the books you can afford (or visit your local library). Read garden magazines and send for all the garden catalogs you can. Due to high printing costs several plant catalogs now charge a small fee, but in most cases it is well worth it. Catalogs are very good sources of information and can keep you updated about new varieties. See the appendix for a partial list of some of my favorite catalogs and books on gardening.

Visit other people's gardens and botanical gardens, and definitely join your local garden club. It's nice to have other garden people to talk to, and you will find new sources for plant swapping and get new ideas.

All these sources will add to your garden knowledge, but the very best place for you to learn is down on your knees in the garden. Here you will see and feel the plant, smell its aroma, and observe its growing cycle.

Your Land Space

You will notice I have my own garden term, "land space," as opposed to the word "landscape." Landscape means a view or vista of scenery on land, for example, a prairie or jungle landscape. Land space means the actual space you have that is devoted to the garden and its relationship to your home.

The best place to start with your personal garden planning is to take inventory of your own land space. This inventory will consist of determining a number of factors: the climate of your particular area and the mini-climate of your special land space; the boundaries of your land; where and what kind of trees are on the property; how light falls through the trees and around buildings; and the soil pH, texture, and moisture content. You will also need to study individual plants and their particular requirements. Fitting every-thing together using this approach will provide you with an attractive and successful garden.

Taking Inventory of Your Land Space

The purpose of an inventory is for us to become intimately involved with and aware of the land space at our disposal. You will need a lead pencil, a set of colored pencils, and a large pad of paper.

I have outlined the steps that work for me; you may need to add or delete certain steps according to your particular situation. For example, in urban ar-eas you may have to contend with underground pipes and buried cables.

Step 1. On one sheet of paper draw the outline of your property. Make three identical copies. With black pencil add all existing structures—the house, sheds, pool, decks, patios, etc. This map does not have to be exact, but try to have everything in proportion.

Step 2. With red pencil, add any planned stationary structures, like a pool, patio, etc.

Step 3. Mark the orientation—north, south, east, west—in relationship to your buildings.

Step 4. With green pencil, color in all existing trees and shrubs. If you plan to add more trees, pencil them in with another color.

Step 5. On your second copy, add where the perennial garden will be located. If you have not decided where to place the garden determine the following conditions:

1. How is the area presently used?

2. Are there any animal or children's paths near your projected garden area? Kids can be trained, but animals may keep right on trekking through your garden anyway.

3. Unless you live alone, determine the needs of other family members. For small children, sand boxes and swings near the garden will keep them occupied while you garden. Older children might appreciate open areas for ball games and other activities.

4. Where are the service areas (or where will they be) placed? These include a spot for trash cans, wood piles, and clotheslines (yes, some of us still have them—we now call them solar dryers!). Older homes will already have these areas established; with new homes you can decide at the beginning where to place them.

Step 6. On the third copy, we are going to record the light factor and soil conditions. To determine where the shade is throughout the day, go into the garden area four times: early in the morning about 8 A.M., at 11 A.M., at 2 P.M., and at 4 P.M. Outline sunny or shady areas with a different colored pencil for each time. This will show you the daily sun pattern for your garden. Keep in mind that in the summer months the sun is higher in the sky than during the winter. Record areas of full sun, partial sun, etc., in your notebook.

Step 7. Check the projected garden areas after a rainstorm to see if there are any wet, puddling areas. These will probably be poorly drained, heavy soil areas.

To find your soil texture, dig down a foot or so in several different spots and check the consistency of sandy or hard clay spots. Keep in mind the soil type can change within a given area. Places where plant life shrivels up after several sunny days may be hardpan areas or ledges just below the surface with a small covering of soil.

Step 8. Take soil samples from your garden area and have them analyzed for pH level and mineral content (see the appendix for the listing of your state agriculture college, where you can have this done). There are also professional companies that specialize in testing soils for a fee. Record your findings in a notebook or on the design sheet.

A notebook is a good companion to your design sheets. Keep an inventory of plants you purchase or have been given. Keep yearly notes on your successes and failures, along with any interesting facts you accumulate along the way. It will be interesting to look back over the years to see how you and your garden have grown and changed as you become more experienced.

Gardeners tend to be changers, planning, planting, and replanting our gardens around at will. We seem to be looking for and working toward the perfection of the Garden of Eden when in reality it's the doing that makes gardening so satisfying. Many of us find working in the garden a good form of exercise and a great mind relaxer—"therapy," as a friend of mine calls it.

Garden Style

We can divide garden styles into three categories: formal, informal, and natural.

The Formal Garden

Elaborate, grand gardens of the past are now left to the botanical gardens, arboretums, and the very rich. Limited time, energy, and money have necessitated smaller gardens for most people. Actually, a smaller version of a grand formal garden may actually be the easiest of all to design; every plant or statue is balanced out by its like.

Formal gardens are characterized by:

1. symmetrical and geometrical pattern designs;
2. boundaries that are strongly defined, often with well-clipped hedges;
3. brick, tile, or wood used for paths or enclosures;
4. less variety but more specimens of a few types of plant;
5. even numbers (two, four, six, etc.) of plants balancing each other;
6. a focal point, either centered or in balance with its like, such as an urn or a statue; and
7. a high level of maintenance to keep the area well balanced and groomed.

The Informal Garden

An informal garden may look like it was planted with no design in mind, but it is actually more difficult to design because it must look unplanned yet be in scale and just as well balanced as the formal garden is. An example of this would be to plant two peonies at one end of your garden and balance the opposite end with a rose bush of equal size. Here not only balance but scale is important. Cottage gardens, herbaceous borders, and island gardens are examples of informal gardens.

Informal gardens are characterized by:

1. a wide variety of different plants, seemingly placed at random;
2. paths that may seem to meander but have a purpose in mind—they may lead to a special focal point hidden somewhere or to a bench in the shade;
3. plants used in odd numbers (one, three, five, etc.); and

A statue makes a good focal point for a formal garden.

4. natural casual materials, including rocks, stone, gravel, bark mulch, or even straw.

The Natural Garden

Also known as the wildflower garden, this type of garden is designed to fit into Mother Nature's scheme. Plantings are used in conjunction with trees and fields. It will look like it has always been there, not interfered with by humans. A good site for a natural garden would be a wooded lot that you clear of underbrush and plant with appropriate plants.

Natural gardens are characterized by:

1. wildflowers and plants that blend with natural design, such as ferns, hostas, bergenia, and columbine (*Aquilegia*);
2. natural materials, like stones, crushed rock, or bark mulch, for pathways;
3. pathways that go somewhere, usually providing an enjoyable stroll through a wooded area; and
4. the sense that they belong where they are and blend with nature.

PHOTO BY BRANDAU/HALL

Meandering paths add interest to informal gardens.

PHOTO BY BRANDAU/HALL

Natural materials like stones, crushed rock, or bark mulch work well on garden paths.

Most of all, when designing your own backyard garden, keep it personal. Make it belong to you; if you are a bird watcher, an informal or natural garden with plants that will attract birds would be in order. If you like very definite lines and neatness, a formal garden is the choice for you.

Line and Form

The line or form of a plant is its physical structure at the time of maturity. It includes its height and width, as well as the shape of the foliage and the flowers.

Vertical Lines

A vertical line is a strong line that we tend to see first. The eye seems to follow the height of a plant before it follows the horizontal lines.

Vertical gardens can be created by using vines and hanging baskets, along with tall perennials and spiking flower lines. Examples of vertical perennials are mullein (*Verbascum thapsus*), snakeroot (*Cimicifuga racemosa*), and anise-hyssop (*Agastache foeniculum*).

Vertical gardens are very effective used on patios and decks and in small garden areas where space is at a premium. Think of a deck area with a 6-by-3-foot garden: mullein, snakeroot, and anise-hyssop could be the main perennials, either planted in front of a clematis vine climbing a trellis, or with flowering plants in hanging baskets that grow down to meet the perennials. This would create a wall of plants, for a pleasing effect.

Horizontal Lines

Low-growing, sprawling plants create horizontal lines. Examples include sundrops (*Oenothera fruticosa*), summer snow (*Cerastium tomentosa*), lily of the valley (*Convallaria*), and clove pinks (*Dianthus caryophyllus*). Horizontal plants can be used to make a small area appear wider.

Flower Head Lines and Form

The form and lines of a plant's flower heads are as important as its foliage in creating an interesting perennial garden. Plan to have different shapes bloom at the same time. Think of including the following flower forms:

Vertical flowers are spike forms, usually elongated; examples are lupine (*Lupinus*), delphinium, liatris, and speedwells (*Veronicas*).

Round shapes appear in the full, tight, clustered circles of the peony and rose (*Rosa*), or in the open-daisy forms of coneflowers (*Echinacea*) and blue flax (*Linum perenne*).

Cluster lines are formed by compound flowers. Some types are tight clusters that look like one flower, like yarrow (*Achillea*) or the dill flower. Others have open panicles like patrinia (*Scabiosifolia nagoya*), lady's mantle (*Alchemilla*) and baby's breath (*Gypsophila*). Clusters can grow on one single stem or branch out on many stems.

Abstract forms can bring a lot of variety to your garden: the bell shapes of campanulas, or the outer-space look of iris and columbine (*Aquilegia*).

Other Lines

Mound-type plants are often used as specimens because of their neat growing habits. These include silver mound (*Artemisia schmidtiana*) and spurge (*Euphorbia epithymoides*).

PHOTO BY GORDON C. PINE

Vertical gardens are very effective on patios and decks, and in small garden areas.

When planning your garden design, combine different types of lines to create an interesting garden. If all the plants were the same height, it would be quite boring. In my sedum garden I have added some taller plants that don't necessarily fit the theme because the low-growing sedums, although pretty, need height to give the garden character.

Scale

Scale is the visual size relationship between the plants in your garden and other plants, trees, and buildings.

A small house surrounded by trees and shrubs will look smaller as the plants outgrow the ideal relationship to the house. Prune trees and shrubs to keep them in scale with the house. With large houses, be generous with plantings. Do not have small skimpy plants and borders; instead use larger, fuller perennials.

In the garden itself, scale refers to plants in relationship to each other. You would not put all the tall full plants on one side of the garden and the tiny ground covers on the other side; this would make the garden look lopsided.

The rounded, arching branches of Linum perenne *create this plant's vertical form.*

Mound-type plants like Artemisia schmidtiana *are often used as specimens because of their neat growing habits.*

Instead you balance the tall plants with other tall plants. With borders, keep the width and length in proportion to each other. A three-foot border will be in scale for a bed up to sixteen feet long; if the bed is longer, make it wider.

Balance

To keep a balanced look in the garden, keep your plants in harmony with the garden and with each other.

Formal gardens are kept in balance by planting the same type of plants opposite each other. Informal gardens will usually have same size plants balanced by a different species of the same height, color, or both. Plants can also be balanced by man-made additions like a statue, bird bath, or trellis. With either type, your planning goal is for the garden to be pleasing and relaxing to the observer without necessarily being obvious.

Rhythm

Rhythm, or repetition, is a movement or recurring pattern created by color, line, or form. Rhythm creates unity and continuity throughout the garden or your entire land space.

To achieve rhythm, use one special color or plant for its distinctive lines, form, or foliage. Place that plant at various places throughout the garden. For example, I use lady's mantle (*Alchemilla vulgare*) throughout my land space. When in bloom you will see the golden flowers everywhere, creating a repetition that makes all the gardens seem to be related by this one plant. When the flowers have passed (usually harvested to dry for winter), then the large pleated leaves give a less obvious rhythm to the land space.

To create rhythm, place the chosen plant at various points in your gardens, pot one up for the patio or deck, and use it as a specimen plant in a prominent spot. It will be the common denominator of your garden. More than one plant can be used as repetition plants; try using plants that bloom at different times so that you have a rhythm plant in bloom all season.

Color used for rhythm or repetition in the garden can begin with a color from the interior of your home. If you have a blue living room, you could

Keep foundation plantings in scale with the house.

PHOTO BY GORDON C. PINE

PHOTO BY GORDON C. PINE

Delphinium, Stachys lanata *(shown here)*, Alchemilla vulgaris, *and* Achillea
are plants with interesting foliage.

continue this color scheme into the garden. On the patio or deck you would
use either blue pots or blue flowers—in the garden beds blue delphiniums
would be towers of blue with blue flax (*Linum perenne*) and blue navelwort
(*Omphalodes*) as blue ground covers.

When planning a rhythm plant use strong foliage or colors. Perennials that
have excellent foliage for the entire season include hostas, ferns, bergenias,
peonies, santolina, and silver mound (*Artemisia schmidtiana*).

Texture

We all enjoy and notice bright colors in the garden, yet we may not always be
as observant of various plant textures. After taking a six-week workshop with
me, one of my students said she now looked at things more carefully, seeing

details that before she just scanned and didn't really see. This happens when you start studying plant life. All of a sudden the fields and forest are full of things you have looked at all your life but didn't really see and couldn't name.

The *foliage texture* is very important; it is the backbone of the garden. Once the flowers have performed their colorful drama, then the foliage is left to fill in for the rest of the season.

You can create a specific "look" in your garden by using plants with different types of foliage. A tropical look will consist of heavier-looking plants like bergenia, yucca, peony, and lady's mantle (*Alchemilla vulgare*); a delicate Victorian look would include the ferny leaves of yarrow (*Achillea*), gold-thread coreopsis, columbine (*Aquilegia*), and baby's breath (*Gypsophila*).

A good variety of foliage in a garden creates interest. Study leaf and foliage patterns and textures as you plan your design. Look at the soft velvet leaves of lamb's ear (*Stachys lanata*), the carefree foliage of columbine, the strong, sturdy leaves of the hostas, and the gray-green leaves of the clove pinks (*Dianthus*).

PHOTO BY GORDON C. PINE

This plant is heavily mulched with a lot of space.

PHOTO BY GORDON C. PINE

How closely you plant your perennials is a matter of personal choice.
Closely spaced drifts are shown here.

Spacing and Drifting

Each individual plant needs the right amount of space for its own particular mature height and width. For example, a peony will require 3½ feet of space per plant, yet in the same 3½ feet you could plant 10 blue flax plants. If you know the mature size of your perennial before planting you can provide it with the necessary spacing.

How close together you plant your perennials is a matter of personal choice. I prefer to fill in every inch of soil—I guess I am hoping the plants will keep out the weeds! My friend likes hers with open spaces between them, mulched heavily. Her plants are almost like single specimens.

Perennials that are fast-spreading will, of course, need more space to roam around in. Fast spreaders are mints (*Mentha*), bishopweed (*Aegopodium podagraria*), and obedient plant (*Physostegia virginiana*). If you do not have a lot of space you may consider not using them at all, planting them in containers, or dividing them twice a year to prevent their spreading.

Growth Rates

The following chart groups perennials according to their growth rate.

FAST SPREADERS
These plants need yearly or every-other-year division.

Allheal (*Prunella*)

Bishopweed (*Aegopodium podagraria*)

Creeping buttercup (*Ranunculus*)

Golden glow (*Rudbeckia*)

Golden marguerite (*Anthemis tinctoria*)

Lily of the valley (*Convallaria majalis*)

Mints (*Mentha* sp.)

Obedient plant (*Physostegia virginiana*)

Pearly everlasting (*Anaphalis margaritacea*)

Silver king (*Artemisia ludoviciana*)

Tansy (*Tanacetum*)

Yarrow, red and white species (*Achillea*)

SLOW SPREADERS
These plants need division every three to four years.

Ajuga

Arabis

Astilbe

Beebalm (*Monarda didyma*)

Bellflower (*Campanula*)

Blue sheep's grass (*Festuca*)

Catnip mussinii (*Hepeta mussinni*)

Chrysanthemum

Cranesbill (*Geranium*)

Delphinium

False lupine (*Thermopsis*)

Flowering onion (*Allium* sp.)

Lamb's ear (*Stachys*)

Lungwort (*Pulmonaria*)

Phlox (all species)

Purple coneflower (*Echinacea*)

Roman wormwood (*Artemisia pontica*)

Sedum

Solomon's seal (*Polygonatum*)

Spiderwort (*Tradescantia*)

Summer snow (*Cerastium*)

Sundrops (*Oenothera*)

Violet (*Viola*)

Yellow loosestrife (*Lysimachia*)

NONSPREADING PLANTS

These neat, slow-growing plants need division every six to eight years if at all. They are ideal plants for low-maintenance gardens.

Basket of gold (*Aurina saxatile*)
Bergenia (*Bergenia cordifolia*)
Candytuft (*Iberis sempervirens*)
Centaurea species
Clematis
Dianthus sp.
Fern sp.
Feverfew (*Chrysanthemum parthenium*)
Hosta sp.
Lady's mantle (*Alchemilla vulgare*)

Lavender (*Lavendula*)
Patrinia (*Scabiosifolia nagoya*)
Peony
Rue (*Ruta graveolens*)
Sea thrift (*Armeria maritima*)
Silver mound (*Artemisia schmidtiana*)
Spurge (*Euphorbia epithymoides*)
Windflower (*Anemone*)
Yucca (*Yucca filamentosa*)

Drifts

"Drift" is a fairly new word in perennial gardening. It means the planting of a very few types of plants—or even just one—in a large space. Drifts are usually associated with annual gardens where one to three plant varieties are used over a large area, but they are also done using perennials. Drifts can be very effective when you wish to have a large area of color at a certain period of time. For example, for a garden-club tour in early spring you might want a slope showing off a design of two different colors of creeping phlox (*Phlox subulata*).

Figure 2-1 shows a drift using three different perennials. Baby's breath (*Gypsophila*) is used in the center, surrounded by hyssop (*Hyssopus officinalis*), bordered by silver mound (*Artemesia schmidtiana*). Hyssop should be clipped in early spring to keep it a low hedge plant. The baby's breath and hyssop will reach their peak color in late June. To add early spring color, plant white tulips among the baby's breath.

Illusions

All is not as it seems! We use foliage, flowers, and color to create illusions in our gardens.

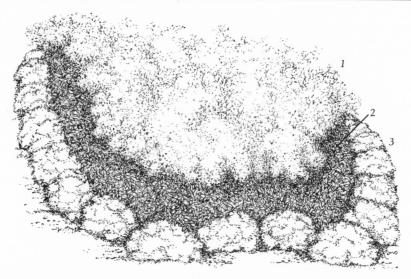

Fig. 2-1: 1. Baby's breath (Gyposophila) *interplanted with white tulips. 2. Hyssop* (Hyssopus) *acts as a hedge; if let grow it will produce attractive purple flowers. Keep clipped to maintain its shape or it will become straggly. 3. Silver mound* (Artemisia schmidtiana) *makes an attractive silver border.*

To create the effect of a larger garden, place bold, large, shiny-leaved plants in the foreground of the garden. Place smaller-leaved plants with blue and purple coloring toward the back to give the impression of depth. For example, in the front of the garden you could place bergenia and lady's mantle (*Alchemilla vulgaris*); in the middle put rue (*Ruta*) with its bluish-green leaves, and in the background use the lighter green, pealike foliage of baptisia.

Color creates illusions. Bright, cheerful warm colors like red, pink, and yellow attract the eye before the cool colors of green, blue, and purple. Placing the bright colors in the front of the garden and the cool colors in the back makes the garden appear larger. But if you want the eye to go to a certain spot, like to a bench placed somewhere in the garden, then plant bright colors around it.

CHAPTER THREE

Working It All Out

Yea, he shall learn from his employ
How God turns mourning into joy,
And from earth's graves calls up at last
His flowers when all the Winter's past.
—Katharine Tynan

Each of us looks at gardens from our own personal perspective. A nongardener might scan the overall picture quickly, appreciating its beauty. That is why balance and scale are so important—the overall picture must be pleasing even to the novice's eye. A plant collector, student of botany, or garden hobbyist will notice individual plants, how they fit into the overall plan, and growing conditions. Some people will notice everything; others will not really see anything other than "a garden."

As gardeners we not only need to see each plant species as an individual character, we have to know how to fit that plant into the scheme of our design.

Mother Nature has taught us the three basic plant schemes: the tall canopy (the trees), the understory (shrubs, hedges, and very tall perennials), and the ground covers (everything else from tiny one-inch plants to tall six-foot herbaceous perennials or annuals). In planning a garden, it helps to place our perennials in three similar categories: the tall canopy will be perennials over three feet tall; the understory will be perennials that grow from one to three feet tall; and the ground covers will be the perennials that are less than 12 inches tall.

Most gardens consist of other plants beside perennials; let us consider what else will be in our gardens.

Trees: Trees are the background and a source of shade for our perennials. If trees are already established, you will work with what you have. If you are landscaping a new area, plan carefully for sun and shade areas. Don't overlook the possibility of using fruit and nut trees, which are useful as well as pretty and often fragrant.

Shrubs: Shrubs can be used to add dimension to the garden, to create backgrounds, or to enclose your gardens. Again, don't overlook small fruit bushes for your perennial garden. In the olden days fruit trees were very much a part of the flower garden. Today interplanting fruits, flowers, and vegetables is called "edible gardening."

Trees and shrubs will provide the winter outline of the garden. Do you prefer the look of green conifers or the skeleton black outlines of deciduous trees against the winter-white snow?

Annual Plants: Annual flowers are also called bedding plants. Annuals are ideal companions to the perennial garden. Use them to fill in between slow-growing perennial seedlings that may take two years to fill in the allotted space provided for them.

Annuals are good for overplanting spring bulbs, covering the decaying foliage as they add beauty to the garden. Annuals also make good potted plants to move where you want color at a certain time, such as when a perennial fails, for whatever the reason.

Many of the annuals will self-seed where they are planted, saving yearly planting. Some self-seeders are love-in-a-mist (*Nigella*), Johnny-jump-ups (*Viola tricolor*), calendula, cornflower (*Centaurea*), and cleome. Some of them self-seed so abundantly you may even be pulling them up as weeds in the spring. Good grief, don't throw them away—pot them up and give them as gifts, sell them at charity plant sales, or even start your own business!

Garden Placement

Living with a smaller land space is typical of our modern life-styles, yet even the smallest spaces can be transformed into attractive garden areas. I like to stress experimenting with plants and ways to use them. Once you develop the basic rules of gardening, you can create your own garden style. Then you can design your space to suit your special likes and dislikes—to become a part of your personality.

Front Yard Plantings

In the United States we have neglected our front yards for too long. When you drive through housing developments you often see house after house with the same unimaginative green foundation plantings, the same pot of petunias or geraniums by the mailbox or lamppost, each one looking very much alike. You will know when you pass by the house of a true garden lover. You will see a well-landscaped garden area with every corner full of flowers and herbs, often intermingled with a few vegetables. In Europe many gardens are in front of the house; they have little grass, but lots of flowers. Just think of the possibilities: you can enclose your front yard with hedges and fences for privacy or build a fantasy garden for the world to enjoy with you. Maybe you will inspire your neighbors to spruce up their front yards as well as their backyards.

Entrance Plantings

I am amazed by some of the rather dull and drab entrances of modern homes. Their owners are very conscious of the inside decor yet neglect the appearance of the area that makes a first impression, the entrance.

Entrances can be as simple or dramatic as you desire. Of course, the first consideration in entrance planning is *safety*. Walkways should be made for walking, out of easy, safe materials. Crushed rock is unsuitable for small toddlers who will stumble and fall on the sharp stones. Women who wear high heels will also find crushed rock hard to walk on. Second, lights should provide safe walking for night visitors. The automatic night lights that come on with movement are a good deterrent against prowlers. The final consideration is *beauty*. The entrance design can be used to project the mood of the home. Hedges and fences and a slightly hidden entrance say "Stay away, we like our privacy" and often discourage solicitors. Open entrances with flowers leading up the pathway to the door say, "Hello, come on in."

Plan your entrance design to coordinate with the building style and color and with other gardens in the land space. Large colonial, brick, Victorian and Tudor homes are attractive with formal entrances and large plantings. For country farmhouses, log cabins, and one-story modern homes, natural or informal gardens are more appropriate.

Matching the scale of plantings with the size of the house is the most important factor. Very large plants seem to dwarf a smaller house; skimpy little plants look silly against a large house.

My own farmhouse entrance is semiformal. Age-worn cement steps are half-clothed in creeping thyme (*Thymus*). More thyme streams over the sides of a black milkcan. On either side of the doorway, dwarf Alberta spruce give a slight formal look to an otherwise informal garden. Thyme, hens and chickens (*Sempervivum*), and blue flax (*Linum perenne*) provide color as they run in and around the spruce. Since my farmhouse is not tall, these small plantings are in scale with the house height. Another house larger than mine actually looks much smaller because it is dwarfed by overgrown large foundation plantings, completely hiding all its windows. The tree-size shrubs seem to swallow up the house.

Foundation Plantings

Evergreen shrubs and trees are excellent as backgrounds for your perennials. Take care that they are kept well pruned and do not outgrow their beauty by dwarfing the house.

Foundation borders should be kept in scale with the house. A large house can use a wide border, four to six feet wide. A small house will be more in scale with a narrower border, perhaps three to four feet wide.

If your house is narrow, you can create an illusion of breadth. At the end of one side add a fence or a line of evergreens, or extend the garden out eight to ten feet from the house. At the end of the fence or garden, plant a tall evergreen.

Silver-colored plants are good contrast plants to use with your evergreens. Silver mound (*Artemisia schmidtiana*), the silver variety of santolina (*Santolina chamaecyparissus*), or Roman wormwood (*Artemisia pontica*) will provide this contrast.

Spring bulbs give a spurt of color in early spring. They can be overplanted with other long-lasting perennials.

Low ground covers around and under evergreens include ajuga variety "burgundy glow" with its variegated pink, green, and cream leaves; sweet woodruff

A smaller house will be more in scale with a narrower border, perhaps 3 or 4 feet wide.

(*Asperula odorata*); "beacon silver" lamium (*Lamium maculatum*), and bishopweed (*Aegopodium podagraria*). All of these are shade-loving and will spread quickly, filling in the space around the evergreens.

In sunny areas try spreaders such as blue navelwort (*Omphalodes*), lady's mantle (*Alchemilla vulgaris*), the white-flowered, silver-gray leaved summer snow (*Cerastium tomentosa*), or the green-gray leaved, pink-scented flowers of the clove pinks (*Dianthus*).

Rain gutters will help prevent large drip lines around your foundation, but check to see if any such lines do appear. Drip lines are grooves worn in the soil where the rain falls from the roof or overflows from the gutters. Keep plants away from this area, or a hard rainstorm will wash away the soil and uproot the plants.

Consider the foundation color when planting your foundation garden. A brick foundation looks nice with contrasting whites and silvers. A monochromatic color scheme with pinks and reds is also attractive (see chapter 7).

Pathways

Pathways must first of all be safe to walk on. They are also necessary in larger gardens where you cannot reach in to weed and clean the garden. There are, however, ways to use paths to create illusions in the garden. Wider paths make the gardens seem most spacious. A straight path can be used to make a garden look longer if you make the entrance slightly wider than the exit; the front could be 4½ feet wide and the exit only 3 feet wide.

If your garden is small and you don't need paths, you can still create the illusion of a larger garden by placing stones to simulate a pathway. When planting a garden of fragrant plants, you might want the pathway narrow so that visitors brush up against the plants, releasing their fragrance while strolling through the garden in the evening with their loved ones.

Path materials might include wood, pine needles, straw, gravel, bricks, flat rocks, tiles, bark mulch, cocoa bean shells, sand, crushed rocks, cement, and grass or other plants. When using grass, be sure the path is wide enough to push a lawn mower through.

Plants used in pathways must be strong enough to tolerate foot traffic. Rupturewort (*Hernaria glabra*) and thyme (*Thymus*) are two plants I have worked

Plants used in pathways, like the thyme shown here,
must be strong enough to tolerate foot traffic.

PHOTO BY BRANDAU/HALL

Wider paths can make gardens seem spacious.

with and found to be excellent path plants. Rupturewort only needs weeding; thyme, however, will need mowing to keep the flowers off. If you let it flower, beware of bees—they will literally cover the plant during the daytime.

Use your imagination when designing your pathways; combine different materials for interest. For example, place flat wood slices in crushed rocks (do *not* use creosote-treated wood—it will damage the plant life). Interplanting grass or herbs between tiles, rocks, or brick is also very attractive.

Gardening under Trees

Many a tree has experienced the accidental nip or cut from a too-close lawn mower. To prevent this type of damage, plant a garden around the tree.

The species of a tree will dictate what you plant around it. Acid-loving trees and shrubs, like azaleas, rhododendrons, and heathers will support acid-loving perennials.

It is difficult to plant around shallow-rooted trees, such as maple (*Acer*)

PHOTO BY BRANDAU/HALL

Stone paths can make a small garden seem larger.

and hemlock (*Tsuga*). These trees do not have large tap roots, but instead have several nearly equal-sized roots that spread out from the base of the tree's trunk. The roots are often contained in the 30 inches of soil just under the surface and can extend beyond the tree's canopy of branches. They greedily use up the available water and nutrients in the soil for their own use.

I like to build a garden in a circle six feet away from the trunk. I mulch inside the circle, using bark mulch, crushed rock, or highly scented cocoa bean shells (they smell like chocolate after a rain—yum). This mulch area also keeps the shallow-rooted trees moist, which they like. Then I add new, well-composted soil to the outer edge, making a three-foot border. Here you can plant shallow-rooted plants such as spring bulbs, ajugas, hens and chickens (*Sempervivum*), thyme (*Thymus*), or coral bells (*Heuchera sanguinea*). If you wanted plants with deeper roots you could build a raised bed in a circle and plant almost any type of plant.

Keep in mind when planting under trees that you may need to provide water at times. The trees' leaves prevent light rains from penetrating the garden area.

Corner Plantings

Brighten up a dull corner area of a fence or building with a corner planting designed for that space. For height, a built-in planter can be used, or you can till up the soil, adding good compost, and plant at the existing ground level.

The design in Figure 3-1 is built up to a height of three bricks (approximately 6 inches), which keeps the soil away from the wood fence. The garden consists of three curved planting strips. Various textures are emphasized for added beauty. One baptisia plant fills the corner. A row of red tulips provides spring beauty; then, as they start to fade away, the baptisia grows and covers their decaying foliage. The second strip is centered with three silver mounds (*Artemisia schmidtiana*) that provide the garden with a stabilizing effect for the entire season. Silver mound peeks above the ground in April and keeps its neat mound shape and shimmering silver foliage until hard frost. On either side, the purple-flowered spike foliage of liatris and the large, almost thornlike leaves and steely-blue globe-shaped flowers of globe thistle (*Echinops rito*) provide texture and contrast. In the front strip, summer snow (*Cerastium tomentosa*) provides a spring glow of white flowers, followed by striking silver foliage. If a really bright color is needed to bring the eye to this area, annuals like golden-

Sand can be used to form a path.

yellow marigolds or brilliant pink petunias would work well.

At both ends of the front strip, another liatris completes the garden.

Freestanding or Island Gardens

A freestanding or island garden bed is one you can walk around completely. It can be as small as a six-foot square or circle or as large as an acre, with paths separating smaller islands within.

In small garden islands, the middle can be raised in a mound to create dimension. Place taller plants in the center of the mound, with lower sizes graduating down to a low edging. If the garden is too large for you to reach in and tend, you will need to make a path for weeding and garden care.

Islands can be in many different forms: round, square, triangular, or free-form. Here I describe two island gardens, the free-form and the infinity garden.

The free-form island garden has an elongated form and contains a mound on the seven-foot-wide end (see Fig. 3-2). Toward the opposite end it narrows to four-and-a-half-feet wide. This particular garden is sort of a mini-mountain and forest. Dwarf conifers are planted at the top, together with perennials under

Pathways are necessary in larger gardens where you cannot reach in to weed and clean the garden.

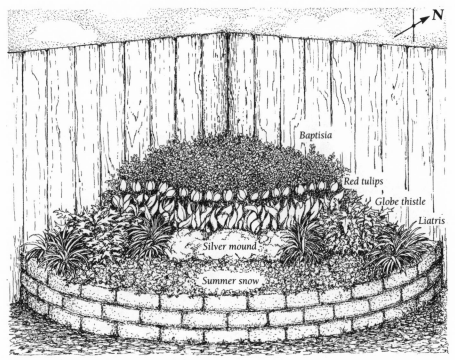

Baptisia

Red tulips

Globe thistle

Liatris

Silver mound

Summer snow

Fig. 3-1. Corner Planting

24 inches tall. Rocks form a chain from the mound to the narrow end of the island. A small water pond would be nice at this end, but a bird bath could also be an effective focal point. Another option is to plant a drift of blue flowers such as navelwort (*Omphalodes*) to simulate the water. Rocks could be used to border the entire garden.

Figure 3-3 shows an infinity garden. Make this garden in sections; it will grow as your time and land space dictate. Start with a six- or eight-foot circle as a central core and focal point. Add three- or five-foot-wide sections that form concentric circles surrounding the central bed. Each new bed becomes longer as it forms a quarter-circle. Leave four openings in each circle and keep pathways large enough to walk and work in. Place a large focal point in the center of the first circle or add a mounded circle for interest.

For example, the center could have a bird bath surrounded by various thyme (*Thymus*) plants. Circle 1 would include low-growing plants like coral bells (*Heuchera sanguinea*) and various sedum species. In circle 2 you could

Fig. 3-2. Free-form Island Bed

have plants of medium height like baby's breath (*Gypsophila*), lady's mantle (*Alchemilla vulgaris*), and lavender (*Lavendula*). Circle 3 would include tall varieties such as yellow loosestrife (*Lysimachia punctata*), peonies (*Paeonia*), and roses (*Rosa*). By planting the tallest plants outside, you will create an intimate space closed off from time and the world—truly an infinity garden.

Slopes and Banks

Areas that are difficult or dangerous for the lawnmower can inspire you to create interesting gardens. There are three easy ways to work out slope gardens.

1. A rock garden is always my first choice; I probably love them because so much of my land is flat. Rock gardens involve hauling and lugging a lot of rocks, unless, of course, you already have a ledge and rock area. If you don't have any rocks, try construction sites. People there may be more than willing to give you their rocks and may even haul them

for you if they are trying to get rid of them. Maine has no lack of rocks. Every year when we till the vegetable garden there seem to be more rocks than the year before, prompting the comment, "We grow rocks in this garden."

Rock garden plants need good drainage and can tolerate dry soil. See the appendix for a sampling of rock garden plants.

2. Terraced gardens can be made with landscaping lumber, creating steps and paths wide enough for walking. If the slope is very steep you will need drains to prevent washouts. Constructing this may be a job for a landscaping company.

3. Ground covers can be planted on the bank or slope without making any major structural changes. Perennials used in this way will help to prevent soil erosion. The slope can

Fig. 3-3. Infinity Garden

become a wild garden with different perennials or planted with all one species of plants. Some quick-covering perennials for an area like this include yarrow (*Achillea*), pearly everlasting (*Anaphalis margaritacea*), silver king (*Artemisia ludoviciana*), Roman wormwood (*Artemisia pontica*), false lupine (*Thermopsis montana*), and, for partially shady to shady areas, hostas and ferns.

Raised Beds

Raised beds have been used throughout history and are still popular today. Many different materials can be used to make a raised bed: landscape lumber, logs, rocks, bricks, or cement blocks. The purpose of a raised bed is to bring the soil up above the ground, for a variety of reasons. I like raised beds with wide borders for easier weeding. You eliminate a problem with poor soil by adding your own special soil mix. Raised beds offer better drainage. As well as

Rock Garden

these practical considerations, they are often used for beauty alone.

When we had to tear down our barn I was able to salvage several huge beams to make raised beds. Some have rotted areas; I dug the rot out and planted hens and chickens in the holes.

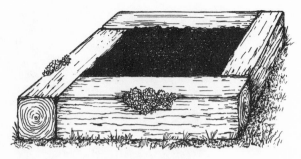

Fig. 3-4. Raised Bed

Mix the soil for your beds to complement your plants. I have included my favorite general soil recipe, with the ingredients listed proportionally. By altering the size of one part—from one cup to one bushel—you can make as small or large a batch as you need.

Homemade Soil Mixture

3 parts good garden soil
3 parts coarse gravel
5 parts peat moss
2 parts rich compost (or
   purchased cow manure)
1 part vermiculite or perlite
1/16 part lime

Perennials As Specimen Plants

A specimen plant is used as a focal point in the garden or placed where there is room for just one plant to be the center of attraction. A specimen plant should have good foliage for the entire season. The following perennials have attractive flowers, but more important, have good foliage for the entire season.

Baptisia: A four- to five-foot perennial with light, pealike foliage and blue flowers. The June flowers are followed by attractive large black pods. These pods can be dried for craft work. This plant always receives compliments in the garden.

Spurge (Euphorbia epithymoides): Even the name sounds interesting. This

Euphorbia epithymoides makes a nice specimen plant.

plant has large mound-shaped, olive-green leaves with some red veins in spring and fall; in June it has bright yellow long-lasting flowers. I have a specimen near the door of my book room.

Hosta: Varieties of this plant are available from dwarf to extra-large sizes. They are excellent for partially shaded or shady areas. No garden should be without at least one or two hostas. They are wonderful as specimen plants.

Lady's Mantle (*Alchemilla vulgaris*): You will see this plant mentioned often in this book; it is one of my very favorites. Its attractive yellow-green flowers bloom in June and are nice for drying, but the large pleated leaves are pretty all year long. In the morning little drops of dew settle on the leaves, sparkling like tiny diamonds caught in the plant's grasp.

Bergenia: I only discovered bergenia a few years ago, but it has since become a rhythm plant for my gardens. Its pink flowers come out very early, along with the tulips. But again, it is the attractive large evergreen leaves that make this plant so nice.

Yucca: Desert or tropical-looking yucca is one of my husband's favorites. It looks nice in the garden, but it is also dramatic as a specimen, alone.

To sum up chapters 2 and 3, the more you learn about your own land space and the plants you want to use in your design, the more success you will have in your final garden. Keep in mind success is what pleases you and not your neighbors—beauty is indeed in the eye of the beholder!

CHAPTER FOUR

Theme Gardening

The garden walks are wet with dew
Fresh gather'd from the rosy hours,
The busy insects hum anew
And stir to life the sleeping flow'rs.
                                    —William Ackerman

Americans seem to be fond of labeling their possessions. We have names for our pets, pet names for our loved ones, and names for our boats, cars, cottages, and farms. Gardeners are no exception to the naming game. We like to name our gardens and sometimes even have a pet name for a particular plant. This naming of gardens is called "theme gardening." A theme garden is a garden that represents a particular idea or design. It can be a special theme that represents a personal hobby, favorite color (a monochromatic garden), or a particular plant species that interests us.

Gardens from the past can be created and recaptured for our modern lifestyle, such as the Victorian, colonial, or medieval garden. A Japanese, French, or old English wort garden can take on an exotic flair.

A hobby or special interest can be turned into a theme garden. This could be a garden of plants mentioned in the poetry we enjoy, a Shakespeare garden, a biblical garden, or a fragrance garden full of scented plants.

At one time I had a whimsical garden I called a zoo garden. It was filled with plants that have animal, bird, or insect names, like catnip (*Nepeta cataria*), cranesbill geraniums (*Geranium* sp.), spiderwort (*Tradescantia virginiana*), and beebalm (*Monarda didyma*). Also included were animal statues to match the plant—a statue of a cat for the catnip and a giant rubber spider for the spiderwort.

A favorite flower can fill a garden with only that species and its varieties; examples are an iris or tulip garden. A favorite color or color scheme can also become the theme of your garden; various color schemes are described in chapter 7. Ideas for theme gardens are only limited by your imagination.

Designing Your Own Theme Garden

Research is the key word in designing your own original theme garden. First you need an idea for a theme; then learn all you can about that subject and the plants associated with it.

Let's pretend you are going to design a Shakespeare garden. You could choose only plants mentioned in his plays and poems or you could use plants of the Elizabethan era. What plants were grown in that particular period? What well-known gardeners were alive at that time? Shakespeare was probably acquainted with such garden greats as John Parkinson, Gervase Markham, and Canon Ellacombe. Your local library will be able to help with histories and biographies from whatever era you choose.

With a Shakespeare garden you could choose either the very formal style of the Elizabethan gardens or the informal front yard garden enjoyed by Shakespeare and his wife, Ann Hathaway. A bench or seat of thyme is a must for this period of time. Back then the rich usually employed gardeners to do the physical work; for themselves, they liked to sit and enjoy the flowers on their strolls through the gardens. And rich and poor alike appreciated the fragrance and soothing power of herbs.

There are numerous plants available from this period appearing under a variety of names. If you have chosen only plants from Shakespeare's works, you will find wormwood (*Artemisia*) called "Dian's bud" as well as "wormwood." Gillyflowers (*Dianthus* sp.) are also mentioned several times.

A nice touch to a Shakespeare garden is to have pieces of slate engraved or painted with the quote that refers to the plant. Next to columbine (*Aquilegia*), for example, you could place this quote from *Love's Labour Lost*: "I am the flower, that mint, that columbine."

The following six designs are planned to get you started on your own theme garden. Your land space will dictate the exact design. The plants suggested are only a partial list of possibilities; plants can be interchanged or substituted according to your own personal taste. The gardens described here are a colonial garden from the early 1700s, a biblical garden, a monochromatic garden in silver and gray, a Victorian garden, a medieval garden, and a wildflower garden.

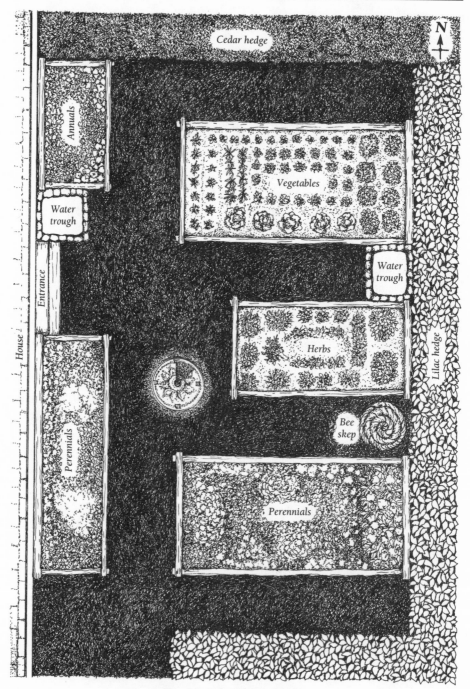

Fig. 4-1. Colonial Garden Plan

The Early Colonial Garden

An early eighteenth-century colonial farmhouse garden was called a "yarb patch." Filled with plants that were necessary for survival, it had no particular design. It was next to the back door or very close to the house, making it easy to go into the garden to collect the vegetables, herbs, and flowers that were planted not so much for their beauty but for their usefulness. Plants were grown for seasoning, for medicines, to scent stuffy homes and repel insects, and for yarn and fabric dyes.

I'm sure flowers were enjoyed for their beauty and dried for decorations, but utility was the first consideration in the early days of hardship and adjusting to a new life-style. Roses, peonies, and lilies were grown as foods as well as for their beauty. Probably those few beautiful flowers were more special in the lives of people back then than they are today with our overabundance of doodads and thingamabobs.

Our re-created colonial yarb patch is well designed and not just planted. The first requirement is to place it near the back door or the stillroom. Trees and shrubs that can surround the garden for protection are red cedar, elderberry, witch hazel, roses (the first shrub to be introduced to America), and lilac (the second shrub to come here from Europe).

In earlier days fences were used around gardens to keep the animals out; today we fence in the animals and leave the gardens open. But for this garden, some sort of fence is needed. A fence at that time might consist of roots dug up while clearing the land or a simple wattle fence, made by driving small trees into the ground and intertwining them with young saplings.

A focal point for this garden might be a bee skep, used to attract bees for their honey, or a wooden or stone trough by the back door where vegetables and herbs could be washed before they were brought into the house.

Designing the Colonial Garden

The house forms the background for the garden's west side; the north side has a cedar hedge for protection from harsh winds. Lilacs bring spring color on the east and south side of the garden, with an opening on the south side. Fruit trees could be planted instead for more productivity.

Although an original yarb patch would have meandering paths, this garden is separated into beds for easy gardening. The raised beds are made of logs in keeping with the old look. Three beds separate the vegetables, herbs, and flowers. A water trough near the door and a bee skep are used for focal points, along with a sundial surrounded by thyme (*Thymus*). Pathways are of natural materials such as gravel, bark mulch, or crushed rocks.

Colonial Garden Plants

In the vegetable garden, any vegetables except corn and vine crops can be used. These two vegetable types would have been field crops. And keep in mind that tomatoes were thought to be poisonous until the early nineteenth century— Thomas Jefferson grew them at Monticello in 1781, but they were not widely accepted until the 1820s. The early tomatoes were ribbed and colored red and yellow.

HERBS

PERENNIALS

Alpine strawberry (*Fragaria*)
Blue flax (*Linum perenne*)
Chives (*Allium Schoenoprasm*)
Costmary (*Chrysanthemum balsamita*)
Feverfew (*Chrysanthemum parthenium*)
Lavender (*Lavendula* sp.)
Rue (*Ruta graveolens*)

Rupturewort (*Hernaria glabra*)
Sage (*Salvia officinalis*)
Soapwort (*Saponaria*)
Southernwood (*Artemisia abrotanum*)
Sweet woodruff (*Asperula odorata*)
Tansy (*Tanacetum vulgare*)
Thyme (*Thymus* sp.)
Wormwood (*Artemisia absinthium*)

ANNUALS

Basil (*Ocimum* sp.)
Borage (*Borago officinalis*)
Calendula (*Calendula officinalis*)

Dill (*Anethum graveolens*)
Mignonette (*Reseda odorata*)
Nasturtium (*Tropaeolum majus*)

BIENNIALS

Caraway (*Carum carvi*)

Parsley (*Petroselinum crispum*)

VINES

PERENNIALS

Honeysuckle (*Lonicera* sp.)   Hops (*Humulus lupulus*)

FLOWERS

PERENNIALS

Baby's breath (*Gypsophila* sp.)   Iris, Jacob's ladder (*Polemonium caeruleum*)
Baptisia (*Baptisia australis*)
Campanulas (*Campanula* sp.)   Lily (*Lilium* sp.)
Candytuft (*Iberis sempervirens*)   Obedient plant (*Physostegia verginiana*)
Columbine (*Aquilegia* sp.)
Cranesbill geranium (*Geranium* sp.)   Pearly everlasting (*Anaphalis margaritacea*)
Delphinium
Dianthus   Peony
Hens and chickens (*Sempervivum* sp.)   Trollius
Hollyhock (biennial) (*Alcea* sp.)   Violet (*Viola* sp.)
    Yarrow (*Achillea* sp.)

The Biblical Garden

Religion has played an important role throughout garden history as well as human history. Early pagan peoples utilized flowers and herbs in their rituals and sacrifices, as well as for food and medicine.

Mythology (another garden theme?) had its part in naming many of our present-day flowers and herbs. Even the name "flower" probably came from the Roman goddess Flora, who was held in high esteem by members of the world's oldest profession, from courtesans down to the lowliest prostitute. A festival of flowers was held on April 28 to worship Flora.

Early Christian priests did not want the layman to use flowers as decorations because of their long association with paganism. But it wasn't long before the wealthy had their own flower gardens and decorations. The Church re-dedicated many flowers for its own religious purposes.

There are several variations of the biblical garden.

1. A Madonna's garden (or Mary's garden) contains all the plants that refer to Mary in some way. Some plants that are appropriate include lady's mantle (*Alchemilla vulgare*), dedicated to all women for their medical problems; Mary's eyes or forget-me-nots (*Myosotis*); and columbine (*Aquilegia*), which is also called Our Lady's shoes.

2. A saints' garden has plants that are dedicated to or named after all the various saints. Some examples would be Herb Robert (*Geranium robertianum*) for Saint Robert, the founder of the Cistercian order; the Michaelmas daisy (*Aster*) for the archangel Michael; and sweet William for Saint William.

3. A monastery garden is created by using the herbs and flowers that were grown during the Middle Ages. We can thank the monks for their careful record-keeping; they preserved much information that would otherwise have been lost from that time. In your monastery garden, grow hollyhock (*Alcea*), lavender (*Lavendula officinalis*), lilies (*Lilium*), lupines (*Lupinus*), peony, and costmary (*Chrysanthemum balsamita*).

Color is often used to signify certain meanings:

white: purity
blue: purity
red: the blood of Christ
violet: royalty
yellow: the sunshine that drives away dark forces of evil

A Biblical Garden Plan

This garden consists of three bedding sections, forming an 18-by-20-foot garden. One part, on the north wall, is backed by a white stockade fence. A statue of Saint Francis is the center focal point, with thyme, the herb of humility, creeping around its base. A holly bush (*Ilex*) on either side represents eternal life. Two climbing red roses symbolize love and the blood of Christ.

The three-and-a-half-foot walkways that separate the three beds are filled with white crushed rock to symbolize purity. In the center of the two raised beds are identical bird baths that create a formal look and provide water for the birds Saint Francis so dearly loved. You could also use statues of angels.

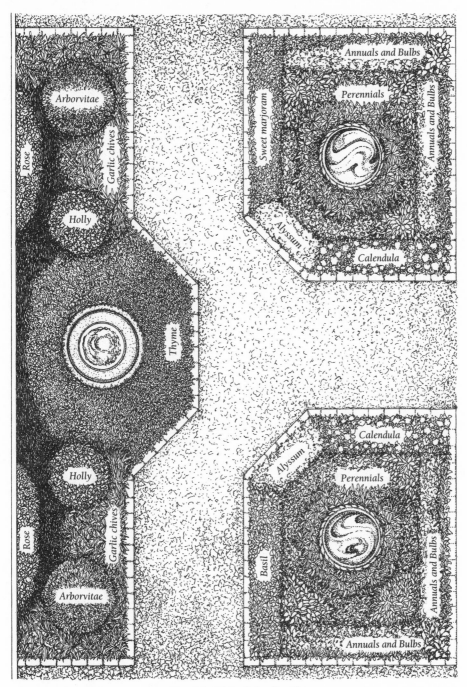

Fig. 4-2. Biblical Garden Plan

Biblical Garden Plant List

PERENNIALS

Bay leaf (*Laurus nobilis*)
Blue flax (*Linum perenne*)
Chamomile, Roman (*Anthemis nobile*)
Chives (*Allium schoenoprasum*)
Costmary (*Chrysanthemum balsamita*)
Herb Robert (*Geranium robertianum*)
Hyssop (*Hyssopus officinalis*)
Ladies' bedstraw (*Galium verum*)
Lady's mantle (*Alchemilla vulgaris*)
Lavender (*Lavendula*)
Lilies (*Lilium* sp.)
Lupine (*Lupinus* sp.)
Marguerite golden daisy (*Anthemis tinctoria*)

Michaelmas daisy (*Aster* sp.)
Peony (*Paeonia*)
Poppy (*Papaver*)
Purple loosestrife (*Lythrum salicaria*)
Rose (*Rosa* sp.)
Rosemary (*Rosmarinus officinalis*)
Rue (*Ruta graveolens*)
Sage (*Salvia* sp.)
Santolina
Shamrock (*Oxalis*)
Spearmint (*Mentha spicata*)
Sweet woodruff (*Asperula odorata*)
Tansy (*Tanacetum vulgare*)
Thyme (*Thymus* sp.)
Valerian (*Valeriana officinalis*)
Wormwood (*Artemisia absintium*)

ANNUALS

Adonis
Alyssum
Basil (*Ocimum basilicum*)
Calendula
Coriander (*Coriandrum sativus*)
Dill (*Anethum graveolens*)
Fennel (*Foeniculum vulgare*)

Johnny-jump-up (*Viola tricolor*)
Larkspur (*Delphinium*)
Leek (*Allium porrum*)
Love-in-a-mist (*Nigella*)
Sweet marjoram (*Marjorana hortense*)

BIENNIALS

Angelica (*Angelica archangelica*)
Hollyhock (*Alcea* sp.)

Parsley (*Petroselinum crispum*)
Sweet William (*Dianthus barbatus*)

BULBS

Crocus
Narcissus

Tulips (*Tulipa*)

SHRUBS

Cedar (*Cedrus*)
Holly (*Ilex*)

Juniper (*Juniperus* sp.)
Pine (*Pinus*)

The Monochromatic Garden Using a Silver-Gray Scheme

A monochromatic color scheme consists of using one basic color with all its tints (the lighter colors) and shades (the darker colors).

Purists will want only the theme color in this garden. However, some white or cream-colored flowers will help contrast and highlight certain flowers.

The following garden design uses silver and gray foliage for its scheme. The flowers will range from pink and yellow to white; in the case of the edelweiss, the flowers will be gray.

Two adjoining sides of the garden are redwood-stained fencing, providing a good contrast color for the background. A brick wall works equally as well. The garden can be planted at ground level, but a sense of depth can be created by raising the level of the back inner corner where the wormwood is planted. The free-form section of the garden can be raised up to 12 inches using wood or brick, with a bench placed next to it in the walkway flanked by two urns. A 4- to 5-foot brick pathway adds deep red contrast to the silver garden.

Silver-Gray Garden Plant List

The only annual in this garden is dusty miller (*Senecio cineraria*), both the delicate-leaved "silver dust" and coarse-leaved "cirrus" varieties.

PERENNIALS

"Beacon silver" lamium (*Lamium*)

Catnip mussinii (*Nepeta cataria mussinii*)

Clove pinks (*Dianthus caryophyllus*)

Edelweiss (*Leontopodium*)

Gnaphalium

Hens and chickens "cobweb" (*Sempervivum arachnoideum*)

Lamb's ear (*Stachys lanata*)

Mullein (biennial) (*Verbascum*)

Pearly everlasting (*Anaphalis margaritacea*)

Rose campion (biennial) (*Lychnis coronaria*)

Santolina, gray (*Santolina chamaecyparissus*)

Silver king (*Artemisia ludoviciana*)

Silver mound (*Artemisia schmidtiana*)

Summer snow (*Cerastium tomentosum*)

Woolly thyme (*Thymus lanuginosis*)

Woolly yarrow (*Achillea tomentosum*)

Wormwood (*Artemisia absinthium*)

Yucca

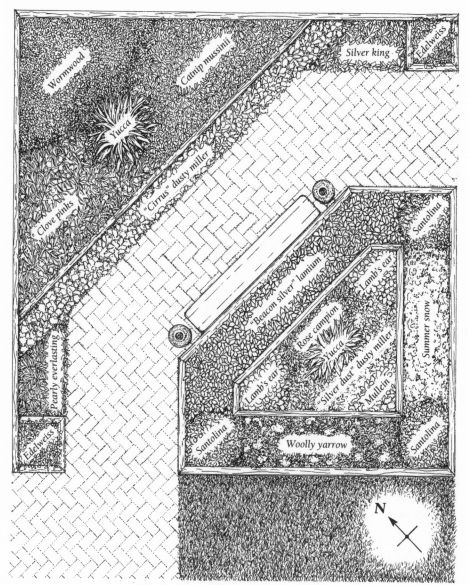

Fig. 4-3. Monochromatic Garden Plan

The Victorian Garden

The Victorian era introduced a new style of beautiful gardens and made many plants that once were the domain of the wealthy available to a broad spectrum of the population. Books on gardening were now being written for middle-class backyard gardeners. Jane Loudon, one of the first women garden writers, wrote several garden guides just for women. Together with her husband, John Claude Loudon, another famous garden author, she printed some of the first garden magazines.

Gardening was the rage of the Victorian era; everyone wanted more and more. Great glass houses called conservatories were built on the estates of the wealthy. The lawn mower was invented and came into general use in 1830, just in time to clip the great lawns of the Victorian era. Croquet and other lawn games, as well as extravagant tea parties, were held on these large lawn areas.

Perennial beds were shaped into fancy outlines like squares, circles, ovals, ribbons, and butterfly shapes. It was not uncommon to have gardens of ten acres or more; of course, hired help was readily available and less expensive than it is today.

Victorian gardens have several characteristics you can emulate. One large unbroken grassy space is necessary for lawn games and tea parties, as well as several areas for sitting to enjoy the vistas and views. Can't you just see those elegant ladies in their long dresses, elaborate hair styles, hats, and parasols? Wide graceful pathways were—and are—ideal for strolling arm-in-arm with a loved one. Summerhouses, tea houses, gazebos, fountains, water gardens, and a greenhouse should dot the landscape wherever possible.

Inside and out, every possible space should be filled with plants, from the living rooms to the gardens and patios and glass houses. And the more exotic the plants, the better. Plant imports were the rage of the day.

Focal points abound, characteristic of an era of opulence. Bee skeps, water fountains, bird baths, statues, and elaborate urns were used profusely. The mode was formal, but exaggeration was also "in." The Victorian motto might have been "the more and the bigger the better."

Designing the Victorian Garden

Over eight thousand new plants were introduced during the Victorian era, so there is no lack of variety in planning a Victorian garden. I have chosen a

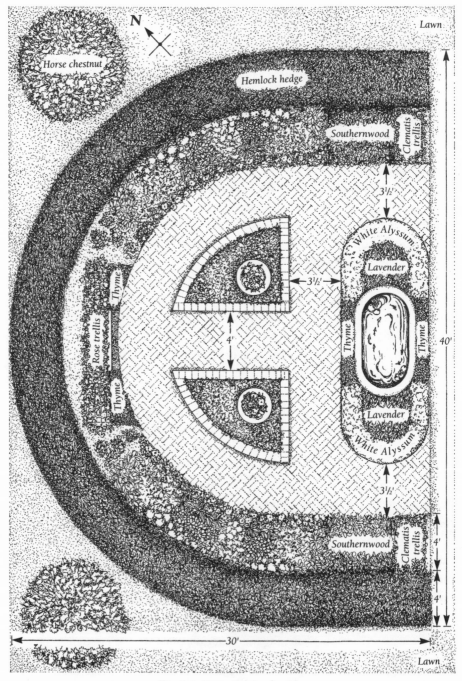

Fig. 4-4. Victorian Garden Plan

half-moon design with a bench on the arc side. It looks out over a large expanse of lawn.

A horse chestnut (*Aesculus*) stands tall on either side of the arc. The arc itself is formed by a hedge of hemlock kept neatly trimmed. Thyme (*Thymus*) is planted around the bench, with a large rose arbor for shade. Inside the arc are two identical raised beds, each with an urn of flowers in the center. At the two ends of the arc trellises are placed, covered by climbing clematis. At the opposite end of the garden from the bench is a bed surrounding a fish pond; a bed of all one kind of perennial could also be used. When planning a fish pond, remember fish need to be wintered over in zones 4 and below.

Victorian Garden Plant List

PERENNIALS

Astilbe

Baby's breath (*Gypsophila*)

Baptisia

Basket of gold (*Aurina saxatile*)

Bay leaf (*Laurus nobilis*)

Bellflower (*Campanula* sp.)

Bergenia

Blue flax (*Linum perenne*)

Chamomile, Roman (*Anthemis nobile*)

Clove pink (*Dianthus* sp.)

Columbine (*Aquilegia* sp.)

Coreopsis

Delphinium

Ferns (many species)

Forget-me-not (*Myosotis*)

Hens and chickens (*Sempervivum*)

Hostas (species)

Hyssop (*Hyssopus officinalis*)

Iris

Ivy (*Hedera*)

Lavender (*Lavendula officinalis*)

Lily (*Lilium*)

Lily of the valley (*Convallaria majalis*)

Meadowsweet (*Filipendula*)

Michaelmas daisy (*Aster* sp.)

Mints (*Mentha* sp.)

Muskmallow (*Malva moschata*)

Peony (*Paeonia*)

Poppy (*Papaver*)

Rose (*Rosa* sp.)

Rosemary (*Rosmarinus officinalis*)

Rue (*Ruta graveolens*)

Shasta daisy (*Chrysanthemum maximum*)

Southernwood (*Artemisia aboratum*)

Spiderwort (*Tradescantia virginiana*)

Stonecrops (*Sedum* sp.)

Sundrops (*Oenothera*)

Thyme (*Thymus* sp.)

Violets (*Viola* sp.)

Yarrow (*Achillea* sp.)

ANNUALS

Ageratum   Larkspur (*Delphinium* sp.)
Alyssum (*Lobularia maritima*)   Lobelia
Begonia   Love-in-a-mist (*Nigella damascena*)
Calendula   Pansy (*Viola* sp.)
Cornflower (*Centaurea*)   Petunia
Dusty miller (*Senecio cineraria*)   Verbena
Fuchsia   Wallflower (*Cheiranthus*)

BIENNIALS

Foxglove (*Digitalis purpurea*)   Mullein (*Verbascum* sp.)
Hollyhock (*Alcea rosea*)

BULBS

All species

VINES

Clematis   Honeysuckle (*Lonicera* sp.)
Grapes (*Vitis* sp.)   Roses (*Rosa* sp.)

The Medieval Theme Garden

The medieval era, or the Middle Ages, was a dark and dim time of destruction, invasions, and warfare. However, this period was not all bleak—it was also a period of political, religious, and economic growth. There was renewed interest in learning, and great universities began to emerge. Literacy spread from the monasteries to the nobility, and the acquisition of classical knowledge became a status symbol.

In Europe at this time, the great castles and cathedrals were being built. Some of our great literature comes from this era, including Chaucer's *Canterbury Tales* and Dante's *Divine Comedy*. Philosophy flowered in the late Middle Ages with Roger Bacon (1214–1294), his teacher Robert Grosseteste (1168–1253), and the great Thomas Aquinas (1224–1274).

Advances in agriculture produced a new heavy plow and harrow, making it possible to plow and plant more land. More workable land meant increased

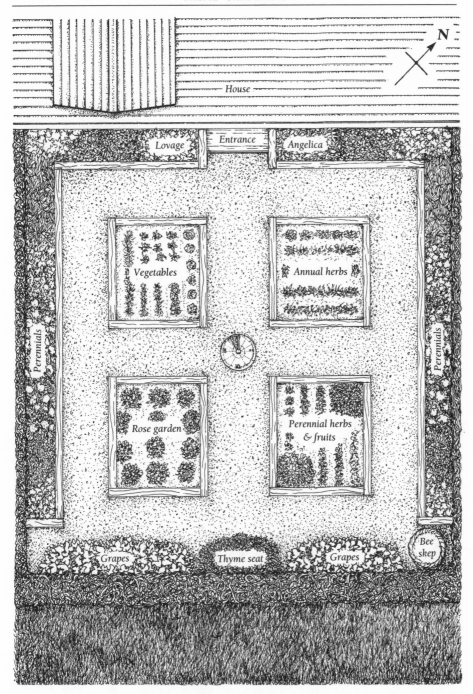

Fig. 4-5. Medieval Theme Garden Plan

income for the nobility and a more comfortable life for the serfs. The wheelbarrow was also invented during this time. As society developed, local warfare decreased and more energy was put into learning and building up instead of tearing down.

Little actual recorded garden history survived those dim times; what little information we have comes from the secluded monasteries, thanks to the record-keeping monks. As we design a medieval garden we should use our imaginations regarding what we think the Middle Ages were like.

Plants were of utilitarian varieties, grown for use in the kitchen and for medicinal purposes rather than for their beauty. But no matter how much we read of their usefulness, I am sure these flowers' beauty was enjoyed by men and women of earlier times just as we enjoy them today. Maybe they enjoyed them even more during the times of war and famine.

Roses were used to make sweet conserves, rosewater, rose vinegar, and rose honey. Rose petals would also be spread around on dirt and stone floors to take away damp musty smells. Remember, little sanitation was available during this period.

In the great feudal castles, protection from enemies was the biggest concern. Sometimes two moats surrounded the castle with the gardens between them. Other gardens were maintained at the back gate for convenience.

Most of us are not going to go to the expense of a moat, but wouldn't it be a different, fun thing to do! Our garden design will be placed at the back door and enclosed by a wall for privacy and protection—even though today's protection may only be from pumpkin-stealing children or corn-stealing raccoons.

During the Middle Ages brick, stone, or even mud and straw would be used for the wall. A wattle fence might be used by poorer people. Inside the enclosed area, smaller individual gardens were symmetrically laid out. A bee skep would be in a corner somewhere to attract bees and provide honey. Mead, a fermented drink made from honey, was popular during that era.

After dinner, the lady of the manor became a lady of leisure. She might stroll in the garden and spend time weaving garlands of roses, thyme, gilly-flowers or clove pinks (*Dianthus*), and lavender (*Lavendula*). A seat was provided, either of stone or a mound of dirt covered with thyme or chamomile, which released their scents as she sat upon it.

Designing the Medieval Garden

The following design is enclosed by a simple wattle fence, easily constructed by pounding young saplings into the ground and interweaving them with soft willow branches or other saplings—a simple, no-cost garden fence.

There is only one entrance, from the house. For practical purposes, you can build in a hidden gate for outside access. Focal points can include the bee skep, a sundial, or a unicorn statue to signify the folklore of that period. The rectangular gardens are raised beds, made from wood or stone.

The lawnmower had not been invented yet, so lawns would be cut by scythe or left to grow into a flowery mead. Around the gardens I have used gravel paths planted here and there with thymes and chamomiles. The vegetables and annual plants are separated into different rectangles. Perennials outline the entire border, and the south wall is covered with grape vines.

Medieval people preferred meat to lowly vegetables, with the exception of garlic, leeks, and onions, which they used to cook and flavor meat dishes.

If you are a purist, keep in mind that vegetables such as tomatoes, corn, squash, and green peppers are New World plants and were unknown in medieval Europe.

The Medieval Plant List

In addition to these plants, include vegetables and annual herbs of your choice.

PERENNIALS

Alpine strawberry (*Fragaria*)

Ajuga

Blue flax (*Linum perenne*)

Chamomile, Roman (*Anthemis nobile*)

Catnip mussinii (*Nepeta cataria "mussinii"*)

Clove pinks (gillyflowers) (*Dianthus caryphyllus*)

Costmary (*Chrysanthemum balsamita*)

Cranesbill geraniums (*Geranium* sp.)

Feverfew (*Chrysanthemum parthenium*)

Garlic (*Allium sativum*)

Gill over the ground (*Hedera*)

Herb Robert (*Geranium robertianum*)

Hyssop (*Hyssopus officinalis*)

Iris

Lavender (*Lavendula officinalis*)

Lily (*Lilium* sp.)

Lovage (*Levisticum officinalis*)
Lupines (*Lupinus* sp.)
Maltese cross (*Lychnis chalcedonica*)
Mints (*Mentha* sp.)
Muskmallow (*Malva moschata*)
Onion (*Allium cepa*)
Poppy (*Papaver*)
Primroses (*Primula* sp.)
Rosemary (*Rosemarinus officinalis*)
Sage (*Salvia* sp.)

Southernwood (*Artemisia abrotanum*)
Speedwell (*Veronica* sp.)
Tansy (*Tanacetum vulgare*)
Trollius
Vervain (*Verbena officinalis*)
Violets (*Viola* sp.)
Wormwood (*Artemisia absinthium*)
Yarrow (*Achillea* sp.)

BIENNIALS
Angelica (*Angelica archangelica*)
Foxglove (*Digitalis purpurea*)

Hollyhocks (*Alcea rosa*)

A Naturalistic Wildflower Garden

We all know the importance of working with nature in order to save the environment. As the world population multiplies out of control and people move into wild areas, clearing away the habitat of our wild animals and destroying yet another patch of wildflowers, we as backyard gardeners must do all we can to provide a space for wild plants and food for wild animals. Every small bit does help.

The Garden Design

This garden is bordered on the southeast side by the house and a rock wall (see Fig. 4-6). The northwest side is bound by a group of evergreen trees. If you do not have trees, it is simple enough to plant the area with the largest trees you can afford. The southwest side can be bordered by either a strip of trees or a fence covered with hop vine (*Humulus lupulus*) or Virginia creeper (*Parthenocissus quinquefolia*). The wooded area could contain a brush pile where rabbits can raise their young and a decaying old log for squirrels and chipmunks (if you don't have a decaying log, find a wooded area and bring one home—with permission from the owner, of course). A picnic table on the edge of the wooded area will give you a place to watch and observe.

The open areas can combine all your favorite wildflowers. I would till the entire area up and plant and seed the flowers I want the first year. A yearly cutting in very late fall will turn the old material into a mulch and enrich the soil. Some weeding may be necessary to keep very invasive weeds from taking over.

This garden is not for neatniks. Weeds and volunteer wildflowers should be welcome. Mother Nature will contribute her own favorites for you. As much as possible, utilize what is already there. If you are not familiar with the native plants of your area, check with your local Audubon Society or extension office. There are several good sources and catalogs to buy wildflower seed. If you want to learn more about wildflowers, join a wildflower society (see appendix for addresses).

You can even be certified as an Official Backyard Wildlife Habitat. For information write to:

National Wildlife Federation
Backyard Wildlife Habitat Program
1412 16th Street N.W.
Washington, DC 20036-2266

I do not condone any digging up of wildflowers, unless the area is going to be devastated by building or roadways. In these cases it is even a good idea to locate these areas and try to save some of the plants that would otherwise be lost forever. Collecting wild seeds or plentiful wildflowers can be fun and advisable, but do not take all the seeds or any seeds from rare plants.

The materials used in your wildflower garden will be wood or rock or other natural products. The open area will have a path made by the lawnmower, two sweeps wide. The wooded area will have paths of pine needles. The features listed below are letter-coded to Figure 4-6.

A raised wooden bed (A) near the deck planted with beebalm (*Monarda didyma*) is an important food source for butterflies and hummingbirds, but does best if weeded periodically. Along the edge of the rock wall, a line of blueberry bushes (B) provides berries for both animals and humans. Their colorful red leaves in the fall are attractive in any garden.

Area C is planted with wildflowers to attract butterflies. The north end includes a row of elderberry (*Sambucus canadensis*) bushes. This area should have a small spot for decaying fruit or perhaps an indentation filled with manure

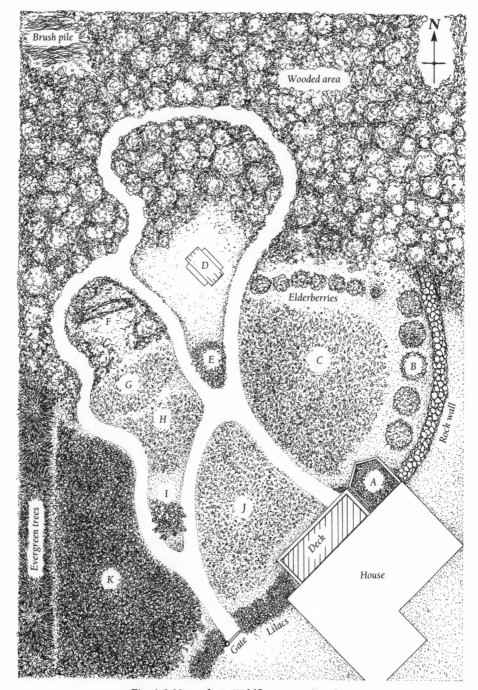

Fig. 4-6. Naturalistic Wildflower Garden Plan

and kept moist. Butterflies will love it—isn't it strange that such a beautiful insect can love such garbage.

The picnic area (D) is set snugly into the edge of the wooded area for us humans to sit, observe, and enjoy the garden and its inhabitants. Baptisia as a herbaceous shrub (E) marks the intersection of the walkway. The decaying log (F) in the wooded area can be a focal point as well as a home for small animals and insects. Mother Nature will probably provide some covering, but this would be a good place to plant small hostas or ferns. And how about a small ceramic elf?

In wildflower beds G and H, plant the taller flowers in the center and graduate down to lower plants for the edging. If you wanted a more formal look, the pathways could be edged with ferns or hostas, but keep in mind that that is not what Mother Nature would do. A mulberry tree (I) provides food for the birds. A small cherry or plum tree would do as well.

Plant a hummingbird garden (J) where you can observe these little beauties from the house and deck (see following list). Area K is the wildest spot in the garden. It will need to be cut back about every three to four years. Blackberry bushes, raspberry bushes, wild roses, teasel (*Dipsacus sylvestris*), bull thistle (*Cirsium vulgare*), and any other wild thistles that grow in your area will thrive here. One of my favorite birds, the little yellow American goldfinch, loves this wild area.

SHADE-LOVING WILDFLOWERS

Baneberry (poisonous) (*Actaea rubra*)
Bloodroot (*Sanguinara canadensis*)
Dutchman's breeches (*Dicentra cucullaria*)
Ferns
Foamflower (*Tiarella cordifolia*)
Goatsbeard (*Aruncus dioicus*)
Jack in the pulpit (*Arisaema triphyllum*)

May apple (*Podophyllium peltatum*)
Solomon's seal (*Polygonatum*)
Snakeroot (*Cimicifuga racemosa*)
Trilliums
Trollius (*Trollius laxus*)
Virginia bluebells (*Mertensia virginica*)
Wild ginger (*Asarum canadense*)

SUN-LOVING WILDFLOWERS

Alfalfa (*Medicago sativa*)
Allheal (*Prunella vulgaris*)
Black-eyed Susan (*Rudbeckia*)
Blue baptisia (*Baptisia tinctoria*)
Buttercup (*Ranunculus*)
Butterflyweed (*Asclepias tuberosa*)
Chicory (*Cichorium intybus*)
Coltsfoot (*Tussilago farfara*)
Columbine (*Aquilegia* sp.)
Coreopsis (*Coreopsis lanceolata*)
Daylilies (*Lilium* sp.)
Elecampane (*Inula helenium*)
Goldenrod (*Solidago* sp.)
Joe-Pye weed (*Eupatorium purpureum*)
Liatris (*Liatris spicata*)

Lupine (*Lupinus*)
Mullein (*Verbascum thapsus*)
Muskmallow (*Malava moschata*)
Purple coneflower (*Echinacea purpurea*)
Purple loosestrife (*Lythrum salicaria*)
Queen Anne's lace (*Daucus carota*)
Queen of the meadow (*Filipendula ruba*)
Stinging nettle (*Urtica dioica*)
St. Johnswort (*Hypericum* sp.)
Tansy (*Tanacetum vulgare*)
Teasel (*Dipsacus sylvestris*)
Valerian (*Valerian officinalis*)
Violets (*Violas*)

PLANTS TO ATTRACT BUTTERFLIES

Baptisia (*Baptisia tinctoria*)
Beebalm (*Monarda didyma*)
Blueberry bushes (*Vaccinium*)
Butterflyweed (*Asclepias tuberosa*)
Chives (*Allium schoenoprasum*)
Coreopsis (*Coreopsis* sp.)
Daylilies (*Lilium* sp.)
Gasplant (*Dictamnus fraxinella*)
Loosestrife (*Lythrum salicaria*)
Lupine (*Lupinus*)
Mallows (*Malva* sp.)

Milkweed (*Asclepias syriaca*)
New England aster (*Aster novae-angliae*)
Pearly everlasting (*Anaphalis margaritacea*)
Purple coneflower (*Echinacea purpurea*)
Queen Anne's lace (*Daucus carota*)
Stinging nettle (*Urtica dioica*)
Turtlehead (*Chelone glabra*)
Violets (*Viola* sp.)

CHAPTER FIVE

The Light Factor

*In its chosen haunts of moist hollows and shaded hill sides
you find the feathery fonds tremulous on their black, glistening stalks,
and in their neighborhood find also the very spirit of the woods.*
—Frances Parson (1899)

Alongside soil and moisture preferences, light is a very important consideration when planning for the health and happiness of your perennial plants. Light is an absolute necessity to the life of any plant. Photosynthesis is the process by which the sunlight enables a plant's leaves to manufacture the carbohydrates that form the plant's energy supply, using inorganic materials of carbon dioxide, oxygen, and water. Without light photosynthesis cannot take place, and the plant dies.

The amount of light a plant requires varies according to the individual species. Because of light differences, Mother Nature has provided us with a large selection of different kinds of plants to choose from. Find the right plant for your own particular light factors, and you will have success in growing plants. Placing a sun-loving plant in the shade will not enable it to photosynthesize the proper amount of energy to thrive. On the other hand, a shade-loving plant placed in a full-sun area will eventually die, its leaves scorched as it slowly withers away from too much light. The sun-loving basket of gold (*Aurinia saxatilis*), the white shasta daisy (*Chrysanthemum maximum*), and the woolly yarrow (*Achillea tomentosa*) will lift their heads to welcome the warmth and bright sunlight that provides for these plants' needs. In contrast, shade-loving plants like lungwort (*Pulmonaria*), the ferns, and hostas need their leaves protected from that same amount of sunlight. They prefer cool shady areas and will thrive in lower light situations.

What is important in planning your light factor areas is to choose the right plant for the right place. Plant your perennials in the proper degree of light for that particular species of perennial. Each plant profile in part 2 of this book suggests what that light requirement is.

Another factor affecting light tolerance is the soil's ability to retain or drain moisture for the plant. Very often plants tolerate more or less light than is recommended because of the moisture content of your soil. Several species of hostas and ferns will tolerate full sun if given rich moist soil and supplied with water when necessary. Sun-loving plants will usually tolerate more shade than is recommended if they are given the good drainage they need. Giving sun lovers some shade often produces fewer flowers, but their color is deeper and they last longer.

As we discuss the light factor and degrees of light, we need a common guide to follow. The following list can serve as a guide to what I mean when I say sun, shade, etc.

Degrees of Light

Full sun: Plants in this category should be in sunlight all day long. All full-sun perennials will need a minimum of six to eight hours of sunlight.

Partial shade: A wide selection of perennials prefer some shade. These plants should receive a minimum of four to six hours of sun, with the remaining daytime in some kind of shade.

Filtered shade: Light under these conditions is filtered through tree foliage. As the sun circles overhead, various patterns of sunlight and shade filter through the leaves of the trees onto the plants below. Under deciduous trees is a good place to plant spring flowers, which can receive more sun before the trees' leaves develop. It is especially good for leopard's-bane (*Doronicum*) and bulbs that lose their own foliage after flowering.

Full shade: The word "full" is deceiving because it suggests the absence of light. With the exception of lichens, fungi, and mosses, very few plants grow in the absence of light. So for gardening purposes, full shade is considered bright light that may or may not have some filtered shade or patches of sunlight. The plants should receive no more than two hours of direct sunlight, if any direct sunlight at all.

Dense shade areas: There are areas on our land spaces that do not have enough light to support *any* plant life, such as a space between two buildings.

Actually, these areas can be fun to decorate—with the help of a vivid imagination. An example might be to cover the area with white rocks, adding a large moss-covered rock or a log that is covered with lichen, moss, or fungi. This area could be turned into a mini-Japanese garden with raked sand and some sort of sculpture as a focal point. An outdoor light could be used to light this area, turning it into an area art form.

Determining Your Own Light Factors

In order to place the plants in the correct amount of light, we first need to know how the sun and shade patterns change over our land space. If you do the initial garden planning in the winter, keep in mind that the sun patterns in the summer, when everything is growing, will be slightly different. The sun is lower in the sky in the winter, and certain sunny areas will be shaded by leafy trees in the summer.

As with most of Mother Nature's plans, her way is the best. The shortest day comes on December 22, the winter solstice, when it is cold and we are busy with the holidays. On June 22, the summer solstice, she provides the longest-light day, just in time for our growing gardens. On both of the solstice days the moon has no apparent motion and is changing to provide us with more or less light.

When you did your land space inventory you checked the light patterns in the garden at four different times of the day. This should give you a good idea of how the sun and shade play out their light drama during a typical sunlit day. You can then evaluate the degrees of light for different areas of your land space.

It is a good idea to take notes on the light factor changes around your land space. This will help you during your winter garden designing or remodeling plans. A notebook can also keep garden records of frost dates, bloom time, and special plants and their cultivation to further help you in planning your garden.

Light Influences

The sun-and-shade patterns of your land space also depend on how the house and other buildings are placed in relationship to the sun. Most of us prefer our gardens placed where they get the eastern morning sun. This helps to dry off night dew and moisture from the plants. The southern side of buildings, especially against foundations, are very hot areas. Plants on the south side appear earlier in spring but may require more frequent watering. The west side often has the hottest sun during the summer months. The north side is usually cooler and plants there are slower to grow in the spring. I have tulips on the north side of my house that bloom two weeks later than those on the south side.

How far your home is located from the equator will influence the brightness of the sun. The closer you are to the equator, the more intense the sunlight. Windy areas will also affect plant growth. Sun-loving plants will appreciate some shade if the wind is very strong and dries out the plants too quickly.

Adding Shade Where There Is None

One complaint I had with Wormwood Farm was its lack of trees. The farm was a dairy before we bought it; its priorities were hay fields and pastures, not shady areas. Since we purchased the farm we have been planting trees for privacy as well as shade—for plants and us—on hot Maine summer days.

However, trees are often slow to produce the shade we want now. Until the ideal situation is achieved, a simple lath frame or trellis can provide shade for shade plants as well as a nice place for people to sit and enjoy a cool spot in the garden. Climbing vines like clematis, ivy (*Hedera*), and grapevines (*Vitis*) will add more shade and beauty for the lath house. With trellis material and a few two-by-fours, a handyperson can erect a lath house in a few hours. Buildings also provide some shade, and fences can be used to create a shady area.

Getting More Light in a Shady Area

Then we have the areas that receive too much shade from trees to plant a wildflower garden. Why is it we always want what we don't have? To open these areas up to the sun, some trees may need to be eliminated. But first try trimming a little here and there. Start with pruning the lower branches and dead limbs.

PHOTO BY BRANDAU/HALL

A lath frame or trellis can provide support for vines and shade for plants.

Evergreens trimmed up two feet from the ground provide a nice area for wildflowers, bulb plants, and low ground covers like sweet woodruff (*Asperula odorata*) and ajuga. Evergreens are usually deep-rooted, so there is no competition for the surface water.

Deciduous trees can have limbs pruned out from the entire tree. If you are a klutz like me, hire a professional tree expert to trim the trees for you, avoiding the possibility of your own broken limbs (pun intended). Pruning and trimming your trees and shrubs not only makes them look better and adds more light, but is actually beneficial to them.

If your shade comes from buildings and fences and you need more light, try painting the fence or building with white paint to reflect light.

I know people who have tried placing aluminum foil behind and under plants to achieve more light. It gives more reflected light, but also confuses insects; it seems they can't tell what is up and what is down. I find that method too expensive, unattractive, and bad for the environment.

Gardening with Shade Plants

Shade alters the air and soil temperature and often increases the humidity in an area. Can you think of a nicer place to be weeding a garden on a hot summer day than under a shady tree? Somehow these shady areas always get the best weeding job.

Different species of trees will produce different degrees of light. The soil under the tree may also be different. Maple and elm are shallow-rooted trees that rob other plants of water and nutrients. These are some of the most difficult trees to plant beneath. I tried several different species under a huge maple in my front yard until finally thyme (*Thymus* sp.) and hens and chickens (*Sempervivum*) took hold and increased, defying the tree's greediness.

One way to deal with shallow-rooted trees is to put bark mulch or crushed stone around its trunk to a distance of about six feet. Then plant your garden around this circle. Keep in mind that plants under a heavily leaved tree may need extra watering. Another solution is to build a wooden raised bed six feet out from the trunk, which can provide both space for plants and a comfortable seat for weeding. Remember that in zones 3 and 4 some plants in containers might need winter protection.

Planting under conifers or evergreens is a little easier. Limbs trimmed a little way up the trunk will provide more light. Bulbs planted under evergreens are pretty in the spring, and the foliage can die back without any interference.

Night Lighting

In recent years the home gardener has been able to choose several inexpensive means of lighting the garden for night use. Floodlights can accent a particular plant or area. Small fixtures mark pathways. There is even solar lighting to help save on the electricity bill. People who work during the day appreciate night lighting because it gives them time to work in the garden after dark. And by using lighting, you can make your garden a focal point and work of art in the evening, enjoyed from the patio or living-room window.

Warning: Before you venture into lighting your garden, check with local inspectors to learn the rules and regulations of outdoor lighting. Every precaution should be taken for safety. Use only recommended wiring and lighting fixtures.

Night lighting will naturally attract insects. I can't recommend those blue-light zappers because they kill both good and bad bugs. But do keep in mind that blue attracts bugs; use yellow bulbs that have had the blue spectrum removed.

How you place the lighting will affect how you see the flowers; one large, powerful light is too bold. A series of smaller low-watt lights will add more drama to the garden.

Plants that show off their best qualities at night are those with white or yellow flowers. Red colors become subdued at night, white and yellow become luminous, and gray becomes dominant. A lighted pathway edged with silver mound (*Artemisia schmiditiana*) or gray santolina (*Santolina chamaecyparissus*) will be quite dramatic.

Before you place your lights, play around with them to see where they will work best. Create silhouettes and shadows against the backgrounds of fences and houses to make the garden appear larger. Do you want to spotlight certain plants, or do they look more interesting with the light placed behind them to silhouette their texture?

Certain flowers produce their scent at night as the natural light fades and the warmth of the daylight encourages them to release their scent. If you enjoy the nighttime garden, you will want to consider adding these plants. The annual flowering tobacco (*Nicotiana sylvestris*) is one of my very favorite night-time scented plants. Perennial carnations (*Dianthus* sp.), hyacinths, evening primrose (*Oenothera biennis*), evening campion (*Lychnis alba*), phlox (*Phlox maculata, Phlox paniculata*) and the daylily species *Hemerocallis flava* are all good choices.

CHAPTER SIX

Preparing the Soil

If Eve had a spade in Paradise and knew what to do with it,
we should not have had all that sad business about the apple.
—*Elizabeth and Her German Garden* (1901)

The soil is where the actual planting takes place, where your plants will spend their entire life. Therefore, finding the right place for the right plant will ensure success in your backyard perennial gardening.

If you plant a moisture-loving *Astilbe* in a lean, arid soil it will soon shrivel up and die. However, plant that *Astilbe* in the rich moist soil it prefers and it will flourish for many years, producing beautiful plumelike flowers. On the other hand, an arid soil-loving *Armeria* would quickly rot away in the same rich moist soil that the astilbe loves. Properly placed in a lean, arid soil in full sun, however, the armeria will produce pretty globe-shaped white, pink, and rose flowers throughout June and off and on during the rest of the season. This chapter furnishes the necessary information for preparing your particular soil type for gardening success.

Soil is a living, breathing, porous structure. It contains air for plants' roots to breathe and the food and water that supply necessary nutrients. In return plants hold the soil together, keeping it from blowing away in the wind or washing away during heavy rainstorms. Soil is full of living organisms, from microscopic bacteria to easy-to-see earthworms, mice, and moles, all providing necessary interaction in Mother Nature's wonderful world.

Knowing your soil's pH and texture will give you the necessary information to make good choices on where to place your perennial plants for successful gardening.

During some of my workshops I hear horror stories about bad soil conditions. A person may buy a new house, dig a few inches into the soil, and find all sorts of junk used as "fill." New housing developments especially are filled in with anything from broken glass and insulation to baby car seats.

If you are having a new home built, check out the soil area and tell the contractor you want good loam for gardening; then oversee the project to make sure it is done the way you want it done. Buying loam to make a garden can become very expensive.

When buying homes already built, tell the real estate agent you want garden areas. We often joke that we bought the land and they threw in the old broken-down farmhouse as a bonus.

Soil Assessment

I remember how my grandfather Prosser, standing in a newly plowed field, would scoop up a handful of soil and squeeze it in his hand, bringing it to his nose and smelling the earth. Then he would open his hand and let the soil crumble to the ground. If it was loose and didn't make a ball, it was sandy soil. If it was a hard-packed ball he would say "potters clay," knowing it would be difficult to work with. But if the soil made a firm ball and slowly crumbled, he knew it was good, workable loam. This is a good basic way to test your soil, but do not do it during a dry spell or right after a rain storm.

Most of us today do not have the natural feel for the earth that the old farmers developed after years of living and working with the soil. We depend on modern technology to tell us exactly what our soil is all about. A number of tests are available that can tell you your soil's mineral content, as well as what is needed to improve its growing ability. There are home test kits available for the hobby gardener, or you can have a professional test done. Your state agricultural extension will do the test for a small fee, and there are private professional testing companies that are more expensive.

What you find growing on your land will often offer clues to what the soil is like. When we were thinking about buying this farm we saw burdock, pigweed, and purslane growing in the fields, a sign of good fertility. When you see pine, hemlock, or oak growing with daisies and hawkweed, the soil is probably acidic, as much of the New England soil tends to be. Acid rain is increasing that acidity every year. If maple, cedar, Queen Anne's lace, and alfalfa predominate in the fields, then the soil probably is alkaline.

The pH Scale Defined

The pH is the amount of potential hydrogen present in the soil. A pH test determines exactly what amount of potential hydrogen is present in the soil, indicating how acid or alkaline the soil is. This test will help you decide just what plants will best grow in a particular area.

The pH scale is read on a scale of 0 to 14; 7 is considered neutral, with everything below it on the acid side and everything above it on the alkaline side. Very little plant life grows in soil with a pH below 4 or above 8.

ACID ——————— ALKALINE
0 ————7———— 14

With gardening, we are working in a small margin of pH 5.5 to 7.5. But this scale is not as straightforward as it seems. The numbers from 1 to 14 do not represent mathematical graduations; each number actually represents ten times the preceding number.

For example, a pH of 6.0 has ten times less potential hydrogen, and is therefore acid, than the neutral pH of 7.0. A soil test of 6.0 is twice as acid as a soil test of 6.2, or the soil test of 6.2 is twice as alkaline as the soil test of 6.0.

Changing Your Soil's pH

But luckily we don't have to live with what we have for soil; it can be improved and changed. Of course if you want the easy way out, just plant perennials that want the type of pH your soil provides—plants like azaleas, sweet woodruff (*Asperula odorata*), and marigolds are happy in acid soil. In alkaline soil peonies (*Paeonia*) and poppies (*Papaver*) will be delighted.

But what if you want alkaline plants in your acid soil? To change your acid soil to alkaline you would add alkaline produces like lime, wood ashes, and bonemeal. On a 500-square-foot area you would generally add 15 to 20 pounds of lime. If your soil is sandy you would need more, because nutrients leach out of sandy soil quickly. Less lime will be needed on heavy clay soil because the clay holds onto its nutrients. Lime also helps break up hard clay particles, improving the structure of the soil.

To make alkaline soil more acid, you would add acidic materials like calcium sulfate, peat moss, and shredded oak leaves. I do not recommend aluminum sulphate because aluminum build-up in the soil is considered potentially carcinogenic.

Soil Texture

Soil texture may be different in different parts of your own land space. At Wormwood Farm we have just about all varieties of soil. In the back field there is a sandy gravel pit that provides us with sand for cement work and the kids' sandbox. The gravelly sand helps to loosen clay areas and fill in low areas. Out back by our man-made farm pond are some heavy, moist clay areas. Rather than try to alter this area, I have planted moist clay-loving perennials like Joe-Pye weed (*Eupatorium purpureum*), mallows (*Malva*), beebalm (*Monarda didyma*), and yellow pseudocarus iris.

In the greenhouse and garden area the soil is rich loam. This is the area where the old barn stood and the old manure pile was located. When we moved here, a 15-foot pile of well-aged, composted manure stood waiting for me to distribute it to my planned garden areas. I called it my black gold; it was so well composted it smelled sweet, nothing like its original smelly state.

As I mentioned earlier, there are three basic soil structures we need to concern ourselves with in backyard gardening: sandy soil, clay soil, and loam.

Sandy soil warms quickly in the spring, stimulating earlier plant growth and allowing us to sow seeds and set plants a little earlier. Its weakness is that it is so porous it leaches away important nutrients and water the plants need. Good drainage is important to some plants, so again, even this characteristic can be beneficial. If we know our soil and what our plants like, we can put the right plant in its proper soil environment.

The structure of sandy soil can be improved by adding all the organic material you can. Peat moss, compost, manures, and grass clippings will all add more structure to the soil. When placing your plants in sandy soil, plant them deeper than you would in loam or clay soil types.

Clay soil takes longer to warm up in the spring. It prevents over-eager gardeners from planting too early and losing their plants to a late frost. Because clay soil is heavy, it holds the nutrients and water longer than sandy soil. However, it also may have poor drainage. Clay soil can be loosened up by adding a large amount of peat moss, compost, and stony gravel. Do not use fine sandy gravel; that only packs in and increases the cementlike quality of the soil. Periods of drought make clay soil very hard. Clay soils should be hand-watered when Mother Nature does not provide sufficient water to keep the soil soft.

Loam is the ideal soil we all strive to have in our gardens. Sandy and clay soils can become good loam with the addition of organic materials.

Loam has a medium texture that drains well yet holds sufficient amounts of water and nutrients to feed the plants. But just because you start with good loam does not mean you can just garden without adding more organic matter. Remember, plants use up nutrients as they grow. Therefore the soil always needs to have more organic matter added.

Improving Your Soil

Basically, plants need the same nutrients and minerals that we require for good health. The three most important plant nutrients are nitrogen (N), phosphorus (P), and potassium (or potash) (K). On purchased chemical fertilizers the nutrient content code is listed, with three numbers representing the three nutrients, always in this order: N-P-K. For example, 5-10-10 means the mixture contains 5 percent nitrogen, 10 percent phosphorus, and 10 percent potassium.

For perennial flowers use a mixture with low nitrogen and a higher phosphorus and potassium content.

When using totally organic materials there are no numbers for us to use. I have found that when I add as many different organic materials as I can that nature takes care of the nutrients in the soil. An occasional soil test will tell you if your soil lacks any of the important nutrients.

Nitrogen builds good leaf structure. When growing foliage plants we want more nitrogen, but with flowers we want less because we are more interested in flower production than leaf production. If our plants are not receiving sufficient amounts of nitrogen they will become spindly, with elongated stems and yellowish leaves. Natural sources of nitrogen include composted manures, cottonseed meal, and bloodmeal.

Without the necessary amount of *phosphorus* in the soil, your perennials will grow slowly and contain some reddish-purple coloring in the leaves. (Know your plants; some perennials such as anise-hyssop [*Agastache foeniculum*] and sundrops [*Oenothera*] have natural purplish coloring when very young.) Phosphorus needs to be added to the soil on a yearly basis to help produce a strong root stalk and stem system and to increase the flower production. Natural sources of organic phosphorus are rock phosphate, bloodmeal, and bonemeal.

Plants that are low in *potassium*, also called *potash*, are slow growers and have yellowish leaves with curled brown spots on the end that look like the plants have been sunburned. For a long time it was not really known why potassium was necessary, only that it was. Scientists now believe that potassium helps to protect plants from extremes of hot and cold weather and aids in disease resistance. Natural sources of potassium include muriate of potash, greensand, granite dust, seaweed, and wood ashes.

Other minor minerals will be present in the soil where sufficient organic materials are used. They include calcium, iron, boron, and manganese. Again, a soil test will tell you what you have and what you need to add.

Soil Builders for Your Garden

Bonemeal: This nutrient decomposes slowly as it releases its nutrients into your soil. Sprinkle around the base of plants, digging lightly into the soil. Add bonemeal to peat moss and other acidic materials to counteract their acidity. I have been told of dogs digging bonemeal up in the garden but have not had that problem myself.

Compost: Every serious gardener needs a compost pile. Because it is a combination of several different organic materials, compost contributes a wide range of nutrients to the soil. Apply all you possibly can. See the section in this chapter on how to make compost.

Cottonseed Meal: Because of its low pH factor, cottonseed meal is ideal for acid-loving plants. It is also high in nitrogen and phosphorus. Work it directly into the soil.

Dried Blood: Sprinkle around plants, digging it into the soil, or add to water when watering. It does not smell very pleasant, but it's a good source of nitrogen and trace minerals. Add sparingly to perennials. Dried blood will also repel deer for a short period of time.

Grass Clippings: Add to the compost pile or use as a mulch for your perennials. Keep this a few inches away from the plants' stems or it will rot them as it decomposes.

Greensand and Granite Dust: Both of these are good sources of potassium. Work directly into the soil or top dress, avoiding the stems to prevent stem damage.

Manures: If you are lucky enough to have access to barnyard manures you can make wonderful compost. My best compost was made when I was raising chickens. You could feel the warmth it generated as it composted, and it smelled very sweet. I think using manures helps other organic materials compost a little faster. Do not use fresh manures directly on plants. The one exception is rabbit droppings, which can be worked directly into the soil. It is worth the trouble of raising a few bunnies just for their droppings. If there is a rabbitry in your area you can probably get the manure free by helping clean out the cages.

Don't overlook race tracks and zoos as manure sources. On a recent television show I saw a new product for gardeners called "Zoo Goo™." Aren't marketing gimmicks and human ingenuity astonishing?

If you have no fresh source of manure, it is available in dried form from garden centers. The dried form can be dug directly into the soil.

Peat Moss: This consists of partially decomposed plants from bogs and swamps. Peat moss does not contain any nutrients, but serves to improve the soil's aeration. It also improves drainage for clay soil and helps to hold moisture in sandy soil. You can never add too much peat moss. Since it is on the acid side you may need to add lime, wood ashes, or bonemeal to increase the soil's alkalinity. Peat moss is a water robber; when adding it to the soil, soak it in water first so it absorbs all the water it can. Do not use it as a mulch because it will prevent water from getting to the plants' roots where it is needed.

Phosphate Rock: Not only is this one of the best sources of phosphates, it also includes several trace minerals. Apply directly to the soil, digging it in.

Pine Needles: Don't be afraid to add plenty of pine needles to your soil. They were once thought to be acid, but garden experts now say they are not. Add to the garden or compost pile. Used as a mulch they break down slowly, helping to aerate the soil. They also make a nice pathway material for woodland garden paths.

Sawdust: Use only well-composted sawdust, whether you add it to your compost pile or let it compost on its own. You may need to accompany it with a boost of nitrogen because it robs the soil of nitrogen as it breaks down and composts. Lime may also be needed to counteract the sawdust's acidity.

Seaweed: Those of us who live near the seashore can gather seaweed for our gardens. It is high in potassium and trace minerals. I hose mine down with water or let the rain leach away salts before adding it to the compost pile or the soil. Once dried it can be pulverized easily.

Sludge: This by-product of sewage waste is on the acid side. I cannot in good faith recommend using sludge. I feel it is not a safe product—I do not believe all the chemicals have been sufficiently processed out. I would have to see more information and testing before I would even try it.

Wood Ash: Since we partially heat by wood stoves, I have a good supply of available wood ash. Apply it directly to the soil or use in the compost pile. Adding it in the spring acts as a dust mulch, discouraging those nasty little slugs. Ashes will add alkalinity to the soil. Be sure the wood ashes are cold before adding them to the soil or you may start a fire.

Wood Chips: These are more often used as a mulch because of their beauty. They can be dug into the soil to help aerate it or used in the compost pile. They may be on the acid side, depending on the species used.

Applying Fertilizers and Soil Builders

These materials can be added to your garden by several methods.

1. They can be tilled directly into the soil when making a new bed.
2. A yearly side dressing of fertilizer can be added as a booster during the growing season. The best time is probably just as the plants are coming into bloom. Place around the base of the plants, keeping it at least 2 inches away from the stems. Placing any fertilizers or mulches too close to the stems may cause them to rot.
3. Apply fertilizer as a liquid solution. You can make this by placing fresh or dried manure in a pail of water and letting it steep for several days. Then use it to water around the plants.
4. There are connections to use on the end of your garden hose that mix in commercial fertilizer as you water. For best results try not to water on the plants, but under them and on the ground.

5. You can add fertilizers and soil builders directly to the compost you will be using around your plants. This saves time by applying the soil builders and compost all at once. Add all the compost or peat moss you have available at any time. Both of these products add energy and texture to all soils.

Keep in mind that soil builders and fertilizers are necessary to keep the soil in good gardening shape. Plants use up nutrients for their growing needs. Each plant will have different needs from other plants. For example, a lavender prefers her soil slightly on the lean side, whereas peonies are heavy feeders and need yearly fertilizing.

Making Compost

Entire books and magazines are devoted to the process of making compost—it seems to be the "in" thing to do today. Not only is composting good for the garden, it also is very good for the environment. We gardeners can keep a lot of waste out of our landfills by returning it to nature in the form of compost.

Being a country gal, I keep my compost pile simple and easy for me to work. It's just a heap at the end of the vegetable garden, made of everything I can add to it. When the pile gets to be about six feet tall I turn it over with the tractor. Of course it could be turned by hand, but I have this thing about the snakes that like to luxuriate in the warmth of my compost pile and garden. When I am on the tractor I can turn the pile without having a screaming fit. When I *know* where the snakes are, I'm okay—it's the fast little buggers that jump out who startle me. And of course the tractor is a lot easier on the back than a pitchfork.

People who want neat little compost piles can make them easily with cement blocks or screens hooked together. There are also commercially

Fig. 6-1. Compost Piles Held in by Cement Blocks

made composters. There is plenty of technological information available on how composting works, but for my backyard garden just knowing it *does* work is enough for me. As my dad always said, "If it works don't mess with it." Very simply, three ingredients are needed to make compost—nitrogen, carbon, and water.

Nitrogen is found in manures, bonemeal, bloodmeal, and cottonseed meal. If nitrogen is not plentiful, the compost pile will not heat up sufficiently to provide the energy needed by all those little bacteria and fungi to do their work and break down materials.

Carbon is necessary to assist the nitrogen. This material is usually plentiful; it is found in grass clippings, seaweed, hay or straw, and vegetable materials from the kitchen and garden.

Water is the third ingredient needed to break down the organic materials. In Maine we usually have sufficient rainfall (sometimes more than sufficient), but where you don't, you need to hand-water. Leave an indentation on the top of the pile so that water can penetrate into the pile and does not just roll off the sides. In dry times, mix your materials with water as you add them to help increase the moisture content. For example, if you have a pail for kitchen scraps, add water to it before dumping it on the pile.

Composting Tips from Wormwood Farm

- Soil added to the compost pile speeds up decomposition. Adding poor soil will enrich that soil.
- Shredding the materials helps them break down faster. Compost time can take from three months to a year.
- Turning the compost pile every few weeks helps the outside material compost faster. The material in the middle will always be composted first.
- Use as many different materials as you can. This increases the nutrient balance of the compost.
- A compost pile is not a trash heap. It is a pile of healthy organic materials that will decompose and be returned to the soil. *Do not add* fats and grease, diseased plant materials, or cat or dog manures (they may carry disease).

Water Content of Your Soil

Water is a necessary part of your garden's health. Plants take in water by the roots and transpire (give off) water from the stems and leaves, adding a small amount of humidity into the air around the plants. Too much water can cause suffocation, especially in clay soils. An insufficient amount of water can cause the plant to dry up and die.

Water is supplied to a garden in two ways. The first is gravitational water, supplied by rainfall or the garden hose. This water normally drains through and passes out of the porous spaces in the soil. In sandy soil it often drains too quickly; in clay soils it can drain slowly, creating poor aeration and even boggy situations. The second source of water is capillary water action that is held by the soil and supplied to the plants as it is needed. A sufficient amount of organic material in the soil will aid the process.

Mother Nature has been very generous by supplying us with a wide selection of plants for every water condition, from water plants that actually grow in water to plants that tolerate windy conditions and dry arid soil on rocky mountaintops—and plants for everything in between.

Familiarize yourself with your own particular soil's structure and pH, its moisture content and how well it drains, and you are one step ahead in planning a successful garden.

CHAPTER SEVEN

Color: The Whole Spectrum

I have a garden of my own
Shining with flowers of every hue;
I love it dearly while alone
But I shall love it more with you.
　　　　　　　　　　—Thomas Moore

An artist selects colors, mixes paints to achieve various shades and tints, and then brushes the paint onto the canvas to create a long-lasting picture. Since the gardener is working with living materials, it is not as easy as it is for the painter to achieve the desired color scheme. The gardener's picture of living color changes constantly, from season to season and even through the different light changes of an average day.

In the early spring we see Mother Nature's wonders appear with fresh, bright, new-green coloring, deepening or graying as the plants mature. Buds form and break into a colorful display of flowers; they fade with age and finally produce seed, either fruit or a seed pod, and die. The foliage is left to provide the texture and coloring for the rest of the growing season. That is why the texture and color of foliage is so important in the perennial garden.

The intensity of light constantly changes our color schemes, from early sunrise to the bright noonday sun to the sunset and darkening night. Low light on cloudy days deepens some colors, making them appear darker to us. Whites and yellows will seem more brilliant on cloudy days. Blues and lavenders will appear brighter on sunny days.

As you stroll through the garden at sunset, you will become more aware of the yellows and whites, seeing the blues and lavenders in a more subdued state. After a rain the silver-gray of lamb's ear (*Stachys lanata*) will look more green; as it dries out, the gray coloring returns. The gray on the lamb's ear is caused by tiny hairs on the leaf that reflect the sunlight. Look closely with your magnifying glass and study its texture.

Witness the constant color changes of the flowers and leaves in your garden by observing them at various times of the day and on sunny and cloudy days. Record your findings.

The oriental poppy (*Papaver orientale*) is a good perennial to observe because of its short lifespan. In early spring it produces a light green, lance-shaped toothed leaf that is slightly hairy in appearance. As the poppy matures you will see its leaves deepen in color; then it will produce a gray-green hairy stalk with a light-green, oval, hairy pod on the end. It will sometimes show a tiny orange spot or, without warning, burst overnight into a beautiful orange papery-looking flower with a black center. Its beauty is there to be enjoyed for only a few days before it drops its petals as quickly as they appeared. Soon a little vase-shaped pod with a lid cover appears. At this time the leaves darken, turning first gray and then yellow as they begin to disappear from sight for the rest of the season. I harvest the pods for decorating purposes and rake away the dead foliage. Annuals or other perennials will fill in the vacant spots. The poppies are then dormant for a month before they begin sending new foliage to the surface for fall.

Color and Your Garden

Color is seen in relationship to other colors and the light factor. This chapter outlines basic principles of using color and describes several color schemes to help you plan how you will use color in your garden.

The colors you choose for your garden plan are, of course, your personal choices and favorite colors. Color combinations for your garden can be much like those you use in choosing color schemes for your wardrobe or interior design. Mother Nature has provided us her favorite color, green, as a background to work with. Study her works to see how adequately she provides beautiful color schemes.

When planning your garden design look at the colors of your backgrounds—buildings, foundations, fences, and trees. For example, a white fence or foundation is going to look drab with white, silver or gray plants next to it. Instead, use bright or dark colors next to the white, with your white flowers in the foreground (see photograph on page 120). A white fence with white flowers in the front border and bright pinks or reds in the center will seem like a picture frame, as Figure 7-1 (page 118) shows.

This garden is backed by a white fence 16 feet long and 5 feet tall. It can be as long as you wish; just keep in mind not to skimp on the width, keeping it in scale with the length.

Here, a row of green ferns are set next to the white fence for good contrast. In front of the ferns red tulip bulbs provide spring color. As the ferns and perennials grow, they cover the decaying foliage of the bulbs. Three cranesbill geraniums (*Geranium sanguineum*) fill the center, with two spurge (*Euphorbia epithymoides*) on either side.

The front border is filled with candytuft (*Iberis sempervirens*), which will provide white coloring in May and June. To keep a white border all summer, interplant white petunias (annuals) with the candytuft.

The Color Wheel

The floral color wheel (Fig. 7-2, page 119) defines how colors work in combination. Use it as a guide to choosing pleasing color schemes for your garden designs. The color wheel consists of three *primary colors*: red, blue, and yellow. These colors are pure, basic colors that cannot be obtained by mixing with any other colors.

The *secondary colors* are orange, purple, and green. They can be obtained by mixing a combination of the primary colors.

Colors are further divided into degrees of heat. *Warm colors* are red, yellow and orange. *Cool colors* are blue, green, and purple. Warm colors are bright and cheerful and in the garden usually characterize the first flowers noticed. They can be very dramatic when placed in large drifts and are good colors to use as rhythm plants.

The cool colors tend to recede, to be the last colors noticed. Cool colors in the garden are relaxing and quiet; they are a good selection for a meditation area.

Color value is determined by the amount of light reflected or transmitted. The colors nearest the white end of the spectrum (the outer rim of the circle of the color wheel) are the lighter colors and are called *tints*. For example, pink is not a color in itself, but a tint of the primary color red.

The colors nearer the blacker end of the spectrum (the inner part of the color wheel) are the darker colors; they are called *shades*. Magenta is a dark shade of the primary color red. For the primary color blue, the light tint is baby blue, a hint away from white, and the dark shade is navy blue, practically black. Then there is a wide range of colors varying in degrees between these two extremes.

The Color Schemes

How colors lie on the color wheel in relationship to each other provides us with various color schemes.

A different color scheme could be used in every garden, or the color scheme can be an extension of the house color scheme.

If you have a white and yellow living room, you could extend these colors onto the patio or deck and into the garden using white and yellow flowers, as well as white and yellow pots and containers.

Monochromatic Color Scheme

The monochromatic color scheme is achieved by using one primary or secondary color as a base, along with all its tints and shades, to produce an all-one-color garden design.

Often white or silver is used to make the other colors appear brighter. In a very large monochromatic garden, some white here and there will keep the theme color from becoming monotonous.

A yellow monochromatic garden might contain:
　　pale yellow primroses (*Primula* sp.)
　　yellow-green lady's mantle (*Alchemilla vulgaris*)
　　golden-yellow black-eyed Susans (*Rudbeckia* sp.)
　　orange-yellow globe trollius (*Trollius*)

Analogous Color Scheme

An analogous color scheme is accomplished by using colors that lie adjacent to each other on the color wheel. For an example we will take blue and purple.

COLORS AND BLOOM TIMES

YELLOW FLOWERS

	May	June	July	Aug.	Sept.
Basket of gold (*Aurinia saxatilis*)	■	■			
Columbine (*Aquilegia*)		■	■		
Coreopsis		■	■	■	
Daylily (*Hemerocallis*)		■	■		
False yellow lupine (*Thermopsis*)		■			
Globe trollius (*Trollius*)		■			
Gnaphalium		■	■	■	
Golden feverfew (*Chrysanthemum parthenium*)			■	■	
Golden glow (*Rudbeckia*)				■	■
Golden marguerite (*Anthemis*)			■	■	
Lady's mantle (*Alchemilla vulgaris*)		■	■		
Leopard's-bane (*Doronicum*)	■	■			
Patrinia (*Scabiosifolia nagoya*)			■	■	
Primroses (*Primula* sp.)	■	■			
Roses (*Rosa* sp.)		■	■	■	
Santolina		■	■		
Sneezeweed (*Helenium*)			■		
Spurge (*Euphorbia epithymoides*)		■	■		
Sundrops (*Oenothera*)		■	■		
Tansy (*Tanacetum vulgare*)			■	■	■
Yarrow (*Achillea*)			■	■	■
Yellow centaurea (*Centaurea macrocephala*)			■	■	
Yellow lamium (*Lamium*)	■	■			
Yellow loosestrife (*Lysimachia punctata*)		■	■		

ORANGE FLOWERS

	May	June	July	Aug.	Sept.
Butterfly weed (*Asclepias*)			■	■	
Chinese lantern (*Physalis*)				■	■
Poppy (*Papaver*)		■			
Wallflower (*Cheriranthus cheiri*)		■	■		

RED FLOWERS

	May	June	July	Aug.	Sept.
Beebalm (*Monarda didyma*)		■	■		
Clematis		■	■	■	
Columbine (*Aquilegia*)		■			
Daylily (*Hemerocallis*)		■	■		
Maltese cross (*Lychnis chaledonica*)			■	■	
Peony (*Paeonia*)		■	■		
Rose (*Rosa*)		■	■		
Yarrow, red (*Achillea millefolium*)			■	■	

PINK FLOWERS

	May	June	July	Aug.	Sept.
Astilbe			▫	▫	
Balloon flower (*Platycodon*)		▫	▫		
Beebalm (*Monarda didyma*)		▫	▫		
Bergenia (*Bergenia cordifolia*)	▫	▫			
Clove pink (*Dianthus*)		▫	▫		
Coral bells (*Heuchera*)		▫	▫	▫	▫
Cranesbill geranium (*Geranium sanguinium*)		▫	▫		
Fleabane (*Erigeron*)			▫		
Forget-me-not (*Myosotis*)		▫			
Foxglove (*Digitalis*)			▫	▫	
Gas plant (*Dictamnus*)			▫	▫	
Hens and chickens (*Sempervivum*)		▫	▫	▫	▫
Lamb's ear (*Stachys lanata*)			▫	▫	
Liatris			▫	▫	
Muskmallow (*Malva moschata*)		▫	▫	▫	
Obedient plant (*Physostegia*)			▫	▫	▫
Painted daisy (*Chrysanthemum coccineum*)		▫	▫		
Peony (*Paeonia*)		▫	▫		
Phlox, border (*Phlox*)			▫	▫	
Phlox, creeping (*Phlox repens*)	▫	▫			

	May	June	July	Aug.	Sept.
Pink centaurea (*Centaurea dealbata*)		▦	▦		
Purple coneflower (*Echinacea*)			▦	▦	▦
Roses (*Rosa* sp.)		▦	▦	▦	
Sea thrift (*Armeria maritima*)	▦	▦			
Showy stonecrop (*Sedum spectible*)				▦	▦
Soapwort (*Saponaria*)		▦	▦		
Thymes (*Thymus* sp.)		▦	▦		

WHITE FLOWERS

	May	June	July	Aug.	Sept.
Astilbe		☐	☐	☐	
Baby's breath (*Gypsophila*)		☐	☐	☐	
Bellflower (*Campanula*)			☐	☐	
Bleeding heart (*Dicentra albus*)	☐	☐			
Candytuft (*Iberis sempervirens*)	☐	☐			
Columbine (*Aquilegia*)		☐	☐		
Feverfew (*Chrysanthemum parthenium*)		☐	☐	☐	
Garlic chives (*Allium tuberosum*)			☐	☐	☐
Gas plant (*Dictamnus alba*)			☐	☐	
Goatsbeard (*Aruncus dioicus*)		☐	☐		
Gooseneck loosestrife (*Lysimachia clethroides*)			☐	☐	
Iris (*Iris* sp.)	☐	☐	☐	☐	
Lily of the valley (*Convallaria majalis*)	☐	☐			
Lupine (*Lupinus*)		☐	☐		
Mat daisy (*Anacyclus depressus*)		☐			
Meadowsweet (*Filipendula*)		☐	☐		
Mints (*Mentha* sp.)		☐	☐	☐	
Obedient plant (*Physostegia*)			☐	☐	☐
Peony (*Paeonia*)		☐	☐		
Phlox, border (*Phlox*)			☐	☐	☐
Phlox, creeping (*Phlox repens*)	☐	☐			

	May	June	July	Aug.	Sept.
Rock cress (*Arabis*)	☐	☐			
Rose (*Rosa* sp.)		☐	☐	☐	
Sea thrift (*Armeria maritima*)		☐			
Shasta daisy (*Chrysanthemum maximus*)		☐	☐		
Snakeroot (*Cimicifuga*)			☐	☐	
Snow in summer (*Cerastium tomentosa*)		☐	☐		
Solomon's seal (*Polygonatum*)		☐	☐		
Sweet cicely (*Myrrhis odorata*)		☐			
Sweet woodruff (*Asperula odorata*)	☐	☐			
Thyme (*Thymus* sp.)		☐	☐		
Violets (*Viola* sp.)	☐	☐			
Yarrow, pearl white (*Achillea*)			☐	☐	☐
Yucca (*Yucca filamentosa*)				☐	☐

LAVENDER FLOWERS

	May	June	July	Aug.	Sept.
Anise-hyssop (*Agastache foeniculum*)			■	■	■
Bellflower (*Campanula*)			■	■	
Catmint (*Cataria nepeta mussinii*)	■	■			
Columbine (*Aquilegia*)		■	■		
Curly or corkscrew onion (*Allium senescens*)			■	■	
Delphinium		■	■		■
Fleabane (*Erigeron*)			■		
Foxglove (*Digitalis*)			■	■	
Iris (*Iris* sp.)	■	■	■	■	
Jacob's ladder (*Polemonium caeruleum*)		■	■		
Lavender (*Lavendula officinalis*)			■	■	■
Lungwort (*Pulmonaria*)	■	■			
Salvia, blue (*Salvia superba*)		■	■	■	
Windflowers (*Anemone* sp.)	■	■			

PURPLE FLOWERS

	May	June	July	Aug.	Sept.
Allheal (*Prunella*)		■	■		
Baptisia (*Baptisia australis*)			■		
Bellflower (*Campanula*)			■	■	
Clematis		■	■		
Columbine (*Aquilegia*)		■			
Delphinium		■	■		■
Hyssop (*Hyssopus officinalis*)			■	■	■
Iris (*Iris* sp.)	■	■	■	■	
Michaelmas daisy (*Aster novae-angliae*)				■	■
Purple loosestrife (*Lythrum salicaria*)			■	■	
Speedwell (*Veronica*)		■	■	■	
Spiderwort (*Tradescantia*)		■	■		
Violet (*Viola odorata*)	■	■			

BLUE FLOWERS

	May	June	July	Aug.	Sept.
Bellflower (*Campanula*)			■	■	
Blue flax (*Linum perenne*)		■	■	■	■
Blue sheep's grass (*Festuca*)			■		
Bugleweed (*Ajuga*)		■			
Cranesbill (*Geranium wallichianum*)		■	■		
Cupid's dart (*Catanache*)			■	■	
Delphinium		■	■		■
Forget-me-nots (*Myosotis*)		■	■		
Globe thistle (*Echinops*)				■	■
Jasione (*Jasione perennis*)			■		
Navelwort (*Omphalodes*)	■	■			
Virginia bluebells (*Mertensia virginica*)		■	■		

Fig. 7-1. A white fence in the back and white flowers along the front border act like a picture frame for the bright pink and red flowers in the center of this garden plot. In spring, this "frame" is created with red tulips and white candytuft (Iberis sempervirens). Shown here is the garden in June, with red cranesbill geranium and white petunias.

Fig. 7-3. A polychromatic color scheme combines all the colors of the color wheel into a garden design.

Fig. 7-2. The Color Wheel

PHOTO BY BRANDAU/HALL

The rhythmic, curving line of this picket fence is echoed in the height and spacing of the plants below.

PHOTO BY BRANDAU/HALL

In this foundation planting, bright, dark colors contrast with the white backdrop, while the white plants in the foreground work with the porch railing to form a "frame" for the garden.

PHOTO BY BRANDAU/HALL

Pathways can be used to create interest in the garden—here the color of the light bark on this curving path contrasts with the green foliage and the tall spires of blue iris and white and rose lupines.

MICHAEL H. DODGE, WHITE FLOWER FARM

"Drifts" of closely planted perennials (Filipendula, Echinacea, and Perovskia) make this summer garden seem to float with clouds of color.

You could choose any blues, from the pale baby blue to a deep, dark navy blue, as well as light lavender to deep purple and all the colors in between. Or you could use just one particular blue and purple.

Perennials for a blue-purple analogous color scheme could consist of the following:

> *lavender* chives (*Allium schoenoprasum*)
> *blue* bellflowers (*Campanula grandiflora*)
> *deep steel blue* globe thistle (*Echinops*)
> *dark purple* violets (*Viola odorata ritro*)
> *light blue* navelwort (*Omphalodes*)
> *light purple* jasione (*Jasione perennis*)
> *bluish-purple* catmint (*Nepeta cataria mussinii*)
> *bright purple* spiderwort (*Tradescantia*)

Complementary Color Scheme

Colors that lie opposite to each other on the color wheel are called complementary colors. We see this color scheme during the various holidays—red and green at Christmas, yellow and purple at Easter.

A spring bulb garden of yellow and purple flowers is a wonderful way to greet spring with a complementary color scheme.

> *yellow* and *purple* crocus
> *purple* grape hyacinth (*Hyacinthus*)
> *yellow* and *purple* iris
> *checkered purple* guinea hen flower (*Fritillaria meleagris*)
> *yellow* daffodils (*Narcissus*)

Multiple Complementary Color Scheme

The multiple complementary color scheme uses two complementary colors plus one color that is analogous to one of the complementary colors.

For example, use blue and orange, which are complementary, and green, which lies next to blue. Since Mother Nature already provides the green, use more foliage plants like fern and hosta in this design.

> *green* ferns, hostas, lungwort (*Pulmonaria*)
> *blue* delphiniums, navelwort (*Omphalodes*), blue flax (*Linum perenne*)

orange butterfly weed (*Asclepias tuberosa*), wallflower
(*Cherianthus cheiri*)

Since there are very few perennial orange flowers, annuals from the geranium, impatiens, and marigold families could also be used.

Polychromatic Color Scheme

The famous English writer and gardener Gertrude Jekyll is well known in the
garden world for introducing this color scheme. She used her talents as an
artist to combine all the colors of the color wheel into a garden design.

To achieve this design, you would start at one end of a bed with one color
and work your way around the entire color wheel. You can use only the primary and secondary colors, or if you are working with a large area, use all their
tints and shades.

In this plan we start with green and end with green (see Fig. 6-3, page 118):
> *greenish-blue* hosta
> *blue* flax (*Linum perenne*)
> *purple* spiderwort (*Tradescantia virginiana*)
> *red* beebalm (*Monarda didyma*)
> *orange* butterfly weed (*Asclepias tuberosa*)
> *yellow* yellow loosestrife (*Lysimachia punctata*)
> *green* hosta

Color and Bloom Time

In designing your garden, it is important to know the bloom time in your
particular area for the perennials you are planting. Suppose you always go on
vacation for the entire month of August; any flowers that come out in this time
would be wasted. Therefore, you would plan your garden to have spring and
early-summer species. If your town has a major celebration day or your garden
club has a tour, you will want to have your garden at its peak during those
times.

Although charts like the one on pages 113–117 are helpful, each of us has
a different mini-climate to contend with. Take out your garden notebook and
keep notes on the bloom time of plants in your garden—as well as plants in

other gardens in your neighborhood that you might want to add in the future.

Something to be careful about regarding bloom time is the location of the early blooming plants that disappear after they produce flowers and seed pods, like leopard's-bane (*Doronicum*), Virginia bluebells (*Mertensia virginica*), and poppies (*Papaver*). These plants should be well marked so you do not accidentally dig up the roots or bulbs. Our memories are not as reliable as a clearly labeled marker! Plant the die-back-foliage plants close to more long-lasting plants, such as fall-blooming perennials, that will fill in that space by midsummer.

The chart on pages 113–117 can serve as a quick reference to color and approximate bloom time. The bloom time given is true for my own zone, 4–5. Remember, bloom time varies depending on your particular zone.

Keeping a personal notebook of conditions in your area and bloom times for your perennials will provide almost exact bloom time for the following year's garden planning.

I am always disappointed when blue turns out to be more purple than what I see as blue; therefore I have listed under blue only those flowers that are true blue, with separate listings for lavender and purple.

CHAPTER EIGHT

Finding and Propagating Your Perennials

If they to whom God gives fair gardens knew
The happy solace which sweet flowers bestow;
Where pain depresses, and where friends are few
To cheer the heart in weariness and woe.

—Anonymous

Your soil is prepared, your design drawn, and you have a list of plants to grow. Now where do you find the plants? Should you buy, ask friends for cuttings and divisions, or start them yourself by seed?

There certainly is no lack of places to find perennials. Farm stands, farmers' markets, greenhouses, garden centers, even chain stores and supermarkets get in on the spring growing rush. By studying your perennials, you will be able to go to any greenhouse and pick out what you want. Keep in mind, however, many greenhouses and garden centers hire temporary, inexperienced summer help who cannot always answer your questions. I personally like to buy from small growers who often have expanded from hobby growers to professional retailers. They are usually very well informed and do it for pleasure as well as profit. And don't forget garden club plant sales.

I don't know how many times I have told someone to buy plants when not in flower and then have gone out and bought some in flower myself. Of course, that is not the best time to buy. The best way is to buy them budded or before flowering; then you get the full benefit of the flowering process. Another reason is that sometimes when you transplant a plant from the pot when it is in flower, the flowers will die so that all the plant's energy can go into making the new root system strong.

Look for healthy plants with no or little insect damage. Remember when dealing with plants that unless they are sprayed to death, you may find a bug or two. Check the bottom of the pot to see how root-bound it might be. If at home you discover that it is very root-bound, take the plant out of the pot, pull the roots out straight, and cut off half of them before planting. This will make the plant stronger. I find many new gardeners very timid about cutting their plants, but this form of pruning is beneficial for the plant.

Another test before you buy a plant is to gently tug at it. If it pops out of the soil, it has not been potted very long and may not have an adequate root system for transplanting.

Plants are most plentiful in May and June, but you can purchase and plant all season.

Plants should be well marked, but beware of little children who like to change markers in the store. Unfortunately some mothers and fathers let their kids run wild while they shop. I am often tempted to put out a sign that reads, "No dogs, and kids on a leash." All the greenhouse people have stories to tell about customers and their little darlings. So if you are not familiar with a plant, always verify its identity with the clerk.

The size of the plants you purchase will depend on whether you are in a hurry. If you want a mature garden quickly, buy the largest plants available. If you are not in a hurry and like to watch the plants develop, buy seedlings and small divisions. Being a very frugal person, I buy small inexpensive plants and can therefore purchase more plants.

Free Perennials

Gardeners, neighbors, friends, and relatives love to share their plants. But beware of introducing disease- and insect-ridden plants into your own garden. A free plant may not come with a name on it—you may have trouble identifying it. I have been given many plants that I had to research to find the correct nomenclature. On the good side, many older established gardeners have perennial species and varieties that are no longer available in the stores.

Starting Your Own Perennials from Seed

If you want only one columbine (*Aquilegia*), then purchasing it will be time- and cost-effective. However, if you want four or more it will pay to start your own from seed.

A well-lighted window will hold a few boxes of seedlings. A fluorescent light is even better.

Roses, iris, bleeding hearts (*Dicentras*), peonies (*Paeonia*), and poppies (*Papaver*) are difficult and slow to start in the home; a greenhouse is really needed. I would recommend you buy established plants for starting those species.

Baptisia, butterfly weed (*Asclepias tuberosa*), bergenia, and snakeroot (*Cimicifuga racemosa*) will take two to four years from seed to flowers, so if you are in a hurry, they also are best purchased.

Perennials that are fairly easy for the home seed-starter include yarrow (*Achillea*), anise-hyssop (*Agastache-foeniculum*), golden marguerite (*Anthemis tinctoria*), sea thrift (*Armeria maritima*), chrysanthemums, clove pinks (*Dianthus* sp.), coral bells (*Heuchera sanguinea*), lavender (*Lavendula*), speedwells (*Veronica* sp.), and Jacob's ladder (*Polemonium caeruleum*).

There is great personal satisfaction in watching those tiny seeds develop into full, mature plants, and it offers a good way to study the plants themselves.

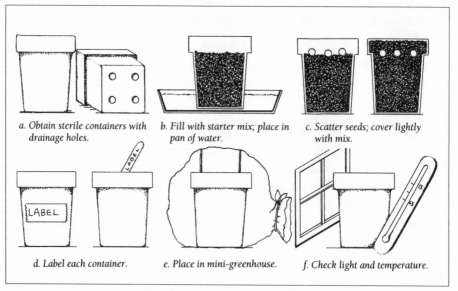

a. Obtain sterile containers with drainage holes.

b. Fill with starter mix; place in pan of water.

c. Scatter seeds; cover lightly with mix.

d. Label each container.

e. Place in mini-greenhouse.

f. Check light and temperature.

Fig. 8-1. Starting Your Own Seeds

Starting Your Own Seeds

The Container: Any container with a depth of 2 to 3 inches and drainage holes will be sufficient. You can purchase flats and trays from the garden center or make your own from milk cartons. The most important factor is that the container be sterile-clean.

The Starting Medium: Nonsoil commercial mixes you buy or those you mix yourself are the best; they are easy to handle and sterile. You can sterilize your own soil, but it is smelly and time-consuming. Soil from your garden is full of bacteria and soil-borne organisms that may kill the tiny seedlings before they start.

Here is the recipe I prefer to use when starting seeds.

Nonsoil Starter Mix

3 parts vermiculite
2 parts wet peat moss
bonemeal (1 Tbsp. to 4
    cups of mix)

Place mix in container; set in a pan of water so that water soaks up into the soil. This is called watering by capillary action.

Scatter seeds lightly (and I mean *lightly*) on top of the soil. Be careful not to seed thickly, or it will overcrowd the container. If you accidently put too many seeds in and you have a mini-forest when they emerge, carefully pluck out excess seedlings or you may lose them all. An overcrowded situation will produce air shortages and damping-off disease (a fungus that attacks small seedlings, causing them to rot at the base and fall over; it is caused by overcrowding, too much water, or soil-borne diseases).

Cover the seeds very lightly with mix. A good rule to follow is to cover them with a layer two times the size of the seed. Read your seed package—some seeds do not like to be covered at all.

Label, Label, Label

If you are growing more than one kind of seed, label them. Small seedlings often look all alike, especially to the beginner. If your memory is as good as mine, you will certainly need to label.

Create a mini-greenhouse for your seedling containers by enclosing each one in a large plastic bag (bread bags work nicely, for economy's sake). Prop the plastic up with sticks so that it does not touch the soil. Check the containers daily; if a fungus starts to grow, the plants are not getting enough air. Open the end of the bag some more or pull the container halfway out to allow more air circulation. The moisture from the plastic should keep it moist enough.

This mini-greenhouse will protect your seeds from cold and provide needed humidity. When seedlings emerge, remove the container from the bag.

Heat and Light

Again, read the seed package. It should have information on the light and heat needs of the plants. On the average, most perennials require a day temperature of 70 to 75° F. and about 65° F. at night.

Greenhouses are in the affordable price range today, and it is nice to have one if you are an avid gardener. A few windows or a fluorescent light will provide light for several flats of seedlings. Keep containers away from windows at night to prevent cold from checking growth or frosting tiny seedlings. Keep seedlings at least one inch away from light bulbs to prevent scorching.

I use a heating pad under my newly seeded flats until green emerges. I believe this hastens and improves the germination rate. Be sure your heating pad is in good condition and do not place it where it may catch on fire.

Care of Seedlings

Once seedlings have appeared, remove the plastic and the heat source. Water regularly—do not let them dry out completely and wilt and do not keep the soil soggy. Watering is one of the most important factors in producing good, strong seedlings.

Check daily for any insects. If you have houseplants growing near the new seedlings, they may be susceptible to red spiders, mealy bugs, and aphids from

Fig. 8-2. Transplanting Seedlings

the houseplants. If your area is dry, provide humidity by misting plants often. Use chamomile (*Anthemis nobile*) or yarrow (*Achillea*) as a tea for watering and misting the plants. This may help ward off disease and insects.

When your seedlings are 1½ to 2 inches tall, transplant them into individual containers or into the garden. Plant outside only when all danger of frost has passed. Watch Mother Nature carefully and be prepared to cover the seedlings if very cold weather returns. Perennials that are mature are hardy, but newly planted tiny seedlings are not.

Other Propagation Methods

Once your perennial garden is established and you have mature plants, you can increase your supply by division, layering, and cuttings. These three methods are asexual methods of propagation, producing clonelike plants, true to the original type. Seeds often are not true to their parentage and may produce slightly different colors than the parent plant.

Divide established plants by pulling apart or cutting roots or rhizomes.

Division

This methods involves separation of the plant's roots. It can be used for fibrous roots, stolens, tubers, and bulbs.

1. Push a spade or garden fork into the soil to loosen the soil and plant. Lift the plant out of the ground.
2. If digging in late summer, cut foliage back to one-third of its former growth so that energy goes into making more roots and less foliage.
3. Pull root pieces apart with your hands if possible. If the roots are tightly entangled, use a sharp knife to cut large sections. Be sure you have left "eyes" or "buds" on each section you cut.
4. Stolens and runners are produced from creeping plants. To divide, simply cut them away from the mother plant and repot. Examples include rock cress (*Arabis*), globe thistle (*Echinops*), and beebalm (*Monarda didyma*).
5. For bulbs and tubers, dig up and separate each eye or bulb section for new plants. Flowering onions are excellent candidates for bulb division.

Stem Cuttings

You can cut young green top stems from the plant and place them in a growing medium to root. As a child I rooted many plants by placing them in a glass of water, but now I prefer the following method for starting new perennials.

1. Cut 2- to 4-inch pieces of succulent new growth from the plant (old stems rarely root themselves).
2. Try to take the cuttings between 10 A.M. and 12 noon, when the stems are full of nutrients, providing better conditions for their taking root.
3. Do not use flowering stems.
4. Remove the bottom leaves, leaving only a few top leaves. The energy should go into producing roots, not into providing energy for the leaves.
5. Dip the stem in a rooting mixture (optional). I do not do this, but several people I know do and say it makes the cuttings root faster.
6. I personally like to use vermiculite as a soilless medium to start cuttings. You can also use the Pro Mix™ type of soil

To propagate by stem cutting, cut 2- to 4-inch pieces of succulent new growth from plant.

mixes or plain perlite. Whatever medium you use, be sure it is well watered.

7. Root several cuttings at one time; some may die for no apparent reason.

8. Wrap the container in plastic to create a mini-greenhouse to create high humidity. As with seeds, keep watch so the container does not become too soggy and die. Provide some air flow inside the plastic.

9. Watch carefully—if cuttings start to brown they are not getting enough water. They should stay green and healthy-looking all the time.

Layering

This asexual method starts new plants from the mother without cutting off the stems. It works well with southernwood (*Artemisia abrotanum*) and lavender (*Lavendula* sp.).

1. Wound a section of the stem by scraping the bark or half-breaking it.

2. Then, bending the stem over, lay it on the ground and cover it with soil. I usually set a brick on it to secure it to the ground. The plant will root at this wound while still receiving nourishment from the mother plant.

3. It usually takes a month or two for the plant to root itself, depending on the species of perennial. It can be left in this condition over the winter for new spring plants.

Fig. 8-3. Layering

Getting to the Root of It All

Learning a little about the root system of your perennials will help you in dividing your plants as well as in planting them. The root system not only anchors the plant in its place, but it is the absorbing mechanism and storage house for food and water.

Roots take in oxygen and nutrients that enter the xylem tissues of the plant. There they are carried upward through the roots and stems to all parts of the plant. The process of photosynthesis then can take place. The flower part of the plant is not designed to please us but to attract insects and bees for pollination and perpetuation of the species.

There are several root systems of interest to perennial growers. I will try to describe them as best I can. To really understand root systems, dig up and examine roots from several different plants.

The *tap root* is a main root that grows straight down. A carrot is a taproot that we eat. This root penetrates deeply into the soil with lateral roots extending along the way. Examples of taproot perennials are baptisia and painted daisy (*Chrysanthemum coccineum*).

Fibrous roots are composed of numerous slender roots. The main roots are nearly the same size as the secondary roots. Examples of fibrous roots are hyssop (*Hyssopus*) and astilbe.

Stolens or *runners* are slender stems rooting at the end of the plant or at a joint as they creep along the ground. Examples include thyme (*Thymus*) and rupturewort (*Herniaria glabra*).

The *rhizome* is a fat root system that grows vertically just below or slightly above the surface of the soil. An example is an iris root.

A *tuber* is a thick portion of an underground root with an eye (bud) from which the stem grows. Examples are creeping buttercup (*Ranunculus*) and windflower (*Anemone*).

Corms, unlike bulbs, shrivel and disappear as the plant grows above the ground. New smaller corms are found on top and at the sides of the old. New corms take two to three years before they produce flowers. An example of this is the crocus.

A *bulb* is a round underground stem that is encased with scales and has a fibrous root at the end. The onion family (*Allium*) and tulips (*Tulipa*) are bulb plants.

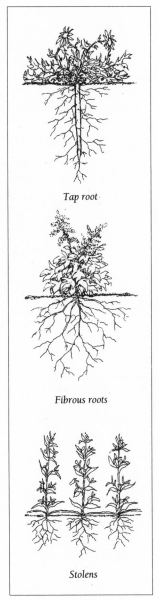

Tap root

Fibrous roots

Stolens

Fig. 8-4. Root Systems

Putting Your Plants in the Garden

Spring is the time most of us are "gung-ho" on gardening, especially adding new plants to the existing garden. If possible, you prepared a new bed the previous fall. If not, let a spring-tilled garden sit a few days before planting to let it settle in. Even though plants are sun lovers, it is best to transplant on a cloudy day or in the evening. This protects the new plants from the sun robbing them of moisture. If you need to plant on a sunny day, place a pot or basket over the plant for a few days so that it can take hold of the soil without it losing too much moisture. A number of plants will wilt when first planted. Protecting them will help them get acclimated more quickly.

Always dig the hole for the plant a little larger than what the plant needs. Spread roots out gently and pack the soil in around the plant.

Plant your perennial at the same level it was in the pot. If you plant it too high, the roots will be sunburned and dry out. If you plant it too low, the stems will suffocate.

If you are planting in the fall, be sure to allow the plant time to adjust before cold weather sets in. It needs to establish its root system before frost, or it will be more susceptible to winter kill.

CHAPTER NINE

Garden Housekeeping

Mark thou thy garden—and not spare
Thyself as honest labourer.
Break thou the earth and turn withal
So the live airs thereon shall fall.
—Katharine Tynan

Without human interference Mother Nature does quite well at providing a landscape of beauty using her own favorite colors and plants. Once we interfere and change the land space, we become responsible caretakers of what we change.

Unfortunately, there is no perfect plant that can be planted and left to care for itself. In nature, the strongest survive. Without our garden housekeeping practices, many plants would be overrun with weeds and insects and succumb to nature's way.

The warm fall days with their fresh, crisp air are perfect for physical exercise in the garden.

As I write this chapter the leaves are falling from the two big maples on my front lawn, covering the rose garden and driveway. In nature they would slowly decay into the ground, providing humus to the soil. But we have to change things to suit our likes and dislikes. The leaves will be raked and hauled to the compost pile to break down, and then in spring we will haul them to the gardens for added enrichment. How we humans love to make extra work for ourselves!

However, this is often part of the fun of our gardening. I find that I cherish the reclusive time alone in my garden. Gardening is a form of mental therapy, curing many a headache or personal problem. A garden is a place away from the trials, stress, and anxiety of today's modern living, a place for the mind to drift off to never-never land, foreign islands, or fairytales, to dream and solve the world's problems as well as our own, a place to practice peaceful existence.

Garden housekeeping can be compared with interior housework. If we did not wash dishes, vacuum floors, make beds, and do laundry, our home would not be a pleasant place to be. Garden work left undone allows the garden to become a jungle of weeds and insects, an unpleasant place to visit.

Some of our garden chores include tilling the soil either by hand or by machine, weeding, watering when necessary, pruning, pinching, and general clean-up. Long-time gardeners can attest to the fact that we often make more work for ourselves than is necessary. I have yet to find too many gardeners who are completely satisfied with their gardens. I know that I change plants around as much as I change the furniture in the house.

A clean, well cultivated, weed-free garden is a joy to look at. However, vacations, illness, or other priorities frequently leave the garden in disarray. Thank goodness most perennials are tolerant of our minor lapses and continue to exist in spite of us.

My advice to you is not to become a slave to your garden. If this year it wasn't all you wanted it to be, there is always next year. Gardens are for enjoying and relaxing.

Weeding

Garden weeding is a chore for some people, while others really enjoy it. The physical exercise combined with the mental relaxation alone in the garden is therapy for many of us.

I like to observe how other people weed their gardens. My 90-year-old friend who wears a back brace bends at the waist for hours on end. I remember my own grandmother (in a dress and nylons) on her knees with a little cushion under them. I even know a local woman who weeds in a dress and high heels. Others sit on little stools, easily bending over to weed. Because I have frequent back pain I plop right down on the ground, sitting on a piece of foam to keep the dampness and dirt away.

There are weeders who wouldn't touch a weed without a pair of gloves, while others can't pull a weed with them on. I usually wear out two pairs a season, one cotton pair for dry weather and a pair of the plastic-coated kind with little nubbies on them. I admit I don't like wearing gloves, and it took me some time to get used to them. However, gloves don't work when weeding the tiny-leaved thyme and rupturewort. It has been said that to weed thyme is a lesson in humility.

Mother Nature protects her soil from wind and rain erosion by filling in all the spots that haven't been planted with something. Nothing keeps weeds away very long, not even those dangerous chemical killers.

One way to prevent weeds and stop erosion is to use a mulch around the plants. I think Mother Nature likes this, and it does break down into nutritious humus after a period of time.

Little kids like to weed for a short period of time. This is a good way to teach them about plants. Make it fun for them, and you will have future gardeners. We often leave a wild daisy or buttercup growing in the garden because kids love them. They are just as pretty as some of the expensive perennials.

If you have space, a small garden just for your kids will be special to them. Include fun plants like alpine strawberries (*Fragaria*), which produce little strawberries all season. Each of my grandchildren has a garden named for them. Jessica has mints (*Mentha*) for her "bellyache," Nicole grows catnip for her kitty, and Zoe likes perennials to pick for a bouquet.

When kids help with the chores, give them a special treat—a cookie, a piece of cake, or a plant of their own to take home.

Mulching

We have talked about mulch in the garden. Mulch in the summer garden helps to keep the weeds at a minimum. In the winter garden mulch acts as an insulator, protecting the plants from alternating between freezing and thawing temperatures, which often damage a plant.

Spring and Summer Mulch: Apply mulch after the soil has thoroughly warmed up in the spring and weed the area well before applying. Mulch tends to keep the soil cooler, and will help keep the moisture in the soil, which is especially helpful during drought periods. Mulch stimulates earthworm activity, which creates new soil and improves the condition of the existing soil. Mulch can be attractive and can help display individual perennials. Add additional mulch all summer as needed.

Winter Mulch: In the spring we wait for the soil to warm up, but in the fall

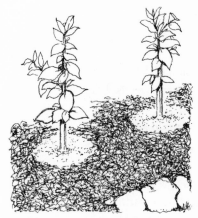

*Fig. 9-1. Keep mulch 2–3"
away from stems.*

we wait for the soil to freeze before adding mulch. If we don't, those pesty little mice and moles will find the mulch an ideal homesite. A good snow cover is the best plant protector, but until we find a way to communicate with Mother Nature to get advance weather predictions, we need to rely on winter mulch.

The type of soil you have will dictate the amount of mulch needed. Add more mulch to sandy soil. Clay soil will need little mulch; in fact, pine or fir boughs may be the best winter protection for clay soil. Mulch that mats down, like leaves or hay, will hold too much moisture in the clay soil and may cause winter rot, as well as delaying the thawing process in the spring.

Mulch Tips

- When using nitrogen robbers like fresh sawdust, hay, or grass clippings as mulch, add a nitrogen fertilizer like fish emulsion or dried manure to counteract the loss of nitrogen in the soil.
- Keep mulch two to three inches away from the perennials' stems to prevent stem rot. Remember that the vegetative mulch will naturally begin to compost itself on the ground.
- Certain types of perennials, including delphiniums and peonies, dislike any mulch. Delphiniums will, however, appreciate a mulch of wood ashes brought up around their roots. Wood ashes will add alkalinity to the soil and repel slugs and snails.
- Find and use inexpensive and available materials for mulching.

Mulch Materials

Cocoa Beans: I discovered cocoa beans only two years ago when they first became available in our area. I love using them—not only do they add humus and beauty, but they have a heavenly aroma when it rains. It makes you want to run to the kitchen for a cup of hot cocoa! But be careful in very wet areas: mildew can be a problem if the soil is not disturbed occasionally.

Grass Clippings: With a large lawn area, we have an abundance of grass clippings. Most of them go into the compost pile. However, there are a few areas where I use the clippings as a mulch. Do not apply thickly or they will rot into a slimy mess. Apply often and lightly, and they will keep the weeds under control. They compost into the ground, adding humus to the area.

Hay: Hay makes good mulching material. I admit I use most of it in the vegetable garden, and sometimes snakes find it a good place to sleep.

Peat Moss: This does not make a good mulch. It robs the soil of necessary water and blows around unless it is kept constantly wet. It is best dug directly into the soil.

Sawdust: Finding a well-rotted sawdust pile is a treasure. When using fresh sawdust you need to add a nitrogen fertilizer because the sawdust will rob the nitrogen from the soil. The level of acidity of sawdust depends on the type of wood the sawdust comes from.

Stones: These are attractive as a mulch but add no nutrients to the soil. They keep the soil moist and cool. Use thick layers of stone to keep weeds away.

Wood Chips: This is the most popular mulch. It is decorative, available at all garden centers, and breaks down slowly into the soil. It is on the acid side, so do add some lime, wood ashes, or bone meal where needed.

Staking Perennials

Stately delphiniums, hollyhocks (*Alcea*), and golden marguerite (*Anthemis tinctoria*) are sometimes blown over after a heavy rain or just lie over when their flowers become too heavy. To prevent this, use some type of staking method. Plants grown against a fence can be staked by placing twine across the front, tacking it on both ends of the fence. Plants standing alone can be staked in groups with bamboo, wood stakes, brush, or commercial cages.

Place stakes in the ground early in the season before major growth begins. Stake them at the projected height of the mature plant and use as many stakes as necessary. One hollyhock will use two or three stakes, while four holly-hocks clumped together will need four or five stakes. When the plants reach their mature height, tie them to the stakes with a soft material. I like pantyhose—you can cut it into pieces and it stretches with the movement of the plant. Yarn and soft twine also work well. Do not use wire because it will cut the plant

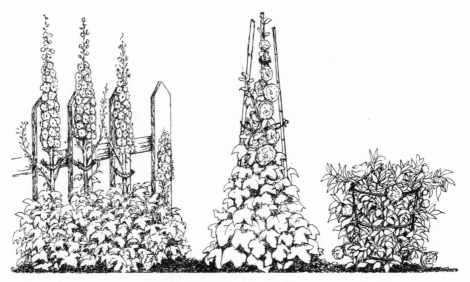

Fig. 9-2. Staking Perennials

when it sways in the wind and as it continues to grow.

Do not tie your plants tightly like a clump of corn stalks set out for decoration. Keep them neat and allow for more growth and wind movement.

Peonies (*Paeonia*) do not always need staking; however, some of mine become so heavy with flowers they sag to the ground. I like wire cages for this type of plant. The wire is hidden with foliage and it holds the flowers up off the ground. For smaller plants that may droop, stick brush in the soil and they will grow to cover it and hold themselves up.

Deadheading

Although not absolutely necessary for the health of the plant, deadheading helps keep the garden neat looking and often encourages new flowers to bloom.

Deadheading involves simply cutting off the flower heads as they go past full bloom. Deadheading also encourages the plant's energy to go into root production instead of seedmaking.

Of course, if you are saving your own seed you would not do this. When planning to save seeds, I tie a ribbon around the biggest and best bloom and then deadhead the other flowers.

Pinching and Pruning

Pinching is simply snipping off the soft tips of a plant using the thumb and forefinger. Pinching ensures a stronger and better plant. This is practiced in growing plants that may be lanky looking, especially chrysanthemums.

Pruning is more often applied to woody plants, but it is also practiced on plants grown for flower shows. Someone who might be going to exhibit at a flower show would prune back all but one or two flower heads. He or she would also prune away a certain amount of foliage so that all the energy would go into making larger flowers for display.

Any special pruning or pinching techniques required by a particular plant will be mentioned in the individual plant profiles in part two.

Dealing with Invasive Perennials

A woman stopped by my house recently, looking *not* for the perfect easy perennial, but something most people would think of as a pest. As she stepped from her blue station wagon she said, "I'm looking for some very invasive plants. Do you know what I'm talking about? I've been to two other greenhouses and they didn't understand what I wanted. Someone said you probably could help me if anyone could."

"Yes," I answered. "I have a backyard full of what I think you want." She went on to tell me she had had her backyard tilled up and wanted to plant lots of wild invasive plants and just let them go. She would mow this garden once a year, but other than that it was on its own. What lived and spread would survive, and what didn't would die out. By the time she left, her station wagon was filled with invasive plants, including anise-hyssop (*Agastache foeniculum*), golden marguerite (*Anthemis tinctoria*), teasel (*Dipacus sativus*), and black-eyed Susans (*Rudbeckia* sp.), all very good self-seeders, and golden glows (*Rudbeckia* sp.), silver king (*Artemisia ludoviciana*), obedient plant (*Physostegia virginiana*), and Roman wormwood (*Artemisia pontica*).

I don't know how her garden turned out. She was from New Hampshire and I have since closed up shop. I like the idea, though. I am turning a back area into a wild garden like that to attract birds and butterflies. It will be mowed clean after the frost kills off the plants, and I will leave the cuttings to enrich the soil.

Just what are invasive plants? They are plants that literally "take over" the garden plot. There are two ways for a plant to be invasive: through a spreading root system and through self-seeding.

A plant with a creeping, spreading root system will spread quickly through an area, pushing out the more fragile plants. Examples are mints (*Mentha* sp.), bishopweed (*Aegopodium podagraria*), and Roman wormwood (*Artemisia pontica*). When grown in an area you want covered quickly, such as a slope or roadside area, these plants are very welcome. However, in a small garden it sometimes gets to be too much work as you keep weeding the excess out. You may want some of these attractive plants in your garden anyway—we all really need at least one mint. At Wormwood Farm we have six different kinds of mint planted at various places. I put some at the edge of a lawn so we can mow down the excess. It sure smells nice when we mow across those sections.

You can use several strategies to cope with invasive-root plants. Plant them in large containers, such as half a wine barrel. Insert a sheet of plastic or metal 24 inches into the ground surrounding the plant and the area where you can tolerate the perennial's invasion. If the barrier is not deep enough, most plants will send their roots under the barrier and back up into the next section. Another option is to dig the plant up each spring and replant only the section you want. This is a lot of work, but you can control its growth that way.

The self-seeding plants include several species that throw their seeds to the wind, drop them near the mother plant, or even have them catch rides on animals and people as they walk around the garden. These are the plants' survival methods. Among the perennial self-seeders are anise-hyssop (*Agastache foeniculum*), golden marguerite (*Anthemis tinctoria*) and many of the biennials.

To control self-seeders, simply weed out the excess or cut off the lower heads before they form seeds. Unfortunately, good intentions or time constraints may not always match up with seed time. If you are swamped with volunteer seedlings, this may be the beginning of a new business! Check your local greenhouses; they often buy plants from small gardeners. They cannot grow everything themselves.

And the last way to deal with invasive plants is to do as my customer did, plant them to go wild for their beauty and for the birds and butterflies.

Spring Cleaning—This and That

Spring is a busy time of the gardening year. We are full of renewed energy and great plans stored up over the long, cold winter months—new ideas to try, new soil to dig, and new plants to buy. The sun is warming up the earth and we are warming up our muscles for a long season of growing.

Winter mulch is slowly removed a little at a time so the frozen soil can warm. Plants that have heaved themselves up out of the soil are gently pushed back. Debris is raked away to the compost pile. Gardens are tilled as soon as the earth permits. Do not try to work the soil too early or when very wet, or you will do more damage than good. Stalks and stems can be cut from perennials that were not cut the previous fall.

Tall plants are staked in anticipation of their mature growth, compost from last year's pile is added to them, and a new pile is started. Spring is my favorite time for dividing plants to increase my gardens. As the spring warms, new plants are bought and added to the backyard perennial garden.

Winter Care—This and That

There are some gardeners who leave the stems and stalks on their herbaceous perennials until spring. Their theory is that this helps protect the plants from winter weather and winterkill. Other gardeners prefer a clean cultivation to get rid of any hiding places for the insects, mulching with evergreen boughs for protection. I have personally tried both methods and can say that both of them work. I always clean the iris, delphiniums, and silver mound (*Artemisia schmidtiana*) before winter. Other plants I leave until spring. Iris tend to rot if a lot of vegetative material is left around them (of course if they were well weeded to begin with, there would be no vegetative materials on them anyway!).

In Maine, many perennials are not frost-hardy and will need to be potted up and brought in the house before a serious frost kills them.

Fall work often depends on the weather. In a warm fall you can accomplish more work than in a cold one. Fall is an ideal time to till up new gardens for the following spring. Gardens that have clay soil will actually be the better for it.

Winter is a good time to repair and paint garden tools. I am forever leaving hand tools in a garden and forgetting where they are. Paint them with a bright color and they will be easier to find.

Finally, when the garden growing season is over and the first snow has fallen, changing the green carpet to a snowy white blanket, the gardener settles back in the rocking chair with a book on gardening. The winter provides us time to reflect on our bounties of the last year and to work out plans for the next. Build your garden library with books and magazines, and dream over those ever-so-colorful pictures in the seed catalogs. See the appendix for suggested reading material, and enjoy!

CHAPTER TEN

Insects, Diseases, and Poisonous Plants

In a lilliputian world, ladybugs, lacewings, and praying mantises flitter
from stem to stem, flower to flower, feasting on diminutive enemies of man—
keepers of the small world in Mother Nature's chain of life.

—P.L.T.

Insects

Any time you are working with members of the plant kingdom, you will sooner or later encounter members of the enormous world of insects. I am not an entomologist, just a curious backyard gardener who has discovered the fascinating world of insects through my gardening adventures. The following information is based on my own experience and that of my gardening friends.

I have found that by working with Mother Nature, not against her, and by avoiding man-made chemicals, the natural chain of life can exist and we can all be healthy and happy.

Too often we humans want a quick-fix solution to all our problems. So what if a few bugs are seen in your garden? If you want to see ladybugs, you first must have a food supply for them.

When I give garden tours I tell my guest that they may see a few bugs, but that they can sample any edibles safely, knowing there are no chemical sprays to poison them. By not using chemicals I believe we have a higher population count of birds, bees, and butterflies at Wormwood Farm. Keep in mind that chemical sprays do not differentiate between the good bugs and the bad bugs—they kill *everything*. The birds and small mammals eat the poisoned bugs and plants, and then become sick or die from chemical buildup. Then everything up the food chain is affected.

The theory that plants cannot be grown without poison sprays is a man-made myth, spread by greed and chemical producers. Through most of time chemicals were not used, and there are too many organic gardeners today who prove it can be done.

The more chemicals sprayed on the land, the more insects build up a resistance to the chemical. As the new chemicals become stronger, it is a lost cause not only for the poisoned insects, but in the end for ourselves as well. Home gardeners are responsible for a large amount of chemical products being used unsafely, adding toxic chemicals to our environment.

Look around and see all the disease and sickness in our country. Everyone knows someone who has had cancer; this is not a disease that is new, but we are killing ourselves with it. Unfortunately we are forced to breathe polluted air from cars and factories, and our waters are all becoming unfit to drink. When are we going to say "enough" and stop using toxic poisons? We can stop using any on our own land and write our president and representatives in government that we want it stopped.

That's enough preaching for now—how are we going to deal with our insect problem without chemicals?

Dealing Naturally with Insects

Practicing good garden housekeeping is a start in controlling insects. Do not leave debris and weeds for them to hide in.

Healthy plants are the most resistant to insect populations. This does not mean your plant is sick if it has bugs. Plants are weaker at certain times in their lifespan, especially when flowering and producing seed pods. At these times they are putting all their energy into these activities. If you observe your plants, you will notice more aphids and other insects on them at these times. You will also notice an increase in ladybugs and other good bugs that eat the bad guys.

The first step in dealing with insects is to buy a good book on insects. If you don't know one bug from the other how can you know who's who, good or bad?

If you must use some kind of spray, use mild insecticides like rotenone or pyrethrin, made from plant products. Simple homemade sprays work for me—here is the recipe for my favorite.

Wormwood Farm Garden Spray

To one quart of boiling hot water, add:
1 crushed garlic glove
1 crushed hot red pepper
1 Tbsp. black pepper
½ cup strong chamomile tea
½ cup strong wormwood tea
½ cup strong yarrow tea

For the teas, use a handful of the leaves and/or flowers of the herb. Let this mixture set overnight to extract all the oils from the herbs. Strain through cheesecloth and add 1 Tbsp. mild dishwashing liquid. Use weekly as a mist on both outdoor plants and house plants to prevent insect build-up.

Who's Who in Bugdom

Some people are repelled by little creepy crawlers and flying fiends, but they are a necessary part of Mother Nature's food chain. Without insects there would be fewer birds, good insects, and small animals. The world would change drastically; soon all the herbivorous animals would deplete the world's food supply. Without insects many crops and flowers could not be pollinated. Already many one-crop farmers need to import bees for pollination because their own poisons have killed off the natural wild bees.

We are going to talk about two groups of insects, the good bugs and the bad bugs. First let's meet the good guys.

THE PREDATORS
Praying mantis: This insect's name can be interpreted two different ways. First, *praying* mantis, the official spelling, refers to the way it holds up its front feet in a praying position, maybe praying for some food to come along. It could also be called the *preying* mantis, for its voracious appetite for other insects. The mantis is a native of China that was introduced to North America in the early 1890s. They eat all other insects, good or bad, and in some mantis species the female even eats her mate. Large insects, one to three inches

long, they do a good job of depleting the insect population.

Lacewing/Aphid Lion: There are various species of lacewings, all with pretty, glasslike wings folded over their backs. The green lacewing in my garden is a voracious devourer of aphids, hence its second name, "aphid lion." Unfortunately lacewings are attracted to light and become victims of those electronic zappers seen in backyards.

Ladybugs: What country child is not familiar with the red-and-black ladybug? Even sophisticated ladies wear little ladybug pins. There are over 5,000 species of ladybugs that are beneficial to our gardens because of their appetite for aphids, thrips, mealybugs, and white flies. Ladybugs can be purchased from garden catalogs, but once placed in the garden they often leave the area because there is not enough food to sustain them. In order for good bugs to survive there must be bad bugs to eat.

Ground Beetles: I admit I am sometimes intimidated by those big fat black beetles when I am tilling the garden by hand and one crawls out of the soil toward me. I have learned to toss them away from me, and they quickly burrow back into the soil. They dislike being disturbed as much as I dislike seeing them. They are, however, welcome in my garden because of their relentless search for ground grubs, ants, caterpillars, slugs, and snails.

Birds and Bats: Although not insects, these creatures are great insect predators for us. Attract birds and bats with bird houses and bat boxes if you do not already have them. I welcome the barn swallows every spring because they harvest the black fly and mosquito population. I know the biting insects are here when I see the first swallow dive-bomb me in the garden. It seems they like to say hello to me when they return each year. I have noticed a great decrease in insects since I have put out bird feeders and nesting boxes. We even have bluebirds returning because they know we are chemical-free here.

THE BAD BUGS

The Chinese theory of yin and yang, or the balance of opposites, is quite correct. For the good bugs we have the opposite bad bugs. In order to have a natural order of things we cannot completely wipe the bad bugs out, but we can take measures to keep their numbers smaller.

In combating these pests it helps to understand how they attack your plants.

The *chewers* eat the flowers and leaves of plants. Chewers include caterpillars (moths and butterflies at the larval stage), flea beetles, and Japanese beetles.

To deal with chewers, hand pick, apply a stomach poison such as the recipe for the homemade spray, or use rotenone or pyrethrin.

The *suckers* suck juice from the plants, yet stomach poisons do not work on them. Sucking insects include aphids, thrips, scale, and flies. Kill by hand picking or washing off with cold sprays of water. Most suckers do not climb around very well. For spray solutions, try a liquid tea made from quassia chips, wormwood, and stinging nettle (*Urtica dioica*).

Ants: Ants are a pest for most of us, even though they are very interesting and live in quite complex, organized communities. They remind me of all the people shuffling here and there in big cities, each doing his or her own little part in the city organization.

Ants become a pest to plants not because they eat them but because they herd aphid populations like a herd of cattle. The aphids emit a sweet honey-dew substance the ants love, so the ants care for the aphids. I guess we can call them "aphid farmers" from the way they move the slow aphids from plant to plant. The problem is that the aphids not only suck the juices from our plants, they transmit diseases from plant to plant.

To prevent ants, we need to prevent aphids. One good method is to spray them often with cold water from the garden hose. Repellents to deter the ants include herbs such as pennyroyal (*Mentha pulegium*), wormwood (*Artemisia absinthium*), and hot red pepper (*Capsicum*). If ants are a problem for you, use branches or cut up pieces of wormwood and tansy (*Tanacetum vulgare*) as mulch for your plants.

Aphids: If you grow any plants at all you will sooner or later encounter a member of the aphid family. They appear in several different colors, usually in the color of the plant's stem or flowers—green or black aphids on stems, pink and whitish-gray on white flowers, and orange on butterfly weed.

Ladybugs will eat aphids. Since the aphids do not move around well without the aid of ants, the best deterrent is to spray cold water on them from the garden hose. If you have a hose with a fertilizing attachment, you can add a teaspoon of dishwashing liquid to help kill them.

Check plants weekly for aphids—they produce a new generation every twelve days.

Cutworms: These ugly, fat little brown or white grubworms are found in the soil. Most common in newly tilled soil, they also appear in soil that has not been well weeded. They eat small seedlings by cutting them off at ground

Japanese beetles damage plants by chewing on leaves.

level. If you have a grub problem in your area, wrap new seedlings with paper collars or till in oak leaves, which the bugs seem not to like. Keep your garden weeded.

Earwigs: Also called pinch bugs. They are not harmful to any great extent but they are annoying, and they *do* pinch if you pick them up. They are easy to trap. They come out at night and like shady dark places during the day. Take a piece of hose, plug one end, and put a little bran or banana peel inside the hose to attract them. They will hide inside, and in the morning you can dump them into a can of kerosene to kill them. Move the trap around to different areas to eliminate the insects.

Flea Beetles: Difficult to see, these little fleas jump off as soon as the plant is touched. When you see tiny pin holes in leaves, it is probably the work of the flea beetle. Horseradish (*Armoracia rusticana*) is susceptible to flea beetles. Adults overwinter in trash and weeds; therefore, keeping the fall garden clean will prevent infestations of the beetle the following year. To deter them, dust leaves with wood ashes (cold ones, please) and spray with wormwood (*Artemisia absinthium*) tea. Make this by soaking wormwood leaves in boiling hot water and letting it set overnight. Keep in mind that when using herbal teas as sprays, you must respray after every rainstorm.

Japanese Beetles: Our personal archenemy at Wormwood Farm ever since they started coming in 1988. They do more damage than any other insect we have seen here, chewing on leaves and even stripping entire plants if not checked. Japanese beetles were introduced to North America by accident in 1916 and have since become a serious pest to commercial and home gardeners alike. Even the birds do not seem to like to eat them. They relish certain types of plants—in my garden they prefer members of the mallow family, roses, potentillas, and hedges. Three methods of eliminating Japanese beetles seem to work:

Fig. 10-1. Handpicking Japanese Beetles

1. *Hand-picking morning or evening.* Kids like to pick what they call "sticky bugs," which cling to their hands when picked up (no one has yet been bitten). The kids call themselves the "sticky-bug hunters." The beetles cannot be caught during the hot part of the day—they will just fly away as you approach. For some reason they are very slow in the morning and in the evening. After you catch them, drop them in a mixture of kerosene and water to kill them.

2. *Commercial yellow traps.* They really do work, using a "smelly" solution that attracts the beetles. Because they do attract them, place the traps away from your plants. Empty the bag every day.

3. *Milky spore disease.* This dust, applied in the spring and fall to the ground, produces a natural disease in the soil that kills the beetle grubs that overwinter in the soils. The disease spore, *Bacillus popilliae,* is mixed with talcum and dusted on lawns. It turns the grubs' blood into a milky-white substance, hence its common name, milky spore disease. It is harmless to animals and humans; however, it will not work on lawns that have been sprayed with herbicides or other

chemicals. This natural approach may not work for several seasons, but you will see a reduction in the beetles. Use according to the manufacturer's directions.

Slugs and Snails: Probably the most often asked question about insects is "How do I get rid of slugs?" During the dry season these nasty, slimy little slugs are nonexistent, but let it rain and it will seem like it rained slugs. Not really insects, but members of the mollusk family, they need moisture to exist. They eat leaves, leaving an iridescent trail of slime behind them. Like the earwigs, they can be easily trapped. They eat at night and hide during the day. Place grapefruit halves or pieces of boards upside down, and gather slugs from them in early morning, putting them in heavily salted water. Slugs also dislike wood ashes and sand, so you can mulch the plants with these products.

Caterpillars: It is hard to generalize about caterpillars. There are some that turn into destructive moths, and some that turn into beautiful butterflies. They all do eat the leaves of certain plants. I always plant plenty of extra members of the Umbelliferae family, which include dill (*Anethum graveolens*), angelica (*Angelica archangelica*), carrots (*Daucus*), and sweet cicely (*Myrrhis odorata*), be-

Green and yellow black swallowtail caterpillars chew rue leaves.

cause I love the black swallowtail. Its caterpillar is an interesting green and yellow, easily detected on the plants. A wild area full of milkweed is left growing for the monarch. My grandchildren gather a few of its caterpillars and feed them, observing nature's wondrous ways as the caterpillar changes from larva to chrysalis to the beautiful black and orange butterfly. Since butterflies are very susceptible to chemicals, the best way to eliminate the bad caterpillars is to hand pick.

Rose Bugs: Chafers, rose slugs, and leaf hoppers are just a sample of the many pests that plague roses, the most susceptible of all the perennials in the backyard garden. To raise roses organically involves constant care. The hose will help keep aphids and white flies away; wash the bushes daily. Slugs and leaf rollers can be hand picked. Planting chives and garlic chives at the base of the rose bushes can help repel some of the insects.

Plant Diseases

Plants are as susceptible to diseases and improper care as we humans are. It would be impossible to cover the entire range of diseases in one short chapter, but I am giving a brief description of some diseases that the backyard gardener might encounter. I have been very lucky during my garden career because I have only been troubled by a few minor disease problems.

Diseases are classified in two basic categories. Some diseases are caused by improper care, the result of either our own actions or conditions beyond our control.

Improper care includes soil nutrient deficiency, wrong pH or texture of the soil, excessive or insufficient water supply, pesticide or chemical injury, and injuries from man or machinery. Events beyond our control include weather and pollution injury.

The other type of disease is that caused by bacteria, parasites, fungi, viruses, or insect damage.

Prevention Tips

We cannot control the weather or most viruses and bacteria but we can, with good care, help prevent many injuries.

- Buy disease-resistant plants.
- Provide good air circulation by not overcrowding plants.
- Keep your garden weed-free. Weeds can be carriers of disease.
- Cut and destroy any plant that you know has a disease. Do not put on the compost pile.
- If you suspect a disease, identify the problem. If you need to take the plant somewhere for identification, place it in an airtight plastic bag so it will not contaminate someone else's plants. Always ask first before bringing diseased plant material to someone else's garden.

Many times a suspected disease is only a soil problem that can easily be corrected. Your local extension office can help you identify the problem and suggest ways of controlling it. See the appendix for the address of your state cooperative extension service.

Diseases

FUNGUS DISEASES, including leaf spot, leaf blight, and black spot.
SYMPTOMS: Definite spots varying in color, size, and shape. Infected leaves may wither and die prematurely.
PLANTS SUBJECT TO ATTACK: All.
CONTROL: Collect and burn infected leaves; control the insects that may spread the disease; practice clean cultivation; provide good air circulation for plants.
BLIGHT (bud rot), a condition caused by pathogenic organisms.
SYMPTOMS: Water-soaked dark spots or streaks on the leaf, stem, or flowers, turning brown or black. Spots may drop out of the leaf, leaving a hole.
PLANTS SUBJECT TO ATTACK: Carnations (*Dianthus* sp.), chrysanthemum species, cranesbill geranium (*Geranium* sp.), delphiniums, poppies (*Papaver* sp.), primrose (*Primula*), and roses (*Rosa* sp.).
CONTROL: Collect and burn all infected parts; blight can be spread by insects or the gardener, especially in damp, wet weather. Practice clean cultivation and provide good air circulation. Buy disease-resistant plants. Difficult to cure once encountered.
MILDEW (downy or powdery mildew).
SYMPTOMS: A powdery feltlike fungus, growing on leaves and/or flowers. It may dwarf plants in early spring. Most mildews appear in late summer when the weather is humid, or in shady areas.

PLANTS SUBJECT TO ATTACK: Artemisia species, yarrows (*Achillea* sp.), astilbe, beebalm (*Monarda didyma*), carnations (*Dianthus* sp.), chrysanthemum species, coral bells (*Heuchera* sp.), coreopsis, delphiniums, fleabane (*Erigeron*), rudbeckia species, liatris, roses (*Rosa* sp.), salvia species, and wallflower (*Cherianthus cheiri*).

CONTROL: Do not plant perennials that are subject to mildew near one another. Cut and burn all infected parts. If I catch mildew early enough I have had success spraying it with a mixture of chamomile and yarrow tea and baking soda. Dusting with fine sulphur will also keep mildew in check. Provide good air circulation.

SMUT

SYMPTOMS: A black, sooty-looking spore appears on leaves, stems, bulbs, or seed. The fungus may enter at the seed stage, but the plant may not show any symptoms until it is mature.

PLANTS SUBJECT TO ATTACK: Windflower (*Anemone*), carnations (*Dianthus* sp.), clematis, columbine (*Aquilegia*), coral bells (*Heuchera* sp.), Maltese cross (*Lychnis chalcedonica*), speedwells (*Veronica* sp.), and violas.

CONTROL: Cut and destroy all infected materials (remember: do *not* place them in the compost pile). Buy smut-resistant seed and plants.

FUSARIUM WILT

SYMPTOMS: A permanent wilted condition that does not improve with watering. Plants are stunted and finally die.

PLANTS SUBJECT TO ATTACK: All.

CONTROL: Dig up and destroy the entire plant; there is no hope of recovery. To prevent recurrence, buy fusarium-resistant plants. Do not replant in the same area. The soil may need to be disinfected; check with your local extension office.

Poisonous Plants

In the world of gardening there are many different side trips to pursue. Two of these related interests are entomology, the study of insects, and toxicology, the study of poisonous plants.

We live with poisonous plants every day of our lives. Some grow on our windowsills and others in our gardens and back yards, as well as those growing wild in the fields and forests.

We can avoid planting poisonous plants in our garden but we cannot control the poisonous weeds growing all around us. For the safety of ourselves, our children, and animals it is a good idea to be acquainted with the plants that are dangerous or the parts of certain plants that are poisonous. For example, the stems and leaves of tomato plants are poisonous if eaten.

The best preventive against plant poisoning is to keep an eye on small children and teach older children about the good and bad plants. Teach children to always check with an adult before eating plants outside. Unfortunately accidents can and do happen, no matter how much education or worrying we provide. Keep the telephone number of your nearest poison control center near the phone. If you have reason to believe that a child has been poisoned by a plant, immediately call the center or your family doctor. Keep in mind that many poisons do not begin to work until five to 20 hours after the poison has been ingested. Do call or write to the poison control center for booklets and information on first aid for poison victims.

Many of our poisonous plants are used as medicinals. Mother Nature has provided man with plants for every need. Digitalis, from foxglove (*Digitalis purpureum*), and morphine, from the opium poppy (*Papaver*), are important medicines. They are poisonous only in improper dosages; however, you should *never* experiment with these plants.

The evil side of poisonous plants being used to commit suicide or murder has been recorded throughout history. Plants range in toxicity from the fatal poisons of belladonna, hemlock, lily of the valley (*Convallaria*), and rhododendron, to rue (*Ruta*) and celandine (*Chelidenium majus*), which may make you very sick but probably will not be fatal. Ancient witches knew the magic of plants and could induce convulsions using the proper amount of certain poisonous plants.

There are over 600 poisonous plants in the United States alone. Some are so bitter, like the irisin in the iris root or the absinth in wormwood (*Artemisia absinthium*), that few people are likely to ingest enough of the poison to kill them.

Safety Tips for Growing Poisonous Plants

If you garden to any extent, you probably will already have some poisonous plants in your garden. To be safe, note the following ideas.

- Know which plants are poisonous and label them.
- Teach children the dangers and what plants not to eat.
- Store seeds and bulbs out of reach of small children and pets.
- Do not plant poisonous plants near animal pens. Some animals are smart enough not to eat certain plants, but others are not.

Poisonous Plants

The following is only a partial list of all of the plants that are poisonous. You will see several that are used medicinally. Those plants are safe only when used in correctly prescribed quantities and should *never* be used without medical supervision.

PLANT	POISONOUS PART
Arnica (all species)	all parts
Baneberry (*Actaea*, all species)	all parts
Baptisia (*Baptisia tinctoria*)	leaves and shoots
Bleeding heart (*Dicentras*)	all parts
Bloodroot (*Sanguinaria canadensis*)	all parts
Buttercup (*Ranunculus* sp.)	all parts
Celandine (*Chelidonium majus*)	all parts
Clematis (all species)	all parts
Columbine (*Aquilegia*)	all parts
Cow parsley (*Heracleum lanatum*)	leaves cause rash similar to poison ivy
Deadly nightshade (*Solanum nigrum*)	berries
Delphinium (all species)	all parts
Euphorbia (*Euphorbia*)	all parts
Ferns (some species)	all parts
Flax (*Linum perenne*)	all parts
Foxglove (*Digitalis purpureum*)	leaves
Ground cherry (*Physalis* sp.)	leaves, unripe fruit
Hyacinths (*Hyacinthus* sp.)	all parts
Hydrangea (all species)	all parts
Iris	all parts

Jack in the pulpit (*Arisaema triphyllum*)	roots
Jimsonweed (*Datura stramonium*)	all parts
Lily of the valley (*Convallaria*)	all parts
Lupine (*Lupinus*)	seeds
May apple (*Podophyllum petatum*)	roots, seeds, leaves, mature stems
Narcissus (*Narcissi* sp.)	juice
Poison ivy (*Rhus radicans*)	leaves, stems, roots
Pokeweed (*Phytolacca americana*)	all parts
Tansy (*Tanacetum vulgare*)	all parts
Windflower (*Anemone* sp.)	all parts
Wolf's bane (*Aconitum napellus*)	all parts

Part Two

Plant Profiles

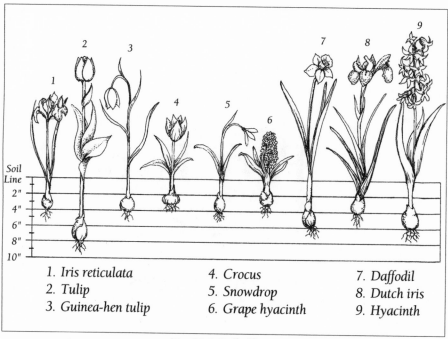

Soil Line	
2"	
4"	
6"	
8"	
10"	

1. Iris reticulata
2. Tulip
3. Guinea-hen tulip

4. Crocus
5. Snowdrop
6. Grape hyacinth

7. Daffodil
8. Dutch iris
9. Hyacinth

Fig. 11-1. Bulb Chart

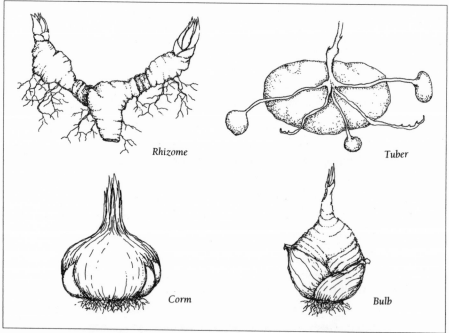

Rhizome

Tuber

Corm

Bulb

Fig. 11-2. Root Systems: Rhizome, Tuber, Corm, and Bulb

CHAPTER ELEVEN

Bulbs

Then the pied wind-flowers and the tulip tall,
And narcissi, the fairest among them all,
Who gaze on their eyes in the stream's recess,
Till they die of their own dear loveliness.
—Percy Bysshe Shelley, "The Sensitive Plant"

This chapter contains a sampling of the more popular bulb plants for the back-yard garden. I have included only the bulbs that stay in the ground year-round, such as crocus, narcissus, etc. Not included are bulbs like canna lilies and dahlias that in zones 3 and 4 need to be taken up at the end of the summer, stored in a cool place, and then replanted in the spring.

I am taking liberties with the word "bulb." Here it will include also the rhizome, tuber, and corm root systems, but each profile will identify the correct type.

These root systems are basically alike in their growth patterns—sort of like underground "buds" waiting for the correct conditions to emerge from the ground and flower. When the bloom period of the plant has passed, its energy is then transferred from the decaying foliage into the root system. Here it produces nutrients for the following year's flower production and the reproduction of new bulbs. I will therefore repeat several times the importance of *not* cutting off the decaying foliage.

My first experience with narcissus was the spring we moved to this farm. A long row of narcissus produced a row of white fragrant heads in the front garden border, which died out in late spring. Being inexperienced (this was before I started studying garden books) I cut that ugly decaying foliage right down to the ground. True to form, the following year I had a lovely display of green foliage with nary a flower.

Hide the unattractive decaying foliage of your bulbs by interplanting them with other perennials, or overplant with annuals.

Bulbs are self-propagating. In the case of the narcissus the original bulb splits, forming new bulbs that in time separate themselves from the mother bulb. The corms of the crocus bulb increase by multiplying themselves. Eventually the mother corm disintegrates, leaving tiny new bulbs in its place.

General Guide to Growing Bulb Plants

Select only healthy bulbs. Carefully examine each bulb before planting. It should be clean and firm, with no blemishes or cut skin. There should be no bruises or soft spongy spots.

Purchase the best bulbs you can afford. Small discounted bulbs are fine if you are not in a hurry for flowers; they may take two to three years before they are large enough to bloom. If you have the space you can make a nursery bed for small bulbs that you can transfer to the regular garden when they are mature enough to flower.

Designing with Your Bulbs

There is nothing more promising than to look out the window in early spring and see the blossoms of windflowers (*Anemone*), crocus, and hyacinths, defying even a light snowfall. Place your bulb garden where you can enjoy it from a window. Planting in clumps is more attractive than single bulbs. Some bulbs can be naturalized; narcissus and daffodils are especially nice naturalized in an unweeded area. If you want to naturalize your bulbs, till the soil first to give them a good start. Then they will take care of themselves.

Bulbs are nice used in your perennial gardens to provide early spring color. They bloom along with early perennials such as rock cress (*Arabis*), lily of the valley (*Convallaria*), and candytuft (*Iberis sempervirens*).

Putting Your Bulbs in the Ground

Unlike other perennials that we generally plant in spring (I personally am not fond of fall plantings) bulbs that bloom in early spring are planted in late summer or early fall. I put my bulbs in the ground in September before the cold weather moves in on us. This gives the bulbs a little time to secure their roots in the soil. I have had several people tell me they lost all their bulbs from late fall plantings. There is always the mice and mole problem, but I believe the bulbs didn't have time to establish themselves before the ground froze.

In southern states bulbs are planted in January and bloom about nine weeks later.

Bulbs are happy in full sun or partial shade (see individual profiles). Good drainage is important; if planted in a poorly drained area, your bulbs will rot.

As a general rule, the depth of planting from the top of the bulb to the top of the soil should be three times the bulb's diameter. Distance between bulbs should be determined by the mature height of the plant. For example, hyacinths like to be about 6 to 8 inches apart, but the small windflowers (*Anemone*) can be placed 3 to 4 inches apart.

Plant the bulbs with the "eyes" looking up. Yes, people have planted them upside down and wondered the next spring where their flowers were. As a child, when I would help my grandfather plant potatoes, he would say, "Make sure the potatoes are looking up toward the sky so they can find their way up through the soil."

Feeding and Caring for Your Bulbs

When you are preparing the soil for the bulbs, add some compost and a fertilizer with bonemeal or another good low-nitrogen fertilizer. When the plant is in the bud stage, add another feeding of fertilizer.

Water is important for bulbs, especially after the flowering period when food is being stored for next year's blooms. Provide water for your bulbs when Mother Nature does not provide at least an inch of water a week.

Take care when weeding your bulb garden—do not injure bulbs as you hoe or dig in the soil. Keep the area marked so you do not disturb the sleeping beauties.

Keep in mind that naturalized bulbs will also need water and fertilizer. Naturalized areas can be mowed after the foliage has decayed sufficiently.

For best results the following spring, always deadhead tulip seedpods.

If you have a heavy crop of older bulb foliage and few flowers, it is probably time to divide your bulbs. I divide mine about every five years.

Bulbs are an important part of the perennial garden, both for early color and for interplanting with other perennials. Plan your design for other perennials to cover the bulbs' decaying foliage without disrupting the garden's beauty.

ALLIUM

(**a**-lee-um)

SYNONYMS: Onion; flowering types

FAMILY: Liliaceae

DESCRIPTION: The foliage ranges from the flat scapes or leafless flower stalks of the garlic chives (*Allium tuberosum*) to the round scapes of the common chives (*Allium schoenoprasum*). Flowers appear as terminal clusters of many little flowers that generally form a globe.

CULTIVATION: Full sun to partial shade. Not fussy about soil conditions as long as there is good drainage and some organic matter. Fertilize once in early spring with low-nitrogen fertilizer. Use care in weeding; some species look like grass when they sprout in the spring.

USES: Fresh or dried arrangements. Chives and garlic chives are edible.

SPECIES:

Allium aflatunense

(**a**-lee-um **a**-fla-tun-**en**-see)

SYNONYM: Flowering onion

HARDY TO ZONE: 4

HEIGHT: 2 to 3 feet

DESCRIPTION: Purple globe-shaped flowers. Other species include *Allium giganteum*, which has large leaves and 6-inch flowers on 3-foot scapes (to zone 5).

BLOOM TIME: May-June

Allium moly

(**a**-lee-um **m**o-lee)

SYNONYM: Yellow flowering onion

HARDY TO ZONE: 2

HEIGHT: 6 to 8 inches

DESCRIPTION: Flat open umbels of yellow, clustered flowers. Plant close together for best results.

BLOOM TIME: June

Allium schoenoprasum

(**a**-lee-um sko-**en**-o-pra-sum)

SYNONYM: Chives

HARDY TO ZONE: 3

HEIGHT: 15 to 24 inches

DESCRIPTION: Hollow round leaves with lavender round globe of many flowers. Scapes are edible.

BLOOM TIME: May-June

Allium senescens

(**a**-lee-um sen-**e**-sens)

SYNONYM: Curly onion

See chapter 12.

Allium sphaerocephalum

(**a**-lee-um sfie-ro-**sef**-a-lum)

SYNONYMS: Drumstick allium

HARDY TO ZONE: 4

HEIGHT: 28 inches

DESCRIPTION: Unusual oblong-shaped flower clusters of reddish purple. Plant bulbs together for best results. Be careful—early growth looks like grass; do not pull out as weeds. My personal favorite of all the alliums.

BLOOM TIME: July-August.

Allium tuberosum

(**a**-lee-um tew-be-**ro**-sum)

SYNONYM: Garlic chives

HARDY TO ZONE: 3

HEIGHT: 18 inches

DESCRIPTION: Flat solid leaves with white, flat-topped, clustered, fragrant flowers. Scapes are edible, with a garlic-onion taste. Roots are more tuberous than bulblike. If flowers are left on the plant, it will self-seed.

BLOOM TIME: August

ANEMONE

(a-**nem**-o-nee)

SYNONYM: Windflower

FAMILY: Ranunculaceae

HARDY TO ZONE: 4

HEIGHT: 3 to 6 inches

DESCRIPTION: The anemone prefers partial shade and does very well at the base of trees. In a rich, well-drained soil it produces early spring colors of pink, white, and purple along with the snowdrops (*Galanthus nivalis*).

Pliny said the flower of the anemone can open only at the bidding of the wind, hence the name "windflower." The daisylike flowers indeed do appear in windy spring weather. Greek and Roman mythology abounds with myths about flowers, many of them named for gods and goddesses. According to the Greeks, the anemone sprang from the tears shed for Venus as she cried over the slain body of the beloved Adonis.

BLOOM TIME: Very early spring

SPECIES:

Anemone blanda

(a-**nem**-o-nee **blan**-da)

DESCRIPTION: These showy plants open their daisy heads when the sun is out and close them tightly on rainy and cloudy days.

Anemone pulsatilla

(a-**nem**-o-nee pul-sa-**til**-la)

DESCRIPTION: Also called pasqueflower, this species has poppylike heads followed by unusual fuzzy seed heads similar to the seed head of the clematis vine flower. Juice of the purple petals will yield a green liquid that can be used to dye Easter eggs but is not a permanent dye.

CONVALLARIA MAJALIS

(kon-va-**lah**-ree-a mah-**yah**-lis)

SYNONYM: Lily of the valley

FAMILY: Liliaceae

HARDY TO ZONE: 2

HEIGHT: 6 to 9 inches

DESCRIPTION: Several wonderfully sweet white bell-like flowers, arranged on separate stems, hang under large, shiny heart-shaped leaves. The rootstalks, called pips, spread invasively. Hard to eradicate once established, it makes an excellent ground cover for slopes or around trees. The heavenly scent from the flowers has kept this plant a garden regular throughout the years. Pretty as a little corsage or mini-arrangement. A pink variety is also available.

BLOOM TIME: June

CULTIVATION: Will grow just about anywhere there is good drainage. Very invasive.

PROPAGATION: Root division

USES: Wonderful small fresh or dried arrangements

CROCUS VERNUS

(**kro**-cus **ver**-nus)

SYNONYMS: none

FAMILY: Iridaceae

HARDY TO ZONE: 4

HEIGHT: 3 to 6 inches

DESCRIPTION: There are over 20 varieties of spring-flowering crocus. I have my crocuses planted under a hydrangea tree where they receive full sun before the tree leaves out. The decaying foliage can be left to die down naturally. The little crocus plants will persist despite neglect. Flowers are yellow, white, and purple.

BLOOM TIME: April-May

CULTIVATION: Crocuses like good, well-drained soil. Do not overfertilize. Use about half the strength you would on other bulbs. In regular gardens, overplant with other perennials. For extra early crocuses, plant near foundations where the soil warms up the earliest.

Mice, moles, rabbits, and squirrels may dig and eat the crocus bulbs. Folks with cats and dogs rarely have that problem.

PROPAGATION: After several years of growth, the roots will become tightly clumped. Dig and separate after foliage has died down.

FRITILLARIA MELEAGRIS

(fri-ti-**lah**-ree-a mel-ee-**ah**-gris)

SYNONYM: Guinea-hen flower

FAMILY: Liliaceae

HARDY TO ZONE: 1

HEIGHT: 12 to 18 inches

DESCRIPTION: I first purchased the bulbs of the guinea-hen flower because at the time I had a pearl-gray guinea that I loved. He would fly to the top of the garage roof and yell like crazy whenever anyone entered the yard. He was the best watchdog we ever had; he would chase away any other animal entering the yard as he watched over the flock of hens. The bloom of the flower proved to be as interesting. In late May and early June the reddish-purple checkered flowers look like giant bells nodding their heads in the wind. There are over 70 species of this plant to choose from.

CULTIVATION: The bulbs are planted 3 inches deep in good soil. They require full sun to partial shade.

USES: A nice addition to fresh arrangements.

GALANTHUS NIVALIS

(ga-**lanth**-us ni-**vah**-lis)

SYNONYM: Snowdrops

FAMILY: Amaryllidaceae

HARDY TO ZONE: 3

HEIGHT: 4 to 5 inches

DESCRIPTION: These frosty-white bell-shaped flowers are the first to appear in the spring garden. The nodding flowers held between two leaves defy the coldest spring weather. They even do well in a heavier soil than most bulbs will tolerate. Snowdrops prefer partial or light shade. A double form, *Galanthus elwesii flore pleno* is an exceptionally pretty plant.

BLOOM TIME: Very early spring

HYACINTHUS

(Hi-a-**sin**-thus)

SYNONYM: Fragrant hyacinth, Dutch hyacinth

FAMILY: Liliaceae

HARDY TO ZONE: 4

HEIGHT: 6 to 8 inches

DESCRIPTION: I can't think of any flower with a more wonderful fragrance. Popular as a late-winter forced house flower, it grows very well in my zone 4 garden. Several clumps of hyacinth set near the doorway will make anyone stop, look, and smell. They come in all colors. Greek mythology says the hyacinth sprang from the blood of a Greek youth named Hyacinthus, who was immortalized by Apollo through the flower.

CULTIVATION: Plant in full sun, sheltered from strong winds in good soil that is well drained. Soil that is too rich does not give the good fragrance that a sandy average loam will. As with herbs, it is the essential oil we want to encourage.

BLOOM TIME: May

IRIS
See chapter 13.

LILIUM
(**lil**-ee-um)
SYNONYMS: Lilies
FAMILY: Liliaceae
HARDY TO ZONE: 3
HEIGHT: 12 inches to 4 feet
DESCRIPTION: With over 200 varieties and continual hybridizing, you can enjoy some type of lily in bloom all season. Lilies have four basic flower types: trumpet, pendulous, bowl, and erect.

The history of the lily goes back to ancient times. Many flowers will come and go at various periods of time throughout our history, gaining and losing favor, but the lily has always remained a favorite. Maybe this is because the lily has been a potent symbol since early times. It was the sacred flower of the Minoan goddess and the Greek goddess Hera. The Madonna lily (*Lilium candidum*) is dedicated to the Virgin Mary. The lily has also been a heraldic device for many different noble families and schools.

Since the lily has such a long history, there are of course many stories surrounding it. Anglo-Saxon folklore says the flower can foretell the sex of an unborn child. A person approaches the expectant mother with a lily in one hand and a rose in the other hand. If the mother chooses the rose the child will be a girl, but if she chooses the lily it will be a boy.

The lily was also considered an herb, and some species are eaten. Dioscorides tells of its use as a medicine: "For a burn, take lily and yarrow, boil them in butter and smear therewith." It was also popular "being beaten with honey to cleareth ye face and maketh them without wrinkles." The closest I have seen lily used on the skin is when the tiger lily and turban lily are in bloom. The kids like to paint their faces with the brown pollen from the stamens to make freckles.

Again, the list of lily species is overwhelming and beyond the scope of this book. The species listed below are some I grow in my garden.

CULTIVATION: Lilies will grow in any average to good soil with good drainage, in full sun to partial shade. Unlike other bulbs, when purchasing lilies, be sure the root system is intact, alive, and healthy-looking. Plant as soon as you get them home. Plant all season long, putting the bulbs 4 to 6 inches below the soil. The exception is the Madonna lily, which should be only an inch below the soil.

Fertilize with low-nitrogen fertilizer in early spring. Use care weeding around your bulbs so you do not injure them. Lilies do not like bare soil, so underplant with other perennial ground covers.

PROPAGATION: Usually by bulbs, but in some cases, such as the tiger lily, the tiny "bulbils" (little seeds) growing at the base of each stem up the stalk can be gathered and planted. They will take two to three years to bloom.

SPECIES:

Lilium canadense
SYNONYMS: Canadian lily, wild yellow lily, fairy-caps
HARDY TO ZONE: 2
HEIGHT: 4 feet
DESCRIPTION: A tall lily with drooping, funnel-shaped yellow blooms, with reddish-brown spots. The leaves are lance-shaped.
BLOOM TIME: June-July

Lilium superbum
SYNONYM: Turk's-cap lily
HARDY TO ZONE: 2
HEIGHT: 3 to 6 feet
DESCRIPTION: Orange-red flowers with purple spots within the large bloom. Each plant contains from six to ten flowers in pyramidal clusters. A North American native, this is the one kids like for painting freckles on their faces, using the six long anthers of the stamens.
BLOOM TIME: July-August

Lilium philadelphicum
SYNONYM: Wood lily
HARDY TO ZONE: 2
HEIGHT: 2 to 3 feet
DESCRIPTION: A strikingly beautiful lily, scarlet-red with spots within its erect, terminal flowers. Multiplies quickly in an enriched garden soil. This lily does best with partial shade.
BLOOM TIME: June

There are so many hybrids that if you are serious about cultivating lilies, I suggest you join the Lily Association listed in the appendix or find a local grower who specializes in the hundreds of available species.

MUSCARI ARMENIACUM
(mus-**kah**-ree ar-men-ee-**ah**-kum)
SYNONYM: Grape hyacinth
FAMILY: *Liliaceae*
HARDY TO ZONE: 1
HEIGHT: 4 to 6 inches
DESCRIPTION: Quickly spreading to fill

an area, these hardy little bulbs hold their own even with neglect. Plant under deciduous trees for color before the trees' leaves come out.

CULTIVATION: Plant in average soil in partial shade or full sun.

USES: The small flowers make good fresh arrangements that last a long time.

NARCISSUS

(nar-**sis**-us)

SYNONYMS: Daffodils, jonquils

FAMILY: Amaryllidaceae

HARDY TO ZONE: 2

HEIGHT: 6 to 8 inches (dwarfs); 14 to 18 inches (standard)

DESCRIPTION: The question is, which is which—narcissus, daffodil, and jonquil? The answer is that narcissus is the name for the entire species, daffodil is the common name for the large cupped narcissus, and jonquil is the name for one species of narcissus (*Narcissus jonquilla*). In the southern states all trumpet narcissi are often called jonquils. Hybridizing has provided the backyard gardener with a wide range of colors and bicolored narcissi.

The story of how this flower got its name is probably the best-known story of the bulb family, but I will repeat it here. The handsome boy Narcissus was so much in love with himself that he drowned while idolizing his own image in a mountain pool. This myth originated long ago when people believed that evil spirits could take a person's very soul by capturing his or her reflection. The narcissus was therefore said to have sprung from the boy's soul where he died.

BLOOM TIME: Early spring

CULTIVATION: A good investment for the backyard gardener, narcissi are very hardy and increase quickly, even surviving neglect. This makes them a good choice for naturalizing an area. My experience shows narcissi planted in partial shade tend to have larger and longer-lasting flowers than those planted in full sun. Although all bulbs like good drainage, the daffodils will tolerate wetter areas than most other bulbs.

TULIPA

(**tew**-lip-a)

SYNONYM: Tulip

FAMILY: Liliaceae

HARDY TO ZONE: 1

HEIGHT: 6 to 24 inches

DESCRIPTION: Ghislain de Busbecq, ambassador to Constantinople, introduced the tulip to Europe over 400 years ago, along with the mock orange (*Philadelphus*) and horse chestnut (*Aesculus*).

During the seventeenth century the famous tulip craze became known as "tulipomania," especially in Holland. Individual tulip bulbs were sold for incredible prices. Stocks were purchased on speculation, and many new varieties were hybridized to get a high return on investments. Finally the government stepped in, and many people lost a considerable amount of money.

That tulip craze and more recent hybridizing have provided an unbelievably wide selection of tulip bulbs for the backyard gardener. Tulips are available in different styles, colors, and bicolors. When someone says "tulips" many of us think of Holland, windmills, and the Darwin type, or single, tulip. Besides the Darwin type there are tulips on multiple flowering stalks, lily-flowering tulips with pointed edges like the lily flower, parrot-type tulips with shaggy edges, and the peony tulip, which looks like the peony flower. The plants range in size from the dwarf kaufmanniana tulips to the taller 20-inch standards.

BLOOM TIME: May to the end of June, depending on the variety.

CULTIVATION: Tulips like well-drained, enriched soil. They prefer full sun; however, tulips grown in partial shade keep their flowers and color for a longer period of time.

PROPAGATION: By bulb division; the size of the bulb does influence the size of the flower. Initial plantings should use bulbs of the 1½-inch size. Tulips are easy to start by seed but take five to seven years before reaching flowering bulb size. Gardeners often get pleasure from starting seeds and watching the entire lifespan of these plants.

Some gardeners lift the tulip bulbs every year after they bloom. However, I prefer adding more bulbs yearly and overplanting with annuals or other perennials.

When adding mulch to the tulip bed, keep it away from the stems. Winter mulch should not be added until the ground has sufficiently frozen, or you may be inviting a mouse for a winter lunch of bulbs.

When cutting tulips for indoor arrangements leave the leaves, which are on the same stem, to provide nourishment for next year's flowers. Deadhead tulip flowers to prevent formation of seed pods.

CHAPTER TWELVE

Low Ground Covers

Plants between 1 and 12 inches high

And the Lord God took the man, and put him
into the garden of Eden to till it and to keep it.
—Genesis 2:15

This chapter covers perennial plants with foliage that grows to between 1 and 12 inches high. In some species, such as coral bells (*Heuchera*), the flowers will be taller than the leaf height. The final mature height of any plant is, of course, determined by your individual soil texture, pH, the light factor, and the moisture it receives—as well as your personal care.

Low-growing perennials can be used in the front of a border, as edging material for walkways, or in rock gardens. Thyme (*Thymus* sp.), rupturewort (*Herniaria glabra*), and the creeping sedums make good plantings for rock walls and between walkways of brick, tile, or stone.

Areas that are difficult to mow can be covered with low-growing creeping perennials. Good types include: for the sun or shade, navelwort (*Omphalodes*); for shade, sweet woodruff (*Asperula odorata*); and for full sun, lamb's ear (*Stachys lanata*), or beacon silver lamium (*Lamium*).

ACHILLEA TOMENTOSA

(ah-**kill**-lee-a toh-men-**toe**-sa)
SYNONYM: Woolly yarrow
FAMILY: Asteraceae (formerly Compositae)
HARDY TO ZONE: 2
HEIGHT: Foliage 2 inches; flowers 6 to 10 inches

Achillea Tomentosa

DESCRIPTION: A ground-hugging perennial with gray-green, lace-patterned foliage. Yellow flowers shoot high above the foliage with bright yellow terminal cluster umbels.
BLOOM TIME: June-July
CULTIVATION: Full sun to partial shade, and well drained, lean to average soil. Keep it weed-free since it does not like competition. Its shallow root system spreads slowly. Cut flower heads off after the bloom period.
PROPAGATION: Seeds or root division.
USES: Rock gardens, edgings, or dried flower gardens. Excellent flowers for both dried or fresh arrangements. Holds color best of all yarrows.
SPECIES: See chapters 13 and 14 for taller species.

AEGOPODIUM PODAGRARIA

(ee-go-**poh**-dee-um pod-a-**gar**-ee-a)
SYNONYMS: Bishopweed, gout-weed, snow-on-the-mountain, Jack jump about, Herb Gerard
FAMILY: Apiaceae (formerly Umbelliferae)
HARDY TO ZONE: 2
HEIGHT: 6 to 8 inches
DESCRIPTION: Cream and green variegated, maple-leaf-shaped leaves. White flat umbel cluster flowers, like dill flower heads. Invasive by creeping root stock and self-sowing.
BLOOM TIME: June-July
CULTIVATION: Color stays best in partial shade, but will grow anywhere from sun to shade. I cleaned out a bed of bishopweed two years ago and I'm still finding new plants trying to catch hold from small pieces of root left undetected. Only merciless weeding will keep it under control.

Aegopodium podagraria

PROPAGATION: Seeds or division.
USES: Excellent ground cover, it spreads quickly to fill in large areas. Will choke out most weeds and can be cut down in fall. If all-green leaves appear cut them off to keep the good variegated strain.
HISTORY: The name *Herb Gerard* comes from its dedication to St. Gerard. The name *bishopweed* comes from its frequent use at monasteries in the Middle Ages where the monks cultivated it for medicinal purposes. The name goutweed comes from its cure for the gout; the Latin word for gout is *podagra*.

AJUGA REPTANS

(a-**joo**-ga **rept**-anz)
SYNONYMS: Bugleweed, carpetweed
FAMILY: Lamiaceae (formerly Labiatae)
HARDY TO ZONE: 3

Ajuga "burgundy glow"

HEIGHT: 3 to 5 inches
DESCRIPTION: Shiny green leaves often with bronze tones in spring and fall. Rosette in habit, it creeps along, rooting as it goes. It is not invasive except in very rich soil. Brilliant 5-inch bluish-purple flowers.
BLOOM TIME: June
CULTIVATION: Average to good soil. Does best in partial shade but will grow anywhere from full sun to shade if well watered.
PROPAGATION: Division of creeping rootstalks.
USES: Under trees or as a ground cover. Medicinal use as an astringent, as a general laxative, and for hemorrhage and consumption.
SPECIES: *Ajuga* **"burgundy glow"** has pretty pink, bronze, and white leaves. For damp moist soils, try

Ajuga pyramidalis, with glossy leaves and royal-blue flowers.

ALCHEMILLA VULGARIS "ALPINA"

(al-ke-**mil**-la vul-**ga**-ris)
SYNONYMS: Mountain lady's mantle, alpine lady's mantle

Alchemilla vulgaris "alpina"

FAMILY: Rosaceae
HARDY TO ZONE: 3
HEIGHT: 6 to 9 inches
DESCRIPTION: Shiny, pleated leaves may be edged in white, depending on the species. A mini-version of the common lady's mantle (*Alchemilla vulgaris*). The flowers are the same green-gold color in a small airy cluster spray. Deep, spreading roots.
BLOOM TIME: June-July
CULTIVATION: Full sun to partial or filtered shade. Soil should be well drained and slightly on the alkaline side—feed a little bonemeal or wood ash now and then. If you don't gather the blooms for dried crafts, cut them off when the bloom period is over.
PROPAGATION: Seeds are slow and need stratification (as many alpine plants do). You can also divide the root system.
USES: Fresh or dried arrangements,

in the garden as edging, or in a rock garden area.
HISTORY: *Alchemilla* comes from the word "alchemy," suggesting that the plant was once believed to have magical powers. This neat little plant is very seldom bothered by pests, so the magic may be its ability to stay insect-free.

ALLIUM SENESCENS GLAUCUM

(**a**-lee-um **sen**-e-cens **glow**-kum)
SYNONYMS: Dwarf curly onion, cork-screw onion, cowlick onion
FAMILY: Liliaceae
HARDY TO ZONE: 3
HEIGHT: 6 to 8 inches
DESCRIPTION: The gray-green leaves turn and twist as they grow, hence its name corkscrew or curly onion. Flowers look like chive blossoms in a pinkish-lavender.

Allium senescens glaucum

BLOOM TIME: August
CULTIVATION: Full sun to partial shade. They like a slightly alkaline soil; add wood ashes or bonemeal every spring.
PROPAGATION: Seeds or root division.
USES: Fresh or dried arrangements; a nice front border plant or specimen in a rock garden.

SPECIES: There is a taller species (18 to 20 inches) with the same name and same appearance; blooms in July.

ARABIS CAUCASICA

(**ar**-a-bis kaw-**kas**-i-ka)
SYNONYM: Rock cress
FAMILY: Brassicaceae (formerly Cruciferae)
HARDY TO ZONE: 4
HEIGHT: 4 to 8 inches
DESCRIPTION: There are over a hundred species of arabis, most of them alpine in nature, but not many are readily available to the general public. This one has oval gray leaves with white (or pink) small fragrant flowers in loose racemes.
BLOOM TIME: May-June
CULTIVATION: Full sun or partial shade, in well-drained lean to average soil. Give plant a good haircut once flowers have finished blooming to make leaves thicker. However, this is not absolutely necessary for the health of the plant.
PROPAGATION: Seeds or division of runners.

Arabis Caucasica

USES: Use in rock gardens, borders, or as a ground cover.
SPECIES: **"Flore-pleno"** is a pretty double variety with long-lasting

flowers. *A. blepharophlla* has carmine-red flowers and is hardy to zone 5.

ARTEMISIA SCHMIDTIANA

(ar-tay-**mis**-ee-a shmit-ee-**ah**-na)
SYNONYMS: Silver mound, angel hair
FAMILY: Asteraceae (formerly Compositae)

Artemisia Schmidtiana

HARDY TO ZONE: 3
HEIGHT: 10 to 15 inches
DESCRIPTION: Very finely divided silvery foliage with insignificant flowers. The plant forms a nice round mound. Slightly aromatic.
CULTIVATION: Full sun to partial shade. Good drainage, or the plant may develop crown rot. Lean to average soil. If the soil is too rich or humidity too high, the plant will open up in the center and lie over.
PROPAGATION: Division or cuttings.
USES: Great as a specimen, a low hedge, or an edging plant. The foliage dries very nicely for a base when making wreaths, or cut up for Christmas potpourri.

ASPERULA ODORATA

(as-pe-**rool**-ah o-do-**rah**-ta)
Also often listed under *Galium odoratum*.

SYNONYMS: Sweet woodruff, wood rove, master of the woods.
FAMILY: Rubiaceae
HARDY TO ZONE: 4
HEIGHT: 8 to 12 inches
DESCRIPTION: Bright green shiny leaves growing in whorls up square stems. Tiny white, starlike flowers cover the plant. The fresh plant has no scent, but once dried it smells of new-mown hay or vanilla.
BLOOM TIME: May-June
CULTIVATION: Partial or filtered shade. Likes acid, moist woodland soil with a lot of composted organic matter. Plant with other acid-loving plants such as rhododendrons, azaleas, pines, etc.

Asperula odorata

PROPAGATION: Seeds are very difficult. They need to be very fresh, with a stratification of about six weeks. Germination rate is low. Ants often eat the very tiny seeds even before they can be gathered. The best propagation method is by division of its creeping root stalks.
USES: Well known as both an herb and a ground cover for shady slopes. Fresh leaves are used in Germany to flavor Rhine wine for the popular May Day drink, *Maibowle*. It's easy to make your own: Steep leaves and/or flowers in Rhine wine for ten days. Serve with strawberries in the glass. It is also used as a medicinal for wounds and cuts. Leaves were used to stuff mattresses as a moth repellent, and as snuff in the olden days. It can be used as a substitute for vanilla. To make, steep leaves and/or flowers in boiling hot water overnight, drain, and use in baking recipes.

AURINIA SAXATILIS

(aw-**rin**-ee-a sax-**ah**-ti-lis)
Also listed as *Alyssum Saxatile* (a-**lis**-sum sax-**ah**-ti-le). Aurinia is the new corrected botanical name. However, many books and catalogs still use the old listing; therefore we have provided both names to prevent confusion. Because of rules of botanical nomenclature (which most of us are not entirely familiar with), the plant was moved from the genus *Alyssum*, under which it has been known since Linnaeus named it in 1753, to the genus *Aurinia*.

Aurinia Saxatilis

SYNONYMS: Rock madwort, basket of gold, golden tuft
FAMILY: Cruciferae
HARDY TO ZONE: 3
HEIGHT: 6 to 10 inches
DESCRIPTION: Lance-shaped, gray-

green sprawling foliage has a matting habit. Bright yellow cluster flowers on many stems.

BLOOM TIME: May-June

CULTIVATION: Full sun or partial shade. It must have very good drainage to prevent root rot and likes a lean, slightly acid soil. Do not fertilize heavily or add lime. When the flowers have finished blooming, cut plant back to one-half its size. It will become stronger and will usually rebloom throughout the summer.

PROPAGATION: This short-lived perennial is easy to propagate by seed or cuttings but, once established, dislikes division or transplanting.

USES: Rock gardens, in hanging baskets, or over a rock wall.

SPECIES: *Aurina saxatilis* "**compactum**" forms a more dense mound that does not spread as quickly—a good dwarf form of aurina for the rock garden. *Aurina saxatilis plenum* is a very pretty double-flower yellow form.

BERGENIA CORDIFOLIA

(ber-**gen**-ee-a kor-di-**fo**-lee-a)

SYNONYMS: Heartleaf bergenia, pig squeak

FAMILY: Saxifragaceae

HARDY TO ZONE: 3

HEIGHT: 6 to 12 inches

DESCRIPTION: Large spoon-shaped, cabbagelike leaves; semi-evergreen. It forms a dense, slow-spreading clump of thick leaves that overpowers most weeds. A good plant for low-maintenance gardens. Leaves have a slight reddish color in fall. In early spring, thick stalks produce pink flowers.

BLOOM TIME: May-June

CULTIVATION: Partial or filtered shade, full shade. It will tolerate full sun if plenty of moisture is provided. Likes rich soil with plenty of organic matter. Fertilize every spring. It may need division every three to four years. Slugs may be a problem in very moist areas; spread some wood ash around plants to discourage slugs.

Bergenia cordifolia

PROPAGATION: Seeds or division.

USES: As a specimen, edging, or ground cover. Nice with early spring bulbs.

SPECIES: *Bergenia crassifolia* is the one called pig squeak; it has smaller leaves.

CAMPANULA CARPATICA

(kam-**pan**-yoo-la kar-**pa**-ti-ka)

SYNONYMS: Harebell, bellflower, Carpathian bellflower

FAMILY: Campanulaceae

HARDY TO ZONE: 3

HEIGHT: 6 to 8 inches

DESCRIPTION: Compact clumps with heart-shaped foliage. Bell-shaped flowers (hence the name bellflower) with violet, blue, or white blooms.

BLOOM TIME: June-July

CULTIVATION: Long-lived campanulas enjoy full sun to partial shade (they do dislike hot afternoon sun;

provide morning sun where possible). Well-drained, moderately rich soil, slightly on the alkaline side. Divide every three or four years to keep clumps vigorous.

Campanula carpatica

PROPAGATION: Seeds, cuttings, division.

USES: Borders, rock gardens or walls, ground cover, or baskets. Nice in containers for the patio.

SPECIES: See chapters 13 and 14 for taller varieties. I have found my favorite low growers to be of the blue or white "Chips" species.

CERASTIUM TOMENTOSUM

(ke-**rass**-tee-um to-men-**to**-sum)

SYNONYM: Summer snow

FAMILY: Caryophyllaceae

HARDY TO ZONE: 3

HEIGHT: 3 to 6 inches

DESCRIPTION: Silvery-green foliage with a sprawling habit, covered with ¾-inch white flowers that look like snow.

BLOOM TIME: June-July

CULTIVATION: Full sun in well drained, slightly alkaline lean to average soil. As with most gray or silver foliaged plants, a too rich soil produces more foliage with fewer

MICHAEL H. DODGE, WHITE FLOWER FARM

flowers. If the plant looks weedy and ratty after blooming, cut it back to about two inches above ground. This helps aid in root production. Foliage is tender; plant in area away from foot traffic.

Cerastium tomentosum

PROPAGATION: Seeds or division.
USES: Excellent in rock gardens or as an edging, hanging over logs or rock walls.

DIANTHUS CARYOPHYLLUS

(dee-**anth**-us ka-ree-o-**fill**-us)
SYNONYMS: Clove pink, carnation, gilly flower, sops-in-wine
FAMILY: Caryophyllaceae
HARDY TO ZONE: 3
HEIGHT: To 12 inches
DESCRIPTION: Long, slender gray-green foliage that sprawls and mats down. Fragrant pink flowers smell like cloves.
BLOOM TIME: June-July
CULTIVATION: Full sun. Lean to average well-drained, slightly alkaline soil. Too much standing water will produce crown rot. Deadhead flowers to keep plant blooming. Water during drought periods.
PROPAGATION: Seeds, cuttings, or layering.

USES: Rock gardens, rock walls, or as a specimen. Flowers are edible; cut off the bitter green calyx, discard, and use the petals in punch, as cake decorations, in salads, or with a cream cheese sandwich.
HISTORY: *Dianthus* was first mentioned in the fourth century and then seems to disappear from literature and botanical books until the fourteenth century, when Chaucer mentions it. The dianthus then seemed to become popular in medicine and food. One source suggests using it for the baffling ailment of "melancholy."

Dianthus caryophyllus

SPECIES: There are over four hundred species of *Dianthus*. Some are *D. deltoides*, known as maiden pinks, and *D. plumarius*, the grassy pinks. For *D. barbatus*, sweet william, see chapter 15.

DORONICUM CORDATUM

(doh-**ron**-ik-um kor-**dat**-um)
SYNONYM: Leopard's-bane
FAMILY: Asteraceae (formerly Compositae)
HARDY TO ZONE: 4
HEIGHT: 6 to 10 inches
DESCRIPTION: Heart-shaped, me-

dium-sized leaves in a small clump; leaves extend up the stem producing yellow, daisy-type flowers. Shallow-rooted, the upper part of the plant disappears when bloom time has passed. Mark the area so you do not accidently dig it up.
BLOOM TIME: May-June

Doronicum cordatum

CULTIVATION: Filtered or partial shade to full shade. Be sure to water during drought periods, even when plant is not visible to the naked eye. It likes good loam soil.
PROPAGATION: Seeds are slow and erratic; do not cover seeds. Division in early spring.
USES: Bedding, edging, shade gardens. Pretty with candytuft (*Iberis sempervirens*) in early spring.

HEUCHERA SANGUINEA

(hew-**ker**-uh sang-**gwin**-ee-a)
SYNONYMS: Coral bells, alum root
FAMILY: Saxifragaceae
HARDY TO ZONE: 3
HEIGHT: 6 to 8 inches
DESCRIPTION: Round, scalloped dark-green leaves. Red, pink, or white flowers on tall stems 6 to 10 inches above the foliage.
BLOOM TIME: June-August
CULTIVATION: Full sun, partial or fil-

tered shade. Lean to good soil with good drainage. Has a tendency to push itself up out of the soil. To control this problem, push the plant into the soil in spring and add more soil over the emerging roots. Frequent division keeps it healthy. Deadhead for continuous bloom.

PROPAGATION: Seeds or division.

Heuchera Sanguinea

USES: In garden design, rock gardens, edging, or as a specimen. Flowers for both fresh or dried arrangements. **SPECIES:** White species cultivars that are nice include **H.s. "Snowflake"** or **"Bridal wreath."**

IBERIS SEMPERVIRENS

(Eye-**ber**-is sem-per-**vir**-enz)
SYNONYM: Candytuft
FAMILY: Brassicaceae (formerly Cruciferae)
HARDY TO ZONE: 3
HEIGHT: 12 inches
DESCRIPTION: Evergreen perennial, a spreading subshrub with medium-sized leaves on woody branches and white flowers.
BLOOM TIME: May-June
CULTIVATION: Full sun, rich, well-drained soil. Prune slightly after flowering to keep perennial from becoming too sprawling. In Maine

we need to provide a winter protection of evergreen boughs, which are removed early in spring.

PROPAGATION: Seeds or cuttings.
USES: In any garden, nice as edging or ground cover.

Iberis Sempervirens

SPECIES: *Iberis Gibraltarica*, just over 12 inches high, has violet flowers.

JASIONE LAEVIS (PERENNIS)

(ya-see-**o**-nay **lie**-vis)
SYNONYMS: Sheep's bit, sheep's scabious, shepherd's scabious.
FAMILY: Campanulaceae
HARDY TO ZONE: 4

Jasione laevis (perennis) "blue light"

HEIGHT: 10 to 12 inches
DESCRIPTION: Rosettes of narrow, slightly hairy leaves. This short-lived perennial (in Maine, anyway) has

leafless branched stems with light lavender-blue scabious-type flowers.
BLOOM TIME: June-July
CULTIVATION: Full sun to partial shade. Soil should be lean to average with good drainage. Keep it weeded—it does not like competition!
PROPAGATION: Seeds or division.
USES: Rock gardens, edging, and borders. I am forever buying seeds of perennials I have never tried before. I guess that's part of the excitement—to discover something new for your backyard garden that fits nicely into the scheme of things. I grew *Jasione* from seeds and enjoyed its beauty the first year. Then a friend who had been studying gardening in Scotland returned home and visited me. He was overwhelmed to find *Jasione* growing successfully in my garden; in Scotland it grows everywhere naturally. Although this plant is short lived, it truly should be grown more often in American gardens.

LAMIUM

(**lay**-mee-um)
SYNONYM: Deadnettle
FAMILY: Lamiaceae (formerly Labiatae)
HARDY TO ZONE: 3
HEIGHT: 3 to 12 inches, depending on species.
DESCRIPTION: Medium-sized saw-toothed leaves. Resembles the nonrelated stinging nettle but does not have the sting, hence its name, deadnettle. Flowers look like snapdragons, whorled on stems, and are especially attractive to bumblebees. Pink, white, and yellow colors (see species below).
BLOOM TIME: May-July

MICHAEL H. DODGE, WHITE FLOWER FARM

CULTIVATION: Sun, partial or filtered shade. Soil can be average to rich as long as good drainage is provided. Shear after blooming, and many species will rebloom for you.

PROPAGATION: Seeds, cuttings, or division.

Lamium maculatum

USES: Too often the lamiums are left out of the gardening books. I have four species in my own garden and find them very effective in the spring garden. Use as ground covers and on rock walls. The yellow archangel species can be used in the Biblical garden. It is supposed to be dedicated to the archangel Michael and has been used historically to treat sores and ulcers. Other medicinal uses that go way back were as a tea to promote perspiration for chills and as an external wash for wounds.

SPECIES: The **Lamium album** has white flowers and grows 12 inches high. **Lamium maculatum**, or spotted deadnettle, has pink flowers and variegated leaves and also grows to 12 inches. Cultivars of maculatum are **"Beacon silver,"** a 4-inch tall ground cover, with pink flowers that bloom off and on all season. **"White Nancy"** is a white-flowered cultivar 6 to 8 inches high.

The yellow species of lamium is now sold as **Lamiastrum galeobdolon**, with synonyms of golden archangel, weazel snout, and dummy nettle. It is taller than the other lamiums (12 to 14 inches). It should be clipped right back to the ground after flowering or it gets straggly. It self-seeds and can be invasive in rich soil. It has a shorter bloom time than the other lamiums and has an unpleasant aroma when crushed.

LEONTOPODIUM ALPINUM

(lee-on-toh-**po**-dee-um al-**peen**-um)
SYNONYM: Edelweiss
FAMILY: Asteraceae (formerly Compositae)
HARDY TO ZONE: 3

Leontopodium alpinum

HEIGHT: 3 to 6 inches
DESCRIPTION: Soft gray, slightly green leaves with soft woolly gray and white star-shaped flowers.
BLOOM TIME: June-July
CULTIVATION: An alpine plant, it needs full sun in gritty, well-drained soil. Add lime to increase alkalinity, which it prefers. Short-lived.
PROPAGATION: Seeds. Needs stratification for three weeks before sowing. Division in early spring.

USES: Rock gardens, edging, alpine gardens. Indigenous to the Swiss Alps, edelweiss became popularly known through the Von Trapp family and the musical based on their life, "The Sound of Music."

NEPETA MUSSINII

(**nep**-et-uh mu-**sin**-ee-ee)
SYNONYMS: Catnip mussinii, catmint
FAMILY: Lamiaceae (formerly Labiatae)
HARDY TO ZONE: 3
HEIGHT: 5 to 8 inches

Nepeta mussinii

DESCRIPTION: Aromatic small gray-green leaves, with some purple coloring underneath the leaf. Flowers are bluish-purple.
BLOOM TIME: June-July
CULTIVATION: Full sun to partial shade in well-drained, lean to average soil. Shear off flowers after blooming and the plant will bloom for you again.
PROPAGATION: Seeds or division in spring.
USES: Rock gardens or walls, edgings, and borders.
HISTORY: The plant was probably named by Pliny after the Italian town of Nepi. Even though it is a member of the catnip family, none of my cats care for it.

OMPHALODES VERNA

(om-fa-**loh**-deez **ver**-na)
SYNONYMS: Navelwort, blue-eyed mary, creeping forget-me-not
FAMILY: Boraginaceae
HARDY TO ZONE: 4
HEIGHT: 3 to 6 inches
DESCRIPTION: Medium oval-shaped

Omphalodes verna

leaves, creeping root stalks. Pretty true-blue flowers that look like giant forget-me-nots, hence its name.
BLOOM TIME: June
CULTIVATION: Full sun to partial shade, with well-drained average soil. It will choke out most weeds as it creeps along.
PROPAGATION: Division of the creeping rootstock is easy.
USES: The blue flowers are attractive flowing over a rock wall or as a creeping ground cover under a tree. Interesting in a hanging tree.

PHLOX SUBULATA

(**flocks** soob-ew-**lah**-ta)
SYNONYMS: Moss pink, mossy phlox, mountain pink, rock pink
FAMILY: Polemoniaceae
HARDY TO ZONE: 3
HEIGHT: 4 to 8 inches
DESCRIPTION: Called moss pink because that is just what the tiny-leaved

foliage looks like, a clump of spreading moss. In spring the foliage is literally covered with small five-petaled flowers in pink, white, or lavender.
BLOOM TIME: May-June
CULTIVATION: Full sun to partial shade. Good rich soil, filled with well-composted organic matter, but with good drainage. Shear back after blooming to retain shape and encourage more root growth. Fertilize with a slow-release fertilizer, which is less apt to injure its shallow root system. I think one reason so many people seem to have trouble with this perennial is that they plant it in too lean a soil, which most of the perennials of this rock garden type seem to prefer.
PROPAGATION: Cuttings (not easy) or division. Be sure to keep the division well watered until established.
USES: Rock and wall gardens with good soil, borders, and baskets.

Phlox subulata

HISTORY: The word *phlox* means fire in Greek, which fits the plant well when it is in full bloom. But the fire meaning actually comes from its ancient medicinal use for treating flaming fevers and sore throats (I do not recommend experimenting medicinally with this plant; not

enough modern research has been done to date).

PRIMULA POLYANTHA

(**prim**-yoo-la pol-ee-**an**-tha)

PRIMULA VULGARIS

(**prim**-yoo-la vul-**ga**-ris)
SYNONYM: Primrose
FAMILY: Primulaceae
HARDY TO ZONE: 3
HEIGHT: 6 to 9 inches

Primula polyantha

DESCRIPTION: Deep, crinkly, long oval-shaped leaves. *Vulgaris* is the common primrose and *polyantha* the hybrid, which provides more flowers. Flowers are produced in single and double varieties in vivid colors.
BLOOM TIME: May-June
CULTIVATION: Primroses do best in cool weather, with filtered to full shade. The soil should have plenty of organic material with good moisture-holding qualities but not be soggy. A light mulch will conserve moisture. Do not neglect the care of your primroses; provide water during drought periods and keep well weeded. Watch for red spiders and slugs.
PROPAGATION: Seeds and division every other year after flowering.
USES: Shade gardens, borders, and edging.

SPECIES: We Americans tend to call all the primula species primroses. The following may help clear up who's who: *Primula vulgaris:* the wild English primrose. *Primula veris:* cowslip. *Primula elatior:* oxlip or meadow plant. *Primula polyanthus:* the hybrid primrose.

PRUNELLA GRANDI-FLORA

(proo-**nell**-ah gran-di-**fl o**-ra)
SYNONYMS: Allheal, self-heal, heal-all, brunella
FAMILY: Lamiaceae (formerly Labiatae)
HARDY TO ZONE: 3
HEIGHT: 4 to 12 inches
DESCRIPTION: Grandiflora is a hybrid of the wild prunella (*Prunella vulgaris*) often found in lawns. It has dark creeping root stalks with oval, medium-sized leaves. Flowers are a blue-purple.
BLOOM TIME: June-July

Prunella grandiflora

CULTIVATION: Full sun to partial shade in good soil. It may be invasive to some extent.
PROPAGATION: Seeds or root division.
USES: The wild species is used as a medicinal herb both internally and externally. What medicinal qualities

the hybrids have I do not know.
SPECIES: Other hybrids worth growing in the backyard garden include *Prunella webbiana*, 9 inches high, with lilac flowers, and two cultivars, *P.w.* pink and *P.w.* white, both 12 inches high.

SEDUM

(**see**-dum or **say**-dum)
SYNONYMS: Stonecrops, live forever
HARDY TO ZONE: 3
FAMILY: Crassulaceae
HEIGHT: 2 to 6 inches

Sedum

DESCRIPTION: Fleshy or succulent leaves. Some species are evergreen, others herbaceous. Most spread quite quickly; some, such as *Sedum acre* are invasive but easy to control. Flowers in all colors, depending on species.
BLOOM TIME: Depends on species.
CULTIVATION: Full sun to partial shade. It needs very well-drained soil and does best where weeds are kept under control. Easy to grow and care for.
PROPAGATION: Seeds, cuttings, or division.
USES: Rock gardens, over or between rock crevices, hanging baskets.
SPECIES: *S. acre* (**akh**-ree) (wall-pep-

per or gold moss), to zone 2. Has light-green foliage with long-lasting bright yellow flowers. Grows 2 inches high. Blooms in June-July.
S. album, to zone 3, has dark-green leaves with white flowers in July (several different varieties of foliage are also sold as *S. album*).
S. Hispanicum (hi-**span**-i-kum), to zone 4, has blue-green leaves and pink flowers in July. This one is especially pretty.
S. kamtschaticum (kamt-**sha**-ti-kum), to zone 4, is an evergreen with dark-green leaves and orange-yellow flowers. At 8 inches it is one of the taller sedums.
S. reflexum (re-**fleks**-um), to zone 4, grows to 10 inches. It has blue-green foliage and yellow flowers in July—one of my favorites.
S. sieboldii (see-**bold**-ee-ee). Also called Japanese stonecrop, it is hardy to zone 3, and grows 8 inches tall. This flowers late in August; then the leaves turn bronze-red for fall color.
S. spurium (**spew**-ree-um), to zone 3. Another sedum whose foliage turns bronze in fall. It has pink or yellow flowers in late summer. Grows 6 inches high.

SEMPERVIVUM

(sem-per-**v i**-vum)
SYNONYMS: Hens and chickens, live forever, houseleeks, Jove's beard
FAMILY: Crassulaceae
HARDY TO ZONE: 3
DESCRIPTION: Hardy, succulent rosette with fleshy leaves. There are several different varieties: some have smooth leaves, others a webbed or hairy covering over their leaves. The flowers, from 4 to 8 inches tall,

form a pink, starlike bloom on top of the stem. The plant is mono-carpic, meaning once the flower dies, so does that particular rosette. But the other rosettes fill in the vacant space quickly. Size of rosettes can very from ½ to 6 inches.

BLOOM TIME: June-August

CULTIVATION: Full sun, partial shade, or filtered shade. Good drainage is the main concern, since the rosettes can rot in soggy soil. I like to put sand around the rosettes when planting. The sand dries out quickly and keeps the rosettes dry, preventing rot. Crushed rocks could also be used in this way.

Sempervivum

PROPAGATION: All semps produce rosettes, or stolens. These are easily detached and planted by pushing into the soil. They quickly root themselves. One variety even rolls off its own rosettes to put down roots away from the mother plant. My name for this one is "roly-poly chick."

USES: Endless places to plant: rock gardens, walls, on rocks that have a small indentation (no kidding), an old shoe, or a fancy container. And even on a wreath form for the picnic table. Little soil is required. Only a lack of imagination will fail to find

a place to plant sempervivens. The sempervivens is also a medicinal herb. Apply the juice from one of the leaves to a burn or cut as you would aloe.

HISTORY: This plant has a long history. During the 1500s it was an important medicinal herb for aches and pains. During that time it was grown on rooftops to help keep thatched and straw roofs from leaking (hence the name houseleeks). Maybe we could try this instead of putting on a new roof. Like many of the early plants, sempervivens has a mythological past. The plant is dedicated to Zeus, Greek god of the sky and of thunder. Where houseleeks were growing, the home was safe from his lightning bolts and free from demons.

SPECIES: There are over 50 different species. I hate to admit it—even though I grow over a dozen kinds, I do not know the exact names of all of them.

S. arachnoideum (ah-rak-**noi**-dee-um) is a cobweb variety with gray-green leaves and a lacy-looking webbing on the rosette. Very pretty and stays quite small.

S. tectorum (tek-**to**-rum) is the common green variety almost every gardener knows. It has been used since ancient times.

S. tectorum "**oddity**" is a favorite of mine. It has a rosette but the leaves are long, skinny, open tubes instead of the fat leaves of the succulent. Very different.

S. triste is another form of *tectorum*. Its green rosettes are tipped with a brownish color.

STACHYS BYZANTINA

(**stay**-kiss bi-zan-**teen**-a)

Often sold as *Stachys lanata*

SYNONYMS: Lamb's ear, lamb's tongue, woolly betony, woundwort, mule's ears

FAMILY: Lamiaceae (formerly Labiatae)

HARDY TO ZONE: 4

HEIGHT: 12 inches; flowers to 18 inches.

DESCRIPTION: Light gray-green leaves covered with dense white hairs that give it a silvery-gray appearance when dry. However, after a rain storm the wet leaves look green. Woolly-stalked pink flowers reach above the lower foliage.

BLOOM TIME: July

CULTIVATION: Full sun; will tolerate a small amount of partial shade. Good drainage is most important, as you will find with most gray-leaved plants. Average to good soil. Cut flower stalk down to the ground after bloom period has ended or the plants become raggy looking.

PROPAGATION: Seeds or spring division.

Stachys byzantina

USES: Excellent ground cover or specimen plant. Flowers are good for fresh or dried arrangements. When doing wreaths put the leaves on while fresh; they dry quickly but are very fragile once dried.

I can attest to the leaves' astringent qualities for cuts and bee stings. The name woundwort comes from its ancient use as an absorbent dressing for wounds. My grandchildren have learned to wrap up a cut with the soft lamb's ear leaves. Isn't it nice to grow plants that are useful? This is available whenever you cut a finger or get a bee string.

THYMUS

(**Ty**-mus)
SYNONYM: Thyme
FAMILY: Lamiaceae (formerly Labiatae)
HARDY TO ZONE: 3
HEIGHT: 1 to 12 inches, depending on species.
DESCRIPTION: Tiny fragrant-leaved herbs with creeping root stalks. Flowers are white, pink, or purple.
BLOOM TIME: May to August, depending on species.

Thymus herba-barona

CULTIVATION: Full sun to partial shade. Needs good drainage in lean to average soil. Loses oil content if grown in too rich soil.

PROPAGATION: Seeds, but division is preferable to get true species. Hybrid seeds often revert to other species.
USES: Rock gardens, walls, edging, borders, baskets, ground covers, between cracks of walkways.

Bees love the plant as much as people do and literally cover it when in bloom, so if using it in a walkway keep it mowed to prevent blooming. Mowing over it does not harm it, but only makes the energy go into more root-making. And of course, thyme is a popular culinary herb in everything from soup to teas.

HISTORY: Thyme goes way back in our history. The word *thyme* comes from the Greek meaning to fumigate, because it was used as incense and for strewing on those old dirt or stone floors. It also signified courage; scarves would be embroidered with a bee hovering over a sprig of thyme. They were given to knights as they went to war.

SPECIES: *T. herba-barona* (**her**-ba ba-**ro**-na), called caraway thyme, is a 1-inch creeper with pink flowers. *T. citrioidorus* (kit-ree-o-**do**-rus) **"Doone Valley,"** 3 inches high, has gold-green variegated leaves and a lemon scent. *T. lanuginosus* (lan-u-**gin**-o-sus), or woolly thyme, with soft gray leaves, is a nice creeper. *T. serpyllum* (ser-**pil**-lum), an 8-inch high culinary herb, called "mother of thyme." *T. vulgaris* (vul-**ga**-ris) **"argenteus,"** or silver thyme (to zone 5), is a pretty herb for baskets or gardens.

VIOLA ODORATA

(**vee**-o-la o-do-**rah**-ta; also **vy**-o-la)
SYNONYMS: Sweet violet, blue violet

FAMILY: Violaceae
HARDY TO ZONE: 3
HEIGHT: 3 to 6 inches
DESCRIPTION: Low-growing medium-sized heart-shaped leaves, with a solitary violet or white flower on the end of a slim stalk. There are many hybrid species, but none are as hardy or long-lived as the sweet violets.
BLOOM TIME: May-June
CULTIVATION: Full sun to shade, good soil with a good water supply. Fertilize in early spring and mow back after bloom.

Viola cornuta "Jersey gem"

PROPAGATION: Seeds or division.
USES: Any garden. Flowers can be used in cooking as syrup, as decoration, or in salads. Also can be used in making wine. The leaves and flowers are used medicinally for bruises and urinary complaints.
HISTORY: Greek legend tells us that Zeus changed his love Io into a white heifer because of Hera's jealousy, and then provided the beautiful spring violets for her food. Violets are mentioned frequently in many poems, associated with love as well as with death.

THIRTEEN

Middle-Range Perennials

Plants between 12 inches and 3 feet high

Brave flower—that I could gallant it like you,
And be as little vain!
You come aboard, and make a harmless show,
And to your beds of earth again.
You are not proud: you know your birth:
For your embroider'd garments are from earth.

—Henry King

Perennials that reach a mature height of between twelve inches and three feet are in the middle range or medium-sized plant category.

In a garden design, perennials of this size are placed in the middle of a herbaceous border, used as edgings or borders, placed along walkways and foundations for hedging material, or used alone as specimen plants. Many are good overall ground covers to cover a steep bank or slope area.

You will find a wide variety of heights and colors in this group.

You will find great differences in soil requirements, from a dry lean soil for the pearly everlasting (*Anaphalis margaritacea*) to a rich soil for the moisture-loving astilbe with its colorful, long-lasting plumelike flowers. You will see common, well-known plants like lupines (*Lupinus*) and the rarer patrinia (*Scabiosifolia nagoya*), which has proven satisfactory in my backyard garden. A good companion to patrinia is the sweet-scented lavender.

ACHILLEA MILLEFOLIUM "ROSEUM"

(ah-**kil**-lee-a mee-lee-**fo**-lee-um)
SYNONYM: Red yarrow
FAMILY: Asteraceae (formerly Compositae)
HARDY TO ZONE: 2
HEIGHT: 12 to 18 inches

Achillea millefolium "roseum"

DESCRIPTION: The word *millefolium* means "thousand leaves," which the yarrow certainly has in its fernlike leaf. "Roseum" is a variation of the wild white yarrow. The flowers are full tight clusters on a terminal stem.
BLOOM TIME: July-August
CULTIVATION: Full sun to partial shade. It likes dry, well-drained soil, on the lean side. If the soil is too rich you lose the flower production and get mostly leaves. It can be invasive in rich soil.
PROPAGATION: Seeds or division.
USES: Good ground cover or specimen. Nice in fresh or dried arrangements.
Leaves of yarrow can be made into a tea for spraying on other plants as an insect repellent and to keep them healthy. Yarrow in your bathwater acts as a skin astringent and softener. I find it too bitter as a tea, but sup-

posedly it is good for colds.
And finally, you might want to try your hand at a little witchcraft. To find an omen for success or a new lover, stick a leaf of yarrow up your nose and tickle the nose while saying the following, "Yarroway, yarroway, bear a white blow. If my love doth love me, my nose will bleed now." I haven't tried this spell, but if you do and you get success or a new lover, let me know.
SPECIES: I am very fond of the new "debutante" hybrid. The pastel colors are very attractive and have excellent drying qualities.

ALCHEMILLA VULGARIS

(al-ke-**mil**-la vul-**ga**-ris)
SYNONYMS: Lady's mantle, lion's foot, bear's foot
FAMILY: Rosaceae
HARDY TO ZONE: 3
HEIGHT: 18 to 24 inches
DESCRIPTION: Gray-green large pleated leaves. In the early morning a drop of dew sparkles from the center of each leaf, simulating a small diamond. Yellow-green flowers on fluffy panicle sprays sprawl over the plant. Flowers are long-lasting.
BLOOM TIME: June-July
CULTIVATION: Full sun to partial shade. Average to good loam that is well drained. Give it plenty of room to display its beautiful, sprawling flowers. When flowers have died, deadhead for the health of the plant. It likes a yearly application of wood ash or bonemeal.
PROPAGATION: Seeds (but they take two to three years to flower). Will also self-seed if flowers are not removed from the plant too early. Di-

vision in spring.
USES: This is one of my favorite plants both as an herb and as a perennial flower. Useful in the garden as a specimen, hedge-type planting, or ground cover. The flowers are useful both fresh and dried.
It is a woman's medicinal plant, dedicated by the Virgin Mary to all women's medical problems—from excessive bleeding during menstruation to hot flashes during menopause. Use caution: do not drink more than one or two cups of the tea a day and do not use continuously. Check with your holistic health practitioner before using.

Alchemilla vulgaris

HISTORY: *Alchemilla* was known from the 1500s as a skin cleanser to help clear up acne. The names lion's foot and bear's foot come from the shape of the leaf, and it is called lady's mantle because its pleated scalloped leaves represent the Virgin Mary's mantle or cloak.
SPECIES: See chapter 12 for low-growing alpine lady's mantle.

AQUILEGIA

(A-kwi-**lee**-gee-a)
SYNONYM: Columbine
FAMILY: Ranunculaceae

HARDY TO ZONE: 3
HEIGHT: 8 inches to 4 feet, depending on species.

Aquilegia "rose queen"

DESCRIPTION: Compounded leaves in three sections. Flowers have five sepals, which are normally green in other plants but in the columbine species are showy colors with the flowers nodding on terminal stems. Five petals are prolonged backward into "spurs" of varying lengths. Spurs can be the same or a different color than the sepal.
BLOOM TIME: June-August
CULTIVATION: Full sun to partial shade, with average to good soil. Has deep taproot that resents transplanting when mature.
PROPAGATION: Seeds; some species will self-seed.
USES: Blends beautifully with almost all other plants.
SPECIES: *Aquilegia vulgare* "granny bonnets" has moved with me several times over the past 25 years. This old-fashioned beauty is a velvety purple with almost no spurs. It is 18 to 26 inches tall and self-seeds abundantly.
A. caerulea (kay-**ru**-le-ah) is the state flower of Colorado. Its 24-inch stems support pretty blue flowers.

A. canadensis (kan-ah-**den**-sis) is a native wildflower, also called cluckies (isn't that a wonderful name?) and rock lily because it likes lean, rocky soil. It blooms in May and June and is the only species used as a medicine for diarrhea.
Many hybrids are available. MacKanna giants are especially nice in many color varieties.
Caution: Seeds may be poisonous, especially to children.

ARTEMISIA ABSINTHIUM
(ar-tay-**mis**-ee-a ab-**sin**-thee-um)
SYNONYM: Wormwood
FAMILY: Asteraceae (formerly Compositae)
HARDY TO ZONE: 3
HEIGHT: 24 to 30 inches

Artemisia absinthium

DESCRIPTION: Gray-green foliage with coarsely divided alternate bi- or tripartite leaves. Yellowish flowers in August are barely noticeable.
CULTIVATION: Full sun to shade, with good drainage in lean to average soil. Will become weedy-looking in late summer unless clipped once or twice during the summer. Wear gloves when handling; you may not like the bitter taste it leaves on the skin for several hours. Once I ate a

sandwich right after weeding it and I could taste the bitterness even though I had washed my hands.
PROPAGATION: Seeds or divisions.
USES: Popular with dried flower arrangers. It is used commercially in some medicines for humans as well as animals. A good addition to any garden.
Plant near foundations to repel ants. Wormwood is an old medicinal for stomach and heartburn problems. Although I know people who still use it as a medicine, selling it for such purposes has been banned by the FDA.
HISTORY: In Britain during the Middle Ages, wormwood was used as a strewing herb or hung in bunches to ward off insects, especially ants and fleas, as well as to keep evil spirits away. It is mentioned several times in the Bible as wormwood.

ASTILBE
(a-**stil**-bee)
SYNONYM: Garden spirea
FAMILY: Saxifragaceae

Astilbe "Rheinland"

HARDY TO ZONE: 4
HEIGHT: 20 inches to 3 feet
DESCRIPTION: Rugged fernlike foliage, shiny and sometimes tinted red.

White, pink, peach, and red flowers are colorful and long-lasting, on tall plumes.

BLOOM TIME: July-August

CULTIVATION: Full sun to shade as long as it has good, rich, moist soil. Slightly acid; do not feed alkaline products. Provide organic materials and fertilize each spring. Will need division every three to four years. In the garden, they do best with a little shade to keep the flowers colorful longer.

PROPAGATION: Seeds are slow, with poor germination. Division is easy in the spring.

USES: The flowers are pretty in fresh or dried arrangements. If they fade they take spray paint very well.

SPECIES: *A. chinensis punuta* (chin-**en**-sis poo-**na**-ta), a smaller version (12 inches), flowers later in August. It tolerates dryer soil than other astilbes.

A. tacquetii (ta-**kway**-tee-ee) **"superba,"** 4 feet high, is a more heat-resistant hybrid.

CAMPANULA
(kam-pan-**yoo**-la)

SYNONYM: Bellflower, harebells

FAMILY: Campanulaceae

HARDY TO ZONE: 3

HEIGHT: 18 to 24 inches

DESCRIPTION: Compact clumps with heart-shaped leaves and bell-shaped flowers in white and blue shades, blooming from June to September. Some varieties have starry-eyed flowers facing upward. Many hybrids.

BLOOM TIME: Depends on species.

CULTIVATION: Long-lived campanulas enjoy full sun to partial shade. They dislike afternoon sun, prefer-

ring the less harsh morning sun. Use well-drained, moderately rich soil, slightly on the alkaline side. Divide every three or four years to keep clumps vigorous.

PROPAGATION: Seeds or division, cuttings.

USES: Borders, cut garden.

Campanula persicifolia

SPECIES: *C. glomerata* (glo-mer-**a**-tah) grows 18 to 20 inches high. Its blossoms are a deep violet-blue; it is pretty even when not in bloom.

C. lactiflora (lak-ti-**fl o**-rah), 4 feet tall, has purple blooms that are good as cut flowers.

C. persicifolia (pur-**s i**-kee-fo-lee-ah) **"white pearl,"** 24 inches high, has double flowers in June-August.

CHRYSANTHEMUM COCCINIUM
(kris-**anth**-em-um kok-**kin**-ee-um)

SYNONYMS: Painted daisy, Persian insect flower, pyrethrum

FAMILY: Asteraceae (formerly Compositae)

HARDY TO ZONE: 2

HEIGHT: 12 to 30 inches

DESCRIPTION: Bright green, deeply cut fernlike leaves and an erect simple stem (occasionally forked) with daisylike flowers. White, pink, and

deep red colors, with yellow centers.

BLOOM TIME: June-July

CULTIVATION: Full sun and well-drained soil. It likes fertile soil; water during drought periods. Keep flowers deadheaded for more blooms. Once blooming is over, shear back to about 10 inches to promote reblooming. Divide every three to four years to keep the plant healthy. Group three or more plants for the best effect in the garden.

Chrysanthemum coccinium

PROPAGATION: Seeds are easy but will not produce flowers the first season. Division is easy.

USES: Long-lasting cut flower. The dried and powdered flower head has some insect-repellent qualities. However, the best insect repellent comes from the white variety of *c. cineriifolium*.

CHRYSANTHEMUM PARTHENIUM
(kris-**anth**-em-um par-**then**-ee-um)

SYNONYMS: Feverfew, featherfoil, matricaria, flirtwort

FAMILY: Asteraceae (formerly Compositae)

HARDY TO ZONE: 4

HEIGHT: 14 to 20 inches

DESCRIPTION: Light-green divided

leaves, slightly fragrant, with small, white daisylike flowers, with the center larger than the outer rays.
BLOOM TIME: July-August
CULTIVATION: Short-lived feverfew does best in protected full sun or partial shade and well-drained, average to good loam. Add wood ashes to this alkaline-loving perennial.
PROPAGATION: Seeds, cuttings.
USES: Borders or cut gardens. As a medicinal herb, be sure to use the correct herb plant and not one of its many hybrids. As a general tonic, a mixture of lemon juice, honey, and the bitter feverfew is used for coughs. Feverfew is enjoying a comeback in the medicinal field as scientists prove its worth as a remedy for migraine headaches.

Chrysanthemum parthenium

SPECIES: *C. p.* "golden ball" is a nice solid-yellow flowered feverfew for the border garden. It dries nicely for craft work. A double white form, *C. p.* "ultra white," is also nice.

CHRYSANTHEMUM X SUPERBUM

(kris-**anth**-em-um ex soo-**per**-bum)
SYNONYM: Shasta daisy
FAMILY: Asteraceae (formerly Compositae)

HARDY TO ZONE: 2
HEIGHT: 1 to 1½ feet
DESCRIPTION: Lance-shaped leaves with numerous white ray petals and a central yellow disk.
BLOOM TIME: June-July
CULTIVATION: These short-lived plants like rich, well-drained soil. Deadhead to extend blooming time.

Chrysanthemum x superbum

PROPAGATION: Seeds or division.
USES: Fresh arrangements.
SPECIES: *C. x rubellum* (roo-**bel**-um) "Clara Curtis" is a salmon-pink single daisy that spreads quickly. It blooms in July and August. *Leucanthemum pinnatifidum*, the common daisy, is often overlooked in the garden. It blooms in June.

COREOPSIS

(ko-ree-**op**-sis)
SYNONYM: Tickseed
FAMILY: Asteraceae (formerly Compositae)
HARDY TO ZONE: 3
HEIGHT: 12 to 30 inches
DESCRIPTION: Long slender leaves. The flowers that appear in June-July are yellow daisy-shaped with center disks the same color as the ray petals. Some varieties have slightly orange colorings. The

flowers, on long stems, can be single or double.

Coreopsis

CULTIVATION: Full sun to partial or filtered shade. Not fussy about soil; it likes good drainage but plenty of water. Deadhead for continuous bloom.
PROPAGATION: Seeds or division.
USES: Rock gardens or border. Cut flowers are long-lasting.
SPECIES: *C. lanceolata* "goldfink," grows to 12 inches, with June flowers. *C. lanceolata* "new gold," grows to 30 inches, has double flowers in June. *C. verticillata* "threadleaf," 24 inches high, has ferny foliage and yellow blossoms. *C. verticillata* "moonbeam," 24 inches high, has delicate light-yellow blossoms.

DICENTRA

(die-**sen**-tra)
SYNONYM: Bleeding heart
FAMILY: Fumariaceae
HARDY TO ZONE: 3
HEIGHT: 24 to 30 inches
DESCRIPTION: Finely cut foliage with little heart-shaped or "pantaloons" flowers that, in the white variety, hang under long arching stems. All except the popular Japanese "spectabilis" are native to North America.

BLOOM TIME: May-June

CULTIVATION: Partial or filtered shade, preferring morning to afternoon sun. Good rich soil full of organic matter. Needs good drainage but plenty of water.

PROPAGATION: Division in early spring from root cuttings; be sure there are one or two "eyes" on each piece of root cutting.

Dicentra spectabilis alba

USES: Borders, wildflower gardens.
SPECIES: *D. spectabilis*, an old-fashioned Japanese variety, 2 to 3 feet tall. *D. spectabilis alba*, a white form, shorter than the pink variety. *D. eximia*, or eastern bleeding heart, grows 12 to 18 inches, and has pink flowers in July. Self-sowing. *D. formosa*, or Pacific bleeding heart, grows to 12 inches with pink flowers. It spreads quickly on the Pacific coast, but in the East does not. *D. canadensis* is native to the New England woods. The root was used by Native Americans for a tonic, skin infections, and syphilis.

ERIGERON

(ehr-**rij**-er-on)
SYNONYM: Fleabane
FAMILY: Asteraceae (formerly Compositae)

HARDY TO ZONE: 4
HEIGHT: 20 to 26 inches
DESCRIPTION: Lance-shaped medium-green leaves. The five-petal daisylike flowers have lavender or pink rays and a yellow center disk.
BLOOM TIME: June-July
CULTIVATION: Full sun to partial shade, with good drainage. It will tolerate most soil conditions, from lean to rich. Deadhead for a longer blooming period.

Erigeron

PROPAGATION: Seeds or division.
USES: Borders, cut flowers; also makes a nice overplant for spring bulbs.
SPECIES: *E. aurantiacus*, with double dark-orange flowers, grows 12 to 16 inches high. *E. speciosus* has bluish-lavender flowers that bloom late in the season; grows 18 to 24 inches.

EUPHORBIA EPITHYMOIDES

(you-**four**-bee-ah e-pi-tie-**moi**-deez)
Formerly *E. polychroma*
SYNONYMS: Spurge, milkwort
FAMILY: Euphorbiaceae
HARDY TO ZONE: 4
HEIGHT: 8 to 24 inches
DESCRIPTION: Leaves have a slight purplish tint in early spring and in fall. Yellow bract flowers on a nice round mound.
BLOOM TIME: June
Caution: Milky acrid sap may cause burning of the skin in some people.
CULTIVATION: Full sun to partial shade. Likes average loam with good drainage, but needs a sufficient water supply. Will tolerate heat and drought if necessary.
PROPAGATION: Seeds (need six weeks of stratification), cuttings, or division.
USES: Excellent specimen or border plant. Also mixes well with other plants.

Euphorbia epithymoides

SPECIES: There are over one thousand species of euphorbias. Most are not hardy in Maine's zone 4. I like the blue-green foliage and yellow flowers of *E. myrsinites* (mur-**sin**-ee-teez). It dies out every year; however, it drops its seeds and starts new seedlings each spring. It can be used in a hanging basket as a houseplant and is nice with its sprawling tentacles falling over the edge of a rock wall.

FERNS

We all know what a fern is when we see it, yet few know the correct

MICHAEL H. DODGE, WHITE FLOWER FARM

name of each type. Ferns are ancient plants that go back to the beginning of time. The botanical names are different for different species, as are its common names.

DESCRIPTION: Although delicate looking, ferns are indeed a very hardy species. They have no flowers or insignificant ones.

HARDY TO ZONE: 4, unless specified.

CULTIVATION: Full sun to shade, depending on the individual species. A woodsy good loam is preferred, slightly on the acid side, making them good companions for rhododendrons, azaleas, pines, and oaks. If the soil is not woodsy, add leaf mold and peat moss.

PROPAGATION: Spores or division.

SPECIES: The following ferns are those that are fairly easy to grow in the backyard garden. Of course, there are many more species you can try.

Pteris Aquilina

(**te**-ris ak-**will**-in-uh)

SYNONYM: Bracken fern

HEIGHT: 1 to 3 feet

DESCRIPTION: Widely distributed, it prefers open woods and sunny hillsides, making it ideal for most gardens. It can be gathered from the woods if you can provide it with the same growing conditions in your garden.

Osmunda cinnamomea

(os-**mund**-uh kin-a-**m**o-mee-a)

SYNONYM: Cinnamon fern

HEIGHT: 3 to 6 feet

DESCRIPTION: The name comes from the stiff rusty wool borne on separate stalks at the base of the plant. It needs constant moisture and is found growing wild in boggy areas. Because of its vase shape it is often confused with the ostrich fern, but the cinnamon fern matures much earlier.

Polystichum acrostichoides

(poh-**lis**-tik-um a-kro-sti-**koi**-deez)

SYNONYM: Christmas fern

HEIGHT: 3 feet

DESCRIPTION: The name comes from the evergreen fronds that are often used dried or fresh for Christmas arrangements. It needs well-drained, constantly moist soil. It will tolerate some sun. There are over 225 species of the polystichum ferns.

Fern: *Athyrium goeringianum* "Picturm"

Adianthum pedatum

(ad-ee-**an**-tum ped-**ah**-tum)

SYNONYM: Maidenhair fern

HEIGHT: 1 to 2 feet

The eastern maidenhair fern grows in well-drained, woodsy soil. The green fronds appear on shiny blackish stalks.

Dennstaedtia punctilobula

(den-**stayd**-ee-uh punk-tee-**lob**-ew-la)

(Formerly *Dicksonia pilioiuscula*)

SYNONYM: Hay-scented fern

HEIGHT: 2 to 3 feet

DESCRIPTION: This was Thoreau's favorite among all the ferns. He wrote, "Its fronds are sweet scented when crushed or in drying." This fern prefers shade and will tolerate most well-drained soils. It can be invasive, making it a good ground cover for shady slopes. Susceptible to early frost. Dry some to use in potpourri.

Osmunda claytoniana

(os-**mund**-uh klay-ton-ee-**ah**-na)

SYNONYMS: Interrupted fern, Clay's fern

HEIGHT: to 5 feet

DESCRIPTION: Likes a well-drained, moist, woodsy, slightly acid soil. The vaselike fronds are interrupted in the middle of the sterile leaflets on top and bottom, thus its name, interrupted fern. Clay's fern comes from the botanical name.

Osmunda regalis

(os-**mund**-uh ray-**gah**-lis)

SYNONYM: Royal fern

HEIGHT: to 9 feet

DESCRIPTION: You can grow the royal fern if you have a boggy or swampy area. It needs a very acid soil and will tolerate quite a lot of sun if it has enough moisture.

Polypodium vulgare

(pol-ee-**poh**-dee-um vul-**gah**-ray)

SYNONYM: Common polypody fern

HEIGHT: 3 inches to 3 feet

DESCRIPTION: There are several varieties. This real evergreen spreads over rocks or fallen logs. Most varieties like a moist but gravelly soil. It grows from rhizomes spreading along the ground, unlike most ferns, which reproduce by spores.

Woodsia ilvensis

(wood-**zee**-uh ill-**ven**-sis)

SYNONYM: Rusty fern

HEIGHT: to 6 inches

DESCRIPTION: A small fern for shady rock gardens. The top sides of the

MICHAEL H. DODGE, WHITE FLOWER FARM

frond are green and the undersides a rusty brown, hence its name. A very hardy fern that needs constant moisture; it turns brown in drought conditions, but returns to its green state when moisture is supplied. There are many other varieties of ferns. Check with local greenhouses for species hardy in your area. All the above are hardy in zone 4. And a final note on ferns—they dry nicely for crafts and can be pressed for artwork.

GERANIUM

(jur-**ray**-nee-um)
SYNONYMS: Cranesbill geranium, hardy geranium
FAMILY: Geraniaceae
HARDY TO ZONE: 3

Geranium

HEIGHT: 12 to 15 inches
DESCRIPTION: Round-lobed leaves with flowers in white, blue, or pink. The name cranesbill comes from the beaklike projection on the seed.
BLOOM TIME: June
CULTIVATION: Full sun, partial or filtered shade, with good drainage in lean to good soil. If the soil is too rich you will have fewer flowers. Do not fertilize. It will tolerate droughts.
PROPAGATION: Seeds or division.

USES: Borders, rock gardens, edging.
SPECIES: *G. sanguineum* grows to 12 to 15 inches with magenta-rose flowers. *G. endressii* grows 12 inches high, spreading pink flowers. Nice in a rock garden. *G. album* is small, 8 to 10 inches, with white flowers. *G. wallichianum* "**Buxtom's blue**" grows 15 inches high with blue flowers.

GYPSOPHILA PANICULATA

(jip-**soph**-ill-a pa-nik-ew-**lah**-ta)
SYNONYM: Baby's breath
FAMILY: Caryophyllaceae
HARDY TO ZONE: 3
HEIGHT: 20 to 28 inches
DESCRIPTION: Gray-green light, airy foliage covered with tiny white flowers on many stems.
BLOOM TIME: June-July

Gypsophila paniculata

CULTIVATION: Full sun and well-drained, lean to good soil. Likes alkaline soil; add lime every three years. It does not like to be moved because of its long taproot. May need staking if not supported by other plants.
PROPAGATION: Seeds, but it will not produce flowers the first season.
USES: Good filler in garden or vase.

Fresh or dried arrangements.
SPECIES: Cultivars of *paniculata* include "**Bristol fairy**" and "**perfecta**," both with large flowers. "**Pink fairy**" is an 18-inch pink flower.

HELENIUM AUTUMNALE

(he-**lee**-nee-um ow-tum-**nah**-lee)
SYNONYMS: Sneezewort, Helen's flower

Helenium autumnale

FAMILY: Asteraceae (formerly Compositae)
HARDY TO ZONE: 3
HEIGHT: 30 to 36 inches
DESCRIPTION: Lance-shaped leaves and daisy flowers in yellow, red, or orange. The rays point backward gracefully over the stems.
BLOOM TIME: August to frost.
CULTIVATION: Full sun. Tolerates poor soil, even clay. It will grow in moist soils as well. Pinch to keep bushy and promote more flowering. Stake taller varieties.
PROPAGATION: Seeds.
USES: Borders.
HISTORY: This is supposedly named after Helen of Troy, hence its common name, Helen's flower.
SPECIES: "**Brilliant**," a 3-foot-tall variety with yellow-orange flowers.

MICHAEL H. DODGE, WHITE FLOWER FARM

TALBOT

HOSTA

(**hos**-ta)

SYNONYMS: Funkia, plantain lily

FAMILY: Liliaceae

HARDY TO ZONE: 3

HEIGHT: Dwarfs to 23 inches

DESCRIPTION: Medium to large, lance- to heart-shaped leaves in green, white, cream, or variegated yellow. The flowers on tall stalks are bell-shaped and appear in late summer.

BLOOM TIME: August

CULTIVATION: Partial or filtered shade in good soil with drainage. Plant them close together and they will choke out the weeds. Hostas require little care once planted. Slugs may be a problem in moist areas.

Hosta

PROPAGATION: Division.

USES: Shade gardens, woodland gardens, borders, or as hedges for walkways.

SPECIES: *H. undulata* has wavy thin leaves with a white center outlined in green. At 16 inches high, this is a good edging hosta.

H. lancifolia has narrow, all-green leaves and grows to 24 inches high.

H. sieboldiana has large heart-shaped blue-green leaves. This hybrid should not be heavily fertilized

or it will lose its color. Excellent specimen hosta.

H. fortunei **"aurea"** has leaves of an unusual color—almost gold. Color is best in spring; it darkens as the season progresses.

H. **"Frances William"** has irregular yellow margins on bluish-green leaves; it is popular as a background or specimen plant.

H. **"Ginko Craig"** has lance-shaped frosted leaves with white markings around the edges. It will take some sun and makes a good hedging along a walkway.

There are enormous numbers of hostas and hybrids available. Check catalogs and greenhouses for many other species.

HYSSOPUS OFFICINALIS

(hi-**sop**-us o-fis-i-**nal**-lis)

SYNONYM: Hyssop

FAMILY: Lamiaceae (formerly Labiatae)

HARDY TO ZONE: 4

HEIGHT: 18 inches

DESCRIPTION: A woody bushy perennial with purple flowers, evergreen in zones 7 and above. This perennial found in the herb garden is gradually making its way into the flower garden. The entire plant has an unusual aroma that some people like and others find offensive.

BLOOM TIME: June-September

CULTIVATION: A lean dry soil, but it needs plenty of water until established.

PROPAGATION: Seeds, cuttings, or division.

USES: It grows nicely in rock gardens or borders, and can be clipped like a hedge for walkways or a garden

frame. Used as tea for pleasure as well as an old medicinal for pulmonary disease and bronchitis. It is used to make a gargle for sore throats and as a general tonic.

Hyssopus officinalis

Caution: Pregnant women, epileptics, and persons with high blood pressure should not use this herb.

HISTORY: *Hyssop* is derived from the Hebrew *azob*, the holy herb. Because of its antiseptic qualities it was used to cleanse sacred places.

IRIS

(**Eye**-ris)

SYNONYM: none

FAMILY: Iridaceae

HARDY TO ZONE: 4

HEIGHT: 6 inches to 3½ feet

DESCRIPTION: The iris, next to the tulip, is probably the best known and most widely grown bulb plant. There are many followers of the iris cult who grow the wide selection of iris that are available. It is possible to have an iris in bloom all season—in every imaginable size, shape, and color. Colors are singles, blends, and bicolors. There are even black irises with fabulous names such as Study in Black, Dusty Dancer, Black Dragon, and my personal favorite,

Superstition. There are over two hundred varieties available, most of which are rhizome plants, with a few bulbs and tuberous plants.

Iris

The abstract flowers form six petals. The three top petals are called standards, and the lower three falls. Some species have crests, or beards, on the falls. The classification of irises is complicated and beyond the scope of this book. I have listed only a few of my favorites.

CULTIVATION: The bearded irises need good drainage in average to good soil. The beardless varieties prefer a richer soil with moisture. The light requirement for all irises is full sun, but a little shade in the afternoon keeps the color richer and the flowers last a little longer than in full sun. Set the rhizomes only an inch below the soil; often they rise above the soil, which is fine. Fertilize with a low-nitrogen fertilizer just before flowering. A light mulch of cocoa bean shells or pine needles around, *not on top of*, the rhizome helps retain moisture and keep the bed neat-looking.

SPECIES: the bearded irises include dwarf, intermediate, and tall varieties. They bloom from May to August in order of their height. The tall bearded iris is probably the most widely grown.

The beardless irises include the Siberian, spurious, and Japanese varieties.

Early spring presents the first iris to bloom, the lilliput or dwarf iris. They multiply quickly and are excellent for the front of border or the rock garden.

A special iris I treasure in my garden is the orris root iris. Its botanical name is written in a variety of ways: **Iris florentina**, or **Iris x germanica var. florentina**. With its pretty bluish-white cast to its bloom, this plant is a source of the orris root (*orris* is an ancient form of *iris*) used as a fixative in potpourri making. It blooms in June.

The Siberian and Japanese irises like a richer soil and a lot of water, but not wet feet. The Japanese iris has huge 6-inch petals. The Siberian iris blooms from May to June, the Japanese from July to August.

For a wet boggy area, blue flag (**Iris versicolor**) and yellow flag (**Iris pseudacorus**) will produce yearly color in June and July.

Caution: the root of blue flag may cause an allergic skin reaction on certain people.

LAVENDULA

(la-**van**-dew-la)
SYNONYM: Lavender
FAMILY: Lamiaceae (formerly Labiatae)
HARDY TO ZONES: 4 or 5
HEIGHT: 12 to 24 inches
DESCRIPTION: A woody evergreen that grows as a small shrub with gray-green, slender leaves. Highly fragrant leaves and flowers. The spike flowers range from light lavender to deep purple.

BLOOM TIME: June-September
CULTIVATION: Full sun, with well-drained lean to good soil. If the soil is too rich you will lose the desired oil properties. In zone 4 only the English species do well over the winter. Plant in a protected area away from the wind. In winter cover lightly with evergreen boughs. Lavender loves an alkaline soil; add wood ashes or bonemeal yearly. Don't be afraid to prune in early spring.

Lavendula

PROPAGATION: Seeds, cuttings, division.
USES: A popular perennial with herbalists because of its scent, it is used in potpourri, sachets, and perfumes. Harvest the flowers while still in the bud stage for the best fragrance. During earlier times it was used as a tea and as medicine. Use it in the bath water to relieve rheumatism. In garden design it does well in all gardens, borders, and edgings.
SPECIES: English lavenders are best for zone 4, including **L. augustifolia** (also sold as **L. vera**) and the new popular **L. augustifolia** "**Munstead**" which is a little earlier in flowering

and has lighter flowers. In zones 5 and above you can grow the French lavenders or **L. stoechas**; it has downy gray leaves with dark purple-violet flowers.

Spike lavender **L. latifolia** has broader leaves and a higher oil content than the other lavenders; it is often grown for commercial purposes. Woolly lavender **L. lanata** is especially pretty, with dense white woolly leaves and bright violet flowers. I have grown this one as a house plant with good results.

LIATRIS SPICATA

(lie-**ay**-tris spee-**kah**-ta); also pronounced (lee-**ah**-tris)

SYNONYMS: Kansas gayfeather, blazing star

Liatris spicata

FAMILY: Asteraceae (formerly Compositae)

HARDY TO ZONE: 3

HEIGHT: 24 to 30 inches

DESCRIPTION: Lance-shaped leaves whorling up the stem, topped with lavender-pink spiked flowers. It is unusual in that the flower buds begin opening up from the top down to the bottom. They have a fuzzy look to them.

BLOOM TIME: Late July-August

CULTIVATION: Full sun to filtered or partial shade, in average to good soil that is well drained.

PROPAGATION: Seeds or division of the small bulb-type roots. Self-seeds abundantly.

USES: Fresh or dried arrangements. It fits nicely into any garden scheme and attracts bees and butterflies; attractive with globe thistle (*Echinops*).

SPECIES: **L. ligulostylis "alba"** has white flowers.

LINUM PERENNE

(**lye**-num pe-**ren**-ee)

SYNONYM: Blue flax

FAMILY: Linaceae

Linum perenne

HARDY TO ZONE: 4

HEIGHT: 12 to 30 inches

DESCRIPTION: Dainty delicate-looking stalks are strong and wiry. Sky-blue flowers appear all over the foliage for one day; they die off and others repeat the process every day for most of the summer. The flowers drop quietly, leaving little mess on the ground. They do not show off on cloudy or rainy days, only on the bright sunny days of summer.

BLOOM TIME: All season

CULTIVATION: Full sun to partial shade. Does well in all but soggy soils.

PROPAGATION: Seeds and division. Self-seeds abundantly.

USES: In any garden for *any* reason. Yes—blue flax is one of my favorite perennials.

SPECIES: **L. flavum**, a golden flax, hardy to zone 5. **L. perenne album**, a white flax. **L. grandiflorum rubrum**, an annual red flax.

LOBELIA SIPHILITICA

(lo-**bel**-ee-a si-fi-**li**-ti-ca)

SYNONYMS: Great lobelia, blue lobelia

FAMILY: Lobeliaceae

HARDY TO ZONE: 4

HEIGHT: 2 to 3 feet

DESCRIPTION: The oval-shaped leaves are large at their base and become smaller as they grow up the thick stalk. Showy, five-pointed large blue flowers climb the slightly hairy spike.

CULTIVATION: Partial or filtered shade, in good moist soil. I have grown them in full sun but they will only grow 15 inches tall. In the correct soil and light conditions they will grow to their full height of 3 feet.

BLOOM TIME: August-September

Lobelia siphilitica

PROPAGATION: Seeds or division.

USES: In garden borders or wildflower gardens. This plant, native from New England to Louisiana, was used by Native Americans to treat venereal diseases, diarrhea, and dysentery. The root was used together with mayapple (*Podophyllum peltatum*), but this is *not* recommended.

HISTORY: Traditionally used in love potions. The root was to be finely chopped and fed unknowingly to a quarrelsome couple to ease strife and make them fall in love again.

Caution: Some species of lobelia are poisonous. Know your species before using internally.

LUPINUS

(lo-**pine**-is)
SYNONYM: Lupine
FAMILY: Fabaceae (formerly Leguminosae)
HARDY TO ZONE: 4
HEIGHT: 24 to 36 inches

Lupinus

HDESCRIPTION: Palmate compound foliage on heavy spikes with pealike flowers on the top one-third of the stalk, followed by pea-type pods. Flowers are now available in most colors and some bicolors. The Russell strain is the most widely grown in perennial gardens.
BLOOM TIME: June
CULTIVATION: Wild species will grow in any soil, but the new hybrids prefer a richer soil. They like full sun with a good water supply. Do not add lime or other alkaline products. This short-lived perennial may rebloom if cut back after the first bloom. If you have very hot summers it will probably not rebloom, since lupines prefer cool weather. They resent transplanting at maturity because of their long taproot.
PROPAGATION: Seeds (gather your own seeds from the pods to start new plants in a greenhouse, or let them fall and self-seed, as they do so abundantly).
USES: In a wildflower garden or border. Good in waste areas where you want some color.
ISTORY: Lupines have been cultivated since early Egyptian times. They were once used as a food and medicine, but this is *not* recommended—more research is needed.

MALVA MOSCHATA

(**mal**-vah mos-**kah**-ta)
SYNONYMS: Muskmallow, hollyhock mallow, mallow
FAMILY: Malvaceae

Malva moschata

HARDY TO ZONE: 3
HEIGHT: 2 to 3 feet
DESCRIPTION: Small, light-green oval leaves. The flowers are five-petaled, papery, and long-blooming. I found both the pink and white species here at the farm the spring we moved in. It has been a favorite ever since.
BLOOM TIME: July-August
CULTIVATION: Easy; will grow in full sun or partial shade, in lean to good soil. Tolerates dry season.
PROPAGATION: Seeds; self-seeds abundantly. I just dig up the little seedlings and put them where I want them.
USES: Borders, wildflower gardens.

MENTHA

(**men**-tha)
SYNONYM: Mint
FAMILY: Lamiaceae (formerly Labiatae)
HARDY TO ZONE: 3
HEIGHT: Varies according to species.
DESCRIPTION: Highly scented leaves and purple or white flowers.
BLOOM TIME: July-August
CULTIVATION: Full sun to partial or filtered shade, in lean to good soil. Most species are invasive.
PROPAGATION: Seeds, division, cuttings.
USES: Mints are a popular herb for culinary purposes and are used in potpourri and sachets.

In the garden the invasive species make excellent ground covers.
SPECIES: Two species are good for growing in the perennial garden.

***M. piperita* "white,"** or white peppermint, grows 3 feet tall with white terminal flowers. It is not invasive as other mints are. Its gray-green leaves are very nice in tea.

Pycanthemum pilosum, or mountain mint, although not a true mint, has the same wonderful scent and uses and usually is sold as a mint. Its needlelike foliage mats down. It grows to 24 inches high and spreads slowly.

Mentha piperita

For invasive ground covers try the following mints: **M. suaveolens**, applemint, a 20-inch plant with soft light-green leaves. **M. x gentilis variegata**, ginger mint, 12 inches high. **M. piperita vulgaris**, peppermint, is called the bellyache mint and makes a delicious cup of tea.

MERTENSIA VIRGINICA

(mer-**tens**-ee-a vir-**jin**-i-ka)
SYNONYM: Virginia bluebells
FAMILY: Boraginaceae
HARDY TO ZONE: 3
HEIGHT: 26 inches
DESCRIPTION: Medium-long, oval-shaped leaves with loose clusters of nodding bell flowers. Buds are pink and turn blue as the flowers mature.
BLOOM TIME: May-June
CULTIVATION: Partial to full shade in moist, rich soil. Mulch will help keep the soil moist. It needs early spring moisture. Once the plant flowers, it then loses its leaves and goes dormant. Because of this you will want

to mark the area well so you do not dig it up accidentally. Do not cut the decaying leaves.

Mertensia virginica

PROPAGATION: Seeds; division or roots in the fall. Another good reason to have the area marked is so you can find the hiding roots.
USES: Attractive with spring bulbs, under tree areas, or in a wildflower garden.

MONARDA DIDYMA

(mon-**are**-da **di**-di-ma)
SYNONYMS: Beebalm, bergamot, Oswego tea
FAMILY: Lamiaceae (formerly Labiatae)
HARDY TO ZONE: 4
HEIGHT: 30 to 36 inches
DESCRIPTION: Saw-edged oval leaves, opposite one another on the square stem that is so common to members of the mint family. Highly scented flowers and foliage. Another perennial that is considered an herb first finds itself being enjoyed by perennial lovers as a flowering perennial. Hybrids have improved the flowers and presented new colors of pinks and reds.
BLOOM TIME: July-August
CULTIVATION: Full sun to shade, in

average to good soil that is well drained. Spreads quickly, but has a nasty habit of middling out—the center dies out, leaving a gap. This gap can be dug out and new roots from the edge replanted in the central area.

In drought areas, mildew near the end of summer is common. If caught early enough, a spray of baking soda and water may stop it. Give lots of wood ashes to add alkalinity to the soil.
PROPAGATION: Seeds, division.
USES: In any garden for its beauty; fresh or dried arrangements. Makes a great cup of tea.

Monarda didyma

HISTORY: Named for Nicholas Monardes, the Spanish doctor who first described it. This was one of the earliest plants to be introduced to Europe from America.

The name Oswego came from its Native American name. The early European settlers, introduced to it by the Indians, used it as a tea, especially during the years when the tax on black tea was so high few people could afford it. The name "beebalm" comes from the fact that bees and butterflies dearly love the nectar from the plant. It also is popular with hummingbirds.

MICHAEL H. DODGE, WHITE FLOWER FARM

SPECIES: Cultivars available include:
Adam—red
Cambridge—scarlet red
Croftway pink—pink
Prairie fire—salmon red
Snow white—white
Violet queen—violet

OENOTHERA FRUTICOSA

(ee-nuh-**theer**-uh froo-ti-**ko**-sa)
SYNONYM: Sundrops
FAMILY: Onagraceae
HARDY TO ZONE: 4
HEIGHT: 16 to 20 inches

Oenothera "Alba"

DESCRIPTION: Purplish new growth turns into dark-green leaves, with large yellow, nearly cup-shaped flowers. In fall, leaves again show purple coloring.
BLOOM TIME: June-July
CULTIVATION: Full sun and well-drained soil, from average to rich.
PROPAGATION: Seeds or root division.
USES: In any garden for its beauty.
SPECIES: Over two hundred species, ranging from the biennial evening primroses that the Japanese beetles love to small ground covers.

ONONIS SPINOSA

(o-**no**-nis spin-**o**-sah)
SYNONYM: Restharrow
FAMILY: Fabaceae (formerly Leguminosae)
HARDY TO ZONE: 4
HEIGHT: 24 to 30 inches
DESCRIPTION: Shrubby, with branched stems and thorns. Flowers are like little pink sweet peas.

Ononis spinosa

BLOOM TIME: July-August
CULTIVATION: Any well-drained soil. It has a long taproot that resents any transplanting except for very small species. Plant it where it is to stay; it is hard to eradicate once it becomes established.
PROPAGATION: Seeds and root cuttings.
USES: Very pretty in the garden and not grown as much as it should be. *Ononis spinosa*, the common plant, is used as a diuretic and for kidney and bladder disorders in herbal medicine.
SPECIES: *O. rotundifolia* does not have the thorns; it is pretty in the garden and tolerant of droughts.

PLATYCODON GRANDIFLORUM

(plat-ee-**coe**-don grand-i-**fl o**-rum)
SYNONYM: Balloon flower
FAMILY: Campanulaceae
HARDY TO ZONE: 3
HEIGHT: 20 to 24 inches

DESCRIPTION: Slender to medium-sized leaves on many stems; the flowers are usually blue or white and develop buds that look like balloons. These open up to five-petal, star-shaped flowers. In some hybrids, the balloon stays closed for a long period of time before opening.
BLOOM TIME: Varies according to the species.
CULTIVATION: Full sun, well-drained, sandy, average to good soil. The long, fleshy roots do not like to be transplanted. Stake taller varieties.

Platycodon grandiflorum

PROPAGATION: Seeds.
USES: In fresh arrangements, cut when buds are just beginning to open. In garden design, use in any garden style.
SPECIES: **P. grandiflorum "alba"** has white flowers and grows to 20 inches. **P. komachi** is a favorite of mine. The large balloon buds stay closed for most of the bloom time before opening. Grows to 14 inches. There are also several new pink hybrids.

POLEMONIUM CAERULEUM

(po-lee-**mow**-nee-um kie-**ru**-lee-um)
SYNONYMS: Jacob's ladder, Greek valerian

MICHAEL H. DODGE, WHITE FLOWER FARM

FAMILY: Polemoniaceae
HARDY TO ZONE: 3
HEIGHT: 18 to 20 inches
DESCRIPTION: Divided palmate leaves arranged like rings up a ladder. The blue flowers are long-lasting.
BLOOM TIME: June
CULTIVATION: Full sun to partial or filtered shade, in well-drained, average to good soil.

Polemonium caeruleum

PROPAGATION: Seeds or division.
USES: Good in any garden design. Flowers last a long time in fresh arrangements. Once used as a medicinal for headaches, epilepsy, and hysteria.
SPECIES: **P. lactrum "alba"** has white flowers.

PULMONARIA OFFICINALIS

(pul-mo-**nah**-ree-uh o-fis-i-**na**-lis)
SYNONYMS: Lungwort, soldiers and sailors, blue cowslip, Bethlehem sage
FAMILY: Boraginaceae
HARDY TO ZONE: 3
HEIGHT: 10 to 15 inches
DESCRIPTION: Green oval leaves, spotted with silvery white hairs, give the plant a white blotched appearance. Flowers often first appear pinkish and then turn blue, as often happens

with members of the borage family.
BLOOM TIME: May-June

Pulmonaria officinalis

CULTIVATION: Partial or filtered shade. Prefers soil that is rich and moist, but not soggy.
PROPAGATION: Seeds or division.
USES: For edgings, borders, or wildflower gardens.
Many years ago people thought that if a plant looked like a part of the body it could be used to cure that part. This was known as the doctrine of signatures. Lungwort, with its speckled leaves, looked like a diseased lung; it was therefore used to cure lung diseases. Notice the name *pulmonaria* also means "lung." Today it is still used for pulmonary complaints.
SPECIES: Hybrids to enjoy in the perennial garden include **P. augustifolia**, or blue lungwort; and **P. rubra**, with plain green leaves and rosy pink flowers.

RUTA GRAVEOLENS

(**roo**-ta gra-**vee**-o-lenz)
SYNONYMS: Rue, herb of grace
FAMILY: Rutaceae
HARDY TO ZONE: 4
HEIGHT: 18 to 24 inches
DESCRIPTION: It has a strong, pungent

aroma. Blue-green double compound leaves on a many-branched base; the yellow flowers in July are followed by interesting seed pods.

Ruta graveolens

BLOOM TIME: July
CULTIVATION: Full sun; will tolerate a minimum of shade. Lean to average soil, tolerates drought conditions. Good drainage is necessary. Prune back if plant becomes leggy to make it bushy.
PROPAGATION: Seeds (self-seeds) and cuttings.
USES: Borders or edging. Provides flowers for fresh arrangements and pods for dried arrangements. An old medicinal, but *not* recommended at this time. The name "Herb of Grace" comes from the fact that it was once used in holy water at High Mass in the Catholic Church.
Caution: Some people may get a rash from rue. I have been working with rue for 12 years and only once received a small rash from it.

SANTOLINA CHAMAECYPARISSUS

(san-toh-**li**-nah ka-mie-kew-pa-**ris**-us)
SYNONYMS: Lavender cotton, dwarf cypress, gray santolina

FAMILY: Asteraceae (formerly Compositae)
HARDY TO ZONE: 5
HEIGHT: 24 inches
DESCRIPTION: Feathery, ferny, silver-gray, scented foliage with yellow buttonlike flowers.
BLOOM TIME: July-August
CULTIVATION: Full sun to partial shade, in alkaline, average soil. Protect with evergreen covering in winter.

Santolina chamaecyparissus

PROPAGATION: Seeds, cuttings, or division.
USES: Both flowers and foliage are good for fresh or dried arrangements. Used as a moth repellent in herbalism. Good specimen or border plant.
SPECIES:
S. virens
(s. vi-**rens**)
SYNONYMS: Green santolina, holy flax
HARDY TO ZONE: 5
HEIGHT: 15 to 20 inches
DESCRIPTION: Dark-green scented leaves, similar to rosemary leaves. Yellow flowers same as on gray santolina, but the scent is different.

SCABIOSIFOLIA NAGOYA
(skab-ee-**o**-si-fol-ee-uh na-**goi**-a)
SYNONYM: Patrinia

FAMILY: Dipsacaceae
HARDY TO ZONE: 4
HEIGHT: 28 to 30 inches

Scabiosifolia nagoya

DESCRIPTION: Deeply cut green foliage and bright yellow airy flowers terminal on many stems. Strange aroma.
BLOOM TIME: August
CULTIVATION: Full sun to partial shade, in average to rich well-drained soil.
PROPAGATION: Seeds.
USES: Pretty in the border or as background plant.

SEDUM SPECTABILE
(**see**-dum spek-**tah**-bi-lee)
SYNONYMS: Stonecrop, everlasting
FAMILY: Crassulaceae
HARDY TO ZONE: 3
HEIGHT: 20 to 24 inches
DESCRIPTION: Light-green, succulent, fleshy leaves. Pink flowers in terminal umbels. Clumps spread slowly.
BLOOM TIME: August
CULTIVATION: A very easy plant; it will grow just about anywhere from full sun to shade, in dry or moist soil.
PROPAGATION: Leaf cuttings or division. Simply place a leaf in the soil and it will grow. Probably the simplest perennial to propagate.

USES: Fresh arrangements. Fits just about anywhere in the garden and makes a good specimen. Provides fall color just when you need it; a good companion to chrysanthemums.

Sedum spectabile

SPECIES: *S. spectabile* "**variegated**" in cream and light green grows about 18 inches high.
Cultivars "**autumn joy**" and "**Indian chief**" have different degrees of pink flowers.

THERMOPSIS
(ther-**mop**-sis)
SYNONYM: False lupine

Thermopsis

FAMILY: Fabaceae (formerly Leguminosae)
HARDY TO ZONE: 3
HEIGHT: 24 inches
DESCRIPTION: Pealike foliage and

bright-yellow sweet pea-type flowers. Very invasive.

BLOOM TIME: June

CULTIVATION: Full sun to shade, lean to good soil.

PROPAGATION: Seeds, underground runners.

USES: Good ground cover; they are also nice cut flowers.

TRADESCANTIA VIRGINIANA

(trad-es-**kan**-tee-a vir-jin-ee-**ay**-na)

SYNONYM: Spiderwort

FAMILY: Commelinaceae

HARDY TO ZONE: 4

HEIGHT: 12 to 20 inches

Tradescantia virginiana

DESCRIPTION: Long lance-shaped leaves whorled to the stem, grass-like. Three-petaled flowers in purple, pink, or white. Flowers drop off every afternoon, reappearing the following day.

BLOOM TIME: July-August

CULTIVATION: Full sun to partial shade in moist, well-drained average soil.

PROPAGATION: Seeds or division.

USES: Edging or borders, or as a specimen.

Scientists have found that the blue spiderwort is a good indicator of low levels of radiation and certain chemi-

cals. The blue cells in the stamens turn pink after a week or so of low radiation levels. Some plants are being placed near nuclear plants. But don't confuse the pink or rose species with radiation leaks.

HISTORY: *Tradescantia* was named for John Tradescant (1608–1662), the gardener of King Charles I of England.

TROLLIUS

(**tro**-lee-us)

SYNONYMS: Globe flower, big buttercup

FAMILY: Ranunculaceae

HARDY TO ZONE: 4

HEIGHT: 20 to 28 inches

DESCRIPTION: Deep palmate toothed leaves and large, tight, orange-to-yellow globelike flowers.

BLOOM TIME: May-June

CULTIVATION: Full sun to partial shade. Good to rich moist soil with good drainage.

Trollius europaeus

PROPAGATION: Seeds; needs stratification for three months. Takes about six months to germinate. Also division of plants.

USES: Borders, nice fresh arrangements.

SPECIES: *T. chinensis* "**golden queen**"

has dark-orange flowers and grows to 24 inches. *T. europaeus*, the variety most often seen in backyard gardens, has yellow globe flowers in June.

VERONICA

(va-**ron**-i-ka)

SYNONYM: Speedwell

FAMILY: Scrophulariaceae

HARDY TO ZONE: 3

HEIGHT: 12 to 18 inches

DESCRIPTION: Lance-shaped leaves; flowers on terminal spikes, mostly in lavender blues.

Veronica incana

BLOOM TIME: June-August, depending on variety.

CULTIVATION: Full sun and average to good, well-drained soil. Deadhead for a longer blooming period.

PROPAGATION: Seeds or division.

USES: Borders, ground covers, cut flowers.

SPECIES: *V. incana* grows to 14 inches with silver-gray foliage, very nice. *V. spicata* is 18 inches high with lavender-blue flowers.

V. alpine "**alba**" is only 9 inches high, with white flowers. *V.* "**red fox**" grows to 15 inches and has pink flowers.

FOURTEEN

The High-Growing Perennials

Plants Over Three Feet Tall

Here, in this sequestered close
Blown the hyacinth and the rose;
Here beside the modest Stock
Flaunts the flowing holly-hock.
—Austin Dobson

High-growing perennials are enjoyed for their stately beauty as they tower over the lower plants. When we enter a garden our eye seems to be drawn first to those tall beauties. They are the stability of the garden as a whole picture.

Taller plants are placed in the back of a border with successively shorter plants in front, down to an edging that can be as low as you wish. In an island planting, one you can walk around from all sides, tall perennials are placed in the center and surrounded by shorter plants.

For a summer hedge that will die back in the fall, peonies (*Paeonia*), baptisia, and southernwood (*Artemisia abrotanum*) are excellent selections. Tall perennials can also be used alone as specimens or grouped in a clump. And don't forget their value as screening to cover unsightly areas. I remember how my farmer neighbor used golden glows (*Rudbeckia*) in front of the manure pile, running from the barn to the garage, to screen it from the highway. And he had the tallest golden glows I have ever seen.

ACHILLEA PTARMICA

(ah-**kill**-lee-a **tar**-mi-ka)
SYNONYMS: Sneezewort, pearly white yarrow
FAMILY: Asteraceae (formerly Compositae)

Achillea ptarmica

HARDY TO ZONE: 3
DESCRIPTION: Does not look like the rest of the yarrow perennials; it has thin, lance-shaped leaves instead of the typical fern leaf, and white flowers that look like soft, little, white powder puffs.
BLOOM TIME: June until frost.
CULTIVATION: Dry, lean to good soil with good drainage, in full sun to partial shade. Do not fertilize. The plant is very invasive. I have mine planted in a strip with lawn on either side. This way I can keep its size under control by mowing its creeping roots.
PROPAGATION: Seeds or division.
USES: Excellent for fresh or dried arrangements.

ACONITUM NAPELLUS

(ak-ah-**ni**-tum na-**pel**-lus)
SYNONYMS: Wolfsbane, monkshood, blue rocket, helmet flower, storm-hat, Thor-hat
FAMILY: Ranunculaceae

HARDY TO ZONE: 2
HEIGHT: 3 to 4 feet
DESCRIPTION: Glossy, deeply divided, palmate leaves. Helmet-shaped flowers are mostly blue or white or bicolors of blue and white.
BLOOM TIME: June-August
CULTIVATION: Full sun in short-season zones, and shade in hot-summer areas. Needs rich, moisture-retentive soil. Add lots of organic matter, especially composed manure from the barnyard. Feed wood ashes or bonemeal. Subject to mildew; dust with sulphur.
PROPAGATION: Seeds (two years to bloom) or division. Although it dislikes division, the plant needs it every three to four years to keep it healthy. Division is difficult.
USES: Wildflower gardens or borders.

Aconitum napellus

HISTORY: Because of the poisonous nature of aconitum, the plant has generated several interesting synonyms. According to the herbalist Gerard, the powdered root was used to make poison darts and arrows to kill wolves and tigers; hence its name wolfsbane. It has also been used to murder humans. Most poisonous plants are in some way associated with evil, the devil, or witchcraft. In German history aconitum is said to be sacred to the devil. However, Denmark and Sweden attribute the aconitum plant to Thor, the god of thunder, from which comes the synonyms of Thor-hat and Storm-hat. Our synonyms of blue rocket flower and helmet flower refer to the shape and color of the flowers.
Caution: Aconitum contains a powerful poison, aconitine, which is present in all parts of the plant, especially the root. It can be ingested or absorbed by the skin. Only one-tenth of a grain can kill a small animal. It is interesting that goats and cows will eat the plant, but the tiny field mouse avoids it even when very hungry.

Poisonous plants should not be grown near vegetables, edible herbs, or near animal pens, and are not recommended where very small children play.

AGASTACHE FOENICULUM

(a-**gah**-sta-kee fee-**nik**-ew-lum)
SYNONYM: Anise-hyssop, honey-bee plant
FAMILY: Lamiaceae (formerly Labiatae)
HARDY TO ZONE: 3
HEIGHT: 3 feet
DESCRIPTION: Gray-green foliage with purple overtones in early spring, which changes to greener foliage as it matures. Wonderful licorice-scented foliage and flowers attract people as well as bees and butterflies. Lavender flowers.
BLOOM TIME: July until frost
CULTIVATION: Full sun, partial or fil-

tered shade. Lean to good soil (if soil is too rich you will lose some of the scent). Keep flowers picked and it will bloom continuously until frost.

Agastache foeniculum

PROPAGATION: Seeds (will self-seed abundantly) and division.
USES: Wonderful for tea, potpourri, and fresh or dried arrangements. Fits into any garden style. That's right—it's another of my favorites at Wormwood Farm.

ANTHEMIS TINCTORIA

(**an**-them-is tink-**to**-ree-a)
SYNONYMS: Dyer's chamomile, golden marguerite
FAMILY: Asteraceae (formerly Compositae)
HARDY TO ZONE: 3
HEIGHT: 3 to 4 feet
DESCRIPTION: Gray-green fernlike foliage held stiff and erect. The many-branched stems are covered with yellow daisies.
BLOOM TIME: July-August
CULTIVATION: Full sun to partial or filtered shade. Easy and invasive, it will grow in any soil with good drainage. Deadhead to maintain continuous bloom. When blooming period is over, cut back completely and it will rebloom. It may

need staking in windy areas.
PROPAGATION: Seeds or division.
USES: Fresh arrangements; good tall ground cover for a slope or border. During the Middle Ages, a yellow dye was extracted from its flowers. That's where the name "dyer's chamomile" came from.

Anthemis tinctoria

SPECIES: *A. sancti-johannis* has orange flowers and grows 2½ feet tall. This species's name refers to St. John's Day, June 24, which is its date of blooming in Bulgaria. A cultivar **"kelwayi,"** which grows to 2½ to 3 feet and has lemon-yellow flowers, is especially nice.

ARTEMISIA ABROTANUM

(ar-tay-**m i s**-ee-a a-**brot**-a-num)
SYNONYMS: Southernwood, old man, lad's love
FAMILY: Asteraceae (formerly Compositae)
HARDY TO ZONE: 3
HEIGHT: 3 feet
DESCRIPTION: The gray-green needle-like foliage on woody branches is highly scented. The blooms in August are insignificant, the same coloring as the foliage.
CULTIVATION: Full sun, partial or filtered shade, in well-drained average

to good soil. The richer the soil the less fragrance. In colder areas prune only in early spring to midsummer. Southernwood needs its woody branches to survive the winter months.

Artemisia abrotanum

PROPAGATION: Cuttings or division.
USES: In garden design as a hedging or specimen. Dried, it can be used as an insect repellent.
HISTORY: A longtime herb, southernwood was once burned and the ashes mixed with oil. This was applied to the head as a cure for baldness.
If you observe southernwood, you will notice no insects like it. Its insect repellent qualities gave it the French name *garde-robe*; it was used in closets and trunks to keep insects away.
SPECIES: *A. abrotanum* **"tangerine,"** growing 4 to 6 feet with a vase shape, is good as a specimen or hedge. *A. abrotanum camphor* is the smallest of the southernwoods, at 2 to 2½ feet. It has a very strong camphor aroma.

ARTEMISIA LUDOVICIANA

(ar-tay-**m i s**-ee-a loo-do-vik-ee-**ah**-na)

SYNONYM: Silver king

HARDY TO ZONE: 3

HEIGHT: 2 to 3 feet

FAMILY: Asteraceae (formerly Compositae)

DESCRIPTION: White, slightly woolly leaves, deeply cut. Tiny insignificant silver and yellow flowers.

BLOOM TIME: July

CULTIVATION: Full sun or partial shade in lean to good soil. This invasive plant has no trouble taking over any other plant—it even chokes out mints.

Artemisia ludoviciana

PROPAGATION: Division of roots.

USES: Fresh or dried arrangements; especially nice as a base for wreath makers. Harvest before it starts to turn brown in late summer.

ASTER NOVAE-ANGLIAE

(**as**-tur **no**-vie-**ang**-lee-ie)

SYNONYMS: Hardy aster, Michaelmas daisy, New England aster

FAMILY: Asteraceae (formerly Compositae)

HARDY TO ZONE: 4

HEIGHT: 3 to 6 feet

DESCRIPTION: Lance-shaped leaves clasp hairy stems. Many branches with lavender-pink daisy flowers. Grows wild in New England.

Aster novae-angliae

BLOOM TIME: August-September

CULTIVATION: Full sun to light shade, in well-drained average soil.

PROPAGATION: Seeds or division in spring.

USES: Good late season color, often overlooked because it is so common.

HISTORY: Once used by Native Americans as a fumigating plant. May possibly have properties that will remove poisons of poison ivy (*Rhus*). Was used in other medicines by Native Americans.

SPECIES:

A. novi-belgii "New York aster."

BAPTISIA AUSTRALIS

(bap-**teez**-ee-uh ow-**strah**-lis)

SYNONYMS: Baptisia, false indigo

FAMILY: Fabaceae (formerly Leguminosae)

HARDY TO ZONE: 3

HEIGHT: 4 to 6 feet

DESCRIPTION: Long-lived perennial with cloverlike foliage. Blue-purple blossoms up and down the long, fleshy stalks look like pea flowers and are followed by interesting black pea pods 3 to 4 inches long.

BLOOM TIME: June-July

CULTIVATION: Full sun to partial shade in well-drained soil. As a legume it fixes its own nitrogen in the soil, so do not use a nitrogen fertilizer. Give plenty of room when planting, since it will spread out its branches 3 to 5 feet. Does not need staking except in very windy areas. It has a long taproot that resents any transplanting at maturity.

Baptisia australis

PROPAGATION: Seeds are slow, taking three or more years to bloom. I let the little self-seeded seedlings grow for a year and then transplant them.

USES: Makes a good summer hedge planted four feet apart. Flowers are good for fresh arrangements. Pods make excellent dried material; harvest before the seed pod opens and scatters its seed.

SPECIES: **B. viridis** grows to 2 to 4 feet and has yellow flowers and bluish foliage. **B. tinctoria**, called wild or false indigo, is used as a substitute for the true indigo plant. Blue dye is made from the yellow sap of the woody stems.

CENTAUREA MACROCEPHALA

(cen-taw-**ree**-uh mak-ro-**kef**-a-la)

SYNONYMS: Globe centaurea, yellow cornflower

FAMILY: Asteraceae (formerly Compositae)

HARDY TO ZONE: 3
HEIGHT: 3 to 4 feet
DESCRIPTION: Large, coarse, lance-shaped leaves; sturdy-looking. Yellow thistlelike flowers on interesting pods.

Centaurea macrocephala

BLOOM TIME: July-August
CULTIVATION: Full sun to partial shade. Not fussy about soil conditions as long as it has good drainage. Give some organic matter.
PROPAGATION: Seeds or division.
USES: In borders and for fresh or dried arrangements. The pods dry well.

CLEMATIS
(**klem**-a-tis)
SYNONYM: None
FAMILY: Ranunculaceae
HARDY TO ZONE: 3
HEIGHT: to 20 feet (vines)
DESCRIPTION: Small oval leaves in sets of three, on a long vine with several branching-off vines. It clings to a trellis, but may need some arranging in early stages. Takes about three years to become well established. Many different colors are available.
BLOOM TIME: June
CULTIVATION: Full sun to partial shade, in good soil with lots of or-

ganic matter. Keep roots covered with other plants since they do not like to be exposed to the sun.

Clematis "Nellie Mosher"

PROPAGATION: Buy the plant from your local greenhouse.
USES: As a vine for vertical gardening; the flower pods dry well for craft work.
SPECIES: My favorite is "**Nellie Mosher**," a pink and white 5-inch flower. "**Jackamani**" is popular with its striking purple 5- to 6-inch blooms. There are also small-flowered varieties. Check your plant catalogs for the many different species available for your area.

CIMICIFUGA RACEMOSA
(si-mi-**si**-**few**-ga ra-se-**m o**-sa)
SYNONYMS: Snakeroot, bugbane, black cohosh
FAMILY: Ranunculaceae
HARDY TO ZONE: 2
HEIGHT: 4 to 7 feet
DESCRIPTION: Large-toothed compound leaves. The flowers are tiny white beadlike buds that open from the bottom up into a fringed spike that looks like a white bottlebrush. Heavy foliage at base, with little if any near the flower spike.
BLOOM TIME: July-August

CULTIVATION: Partial or filtered shade; likes a moisture-retentive soil. Water when Mother Nature's supply isn't sufficient. Fertilize once a year with good compost. Mulch to keep soil around roots cool and to hold onto moisture. Spreads slowly. It has no bug problem, hence its name bugbane.
PROPAGATION: Seeds—but slow and erratic. Division.
USES: Back of a border or in a wildflower or herb garden. This North American native is an old medicinal used for whooping cough, rheumatism, and snakebite, and as a diuretic.

Cimicifuga racemosa

SPECIES: *C. ramosa atropurpuree* grows 6 feet tall, with white flowers set off by purple foliage. A rare species. *C. simplex* is smaller, growing 3 to 5 feet tall, with white flowers in September.

DELPHINIUM
(del-**fi n**-ee-um)
SYNONYM: None
FAMILY: Ranunculaceae
HARDY TO ZONE: 2
HEIGHT: 5 to 7 feet
DESCRIPTION: Lobed leaves, large at the base, become scarce as they el-

evate the stalk. Many flowers blooming on a thick terminal stalk, mostly in blue and purple.

BLOOM TIME: July

CULTIVATION: Full sun in rich soil. It seems you can't feed delphiniums enough; give them all the organic matter you can. Will tolerate either slightly acid or slightly alkaline soil. They are fussy and difficult but worth the trouble because they are so beautiful. Fertilize in early spring, when they come into flower, and again when you cut them back.

Delphinium

Delphiniums will need staking, which should be done just as they break through the ground in spring. After blooming cut back to the ground and you may get a second bloom in the fall. They need good air circulation and dislike too much water on their leaves. When watering, water at the base; do not spray the plant.

Mulch to keep the soil moist, but keep it about 3 inches away from the stalk to prevent crown rot. Division every three or four years will keep the plant healthy. For winter care, a mulch of sand or wood ashes helps keep them dry. Delphiniums are susceptible to many problems,

including crown rot, powdery mildew, and other fungal diseases, and those slimy slugs enjoy eating the leaves.

PROPAGATION: Seeds or division.

USES: Beautiful as a specimen or as background plants. The flowers are good for fresh or dried for arrangements.

SPECIES: There are basically two types: *Elatum,* which includes most of the giant pacifics, and *Cheilanthum,* which includes the belladonnas. The belladonnas flower more freely but are not as long-stemmed. There are also several new dwarf species.

Caution: All 250 species of delphiniums and larkspurs (the annual ones) are poisonous. The entire plant is poisonous.

ECHINACEA PURPUREA

(e-kee-**nah**-shee-a pur-**pew**-ree-a) Often listed incorrectly under Rudbeckias—this is an outdated classification.

Echinacea purpurea

SYNONYMS: Red coneflower, purple coneflower

FAMILY: Asteraceae (formerly Compositae)

HARDY TO ZONE: 3

HEIGHT: 3 to 4 feet

DESCRIPTION: Dull, coarse gray-green leaves, heavy at base. Many-branched stalk bearing 3- to 4-inch lavender to pink flowers with bristly cone-shaped brown centers. As rays of the flower mature, they turn backward away from the center.

BLOOM TIME: July-August

CULTIVATION: Full sun to partial shade in average to good, well-drained soil. Divide every three to four years to keep in bounds and healthy.

PROPAGATION: Seeds or division.

USES: For cut flowers. Pods dry well. The root is used medicinally as a blood purifier, antibiotic, and antiseptic. Capsules are available at health stores.

Caution: The overharvesting of wild Echinacea is a serious problem. Since the plant is very easy to grow, raise your own supply to save the environment and to have your own unlimited supply.

ECHINOPS RITRO

(e-**kee**-nops **rit**-ro)

SYNONYM: Globe thistle

FAMILY: Asteraceae (formerly Compositae)

HARDY TO ZONE: 3

HEIGHT: 3 to 4 feet

DESCRIPTION: Large, strong, spiny-looking leaves, deep green on top and whitish underneath. Blue globelike flowers. Spreads quickly in good soil.

BLOOM TIME: July-August

CULTIVATION: Full sun to partial shade in well-drained, lean to good soil. It appreciates some wood ashes or bonemeal every year. Has a deep taproot, but spreads, providing plenty of root cuttings for new plants.

PROPAGATION: Seeds or root cuttings.

Echinops ritro

USES: Pretty in any garden design. Flowers can be used for fresh or dried arrangements. Harvest flowers before they are mature for best results.

EUPATORIUM PURPUREUM

(ew-pa-**to**-ree-um pur-**pew**-ree-um)

SYNONYM: Joe-Pye weed

FAMILY: Asteraceae (formerly Compositae)

HARDY TO ZONE: 4

HEIGHT: 4 to 6 feet

DESCRIPTION: Large straplike leaves, gray underneath. Flowers on many branches in terminal mauve-colored clusters.

BLOOM TIME: July-August

CULTIVATION: Full sun or partial shade. This is a plant for very moist areas. My Joe-Pye weed grows near the farm pond where it is very damp, but it does very well in a garden situation as long as it receives sufficient water.

PROPAGATION: Seeds or division.

USES: In a bog area or the wildflower or herb garden. Good tall background plant. Fresh or dried arrangements. Harvest for drying in the budded stage so it does not fluff out and scatter its seeds. Leaves and flowers have been used medicinally as a laxative, in small doses.

Eupatorium purpureum

SPECIES: *E. rugosum* produces white flowers to zone 3. *E. fistulosum* has hollow stems. *E. maculatum* has spotted leaves, for marshy areas to zone 2.

HEMEROCALLIS

(hem-er-oh-**kal**-is)

SYNONYM: Daylily

FAMILY: Liliaceae

HARDY TO ZONE: 3

HEIGHT: 3 to 4 feet

DESCRIPTION: Long, grassy, swordlike leaves. Flowers of assorted colors grow on "scapes" (like the alliums). Many buds keep the long flowering period going; each flower lasts only a day and then dies.

BLOOM TIME: Varies according to species.

CULTIVATION: Full sun, in almost any well-drained alkaline soil. Give a good yearly supply of wood ashes from that winter stove. Only use a low nitrogen fertilizer or you will have a lot of foliage at the expense of flower production. Provide water during droughts, especially when in bloom.

Hemerocallis "Annie Welch"

PROPAGATION: Division of roots.

USES: A good plant for naturalizing as well as for the garden. An old medicinal to reduce fever and as a diuretic. The flowers are edible.

SPECIES: Many new cultivars are developed every year; at present there are over 3,000 registered. It is possible to have a daylily in bloom all season. *Hemerocallis fulva* and *Hemerocallis aurantiaca* are edible species—in Chinese cooking daylily blossoms are called *gum jum* (golden needles). The bud is dried and then soaked 30 minutes in water when needed in a recipe. You can also purchase the dried daylily buds in a Chinese food store.

LYSIMACHIA CLETHROIDES

(ly-si-**mack**-ee-ah kleth-**roi**-deez)

SYNONYMS: Gooseneck loosestrife, Japanese loosestrife

FAMILY: Primulaceae

HARDY TO ZONE: 3

HEIGHT: 3 to 4 feet

DESCRIPTION: Lance-shaped dark

MICHAEL H. DODGE, WHITE FLOWER FARM

leaves in dense clumps. The slender arching spike bears many branches with white flowers.
BLOOM TIME: July-August
CULTIVATION: Sun or partial shade; likes moist rich soil. Divide every two to three years to keep under control.

Lysimachia clethroides

PROPAGATION: Seeds or division.
USES: Good in any garden design and for fresh arrangements.

LYSIMACHIA PUNCTATA
(ly-si-**mack**-ee-ah punk-**tah**-ta)
SYNONYMS: Yellow loosestrife, circle flower

Lysimachia punctata

FAMILY: Primulaceae
HARDY TO ZONE: 4
HEIGHT: 30 to 36 inches
DESCRIPTION: Oval green leaves. Whorls of flowers climb loosely up the stalk between leaves. The lemon-yellow flowers have a circle of light-brown at the throat, hence its name circle flower.
BLOOM TIME: June-July
CULTIVATION: Full sun to partial shade; tolerates most soil conditions, but does not like extreme dry conditions. Mulch to keep soil cool.
PROPAGATION: Seeds or division.
USES: In any garden style, especially old-fashioned gardens.

PAPAVER ORIENTALE
(pa-**pah**-ver o-ree-en-**tah**-lee)
SYNONYM: Oriental poppy
FAMILY: Papaveraceae
HARDY TO ZONE: 3
HEIGHT: 1 to 4 feet

Papaver orientale

DESCRIPTION: Once established, the oriental poppy is hardy to the point of being invasive. Toothed, lance-shaped hairy leaves. The flower petals are paper-thin, in pinks, reds, and oranges. The flowers are short-lived, followed by interesting pods.
BLOOM TIME: June
CULTIVATION: Full sun in well-drained, average to good soil. Once the flowering is over, the foliage becomes ratty-looking and will disappear. I usually cut it back after the pods are ready to harvest for drying. This area can then be overplanted with colorful annuals. A light fertilizer is added at this time for both the annuals and the newly forming foliage of the poppies.
PROPAGATION: Seeds. Division should be done in late summer when new foliage has appeared. You may want to mulch well the first year to protect the new plants.
USES: As a cut flower, harvest just when buds are ready to open; sear stem end of stalk with flame of match or candle to prevent it from losing all its milky sap.
The dried pods look like little vases with lids on top. I am often asked about the opium from poppies. The oriental poppy grown in our gardens is not the poppy that produces opium gum. Opium comes from a variety of Papaver somniferum.
Caution: Poppies can be toxic if eaten in large amounts.

PAEONIA
(pie-**on**-ee-a; also pee-**o**-nee-a)
SYNONYM: Peony
FAMILY: Paeoniaceae (formerly Ranunculaceae)
HARDY TO ZONE: 2
HEIGHT: 2 to 4 feet
DESCRIPTION: One of the longest-lived sturdy perennials. It has shiny compound leaves and large fragrant flowers that grow to 6 to 7 inches, in single and double forms. Colors are red, pink, and white. The foliage looks good all season, making this a good specimen plant.
BLOOM TIME: June-July
CULTIVATION: Full sun to partial or filtered shade. When first planting, dig a large hole and provide plenty of good, composted organic matter.

A heavy feeder, it likes a yearly application of high-phosphate fertilizer. Add peat moss if the soil becomes too alkaline. Feed twice a season. Leaves produce foods for following year's flowers. Do not plant too deeply or it will not bloom. On species with extra-large flowers, I use the commercial wire cages for support. Cut the flower stalks after blooming and cut foliage when it dies in fall.

Paeonia

PROPAGATION: Division after blooming period in late summer.
USES: Excellent in any garden. Nice as a border plant or specimen. Flowers make beautiful fresh arrangements. I dry the petals for my potpourri mixes.
Ants and Peonies: Every so often someone complains to me about ants eating their peonies. I laugh as I tell them the ants we so dislike are actually helping the peonies by eating the sweet syrup on the buds; this helps open up the blossom. I have noticed where there is a lack of ants the buds often do not open, they just rot. Mother Nature has truly provided for every need—we only have to open our eyes to see it.
HISTORY: From early Greek times, shepherds thought that the peony was of divine origin, possessing potent magic to drive away evil spirits. It is interesting that in ancient times there was a country called Paeonia, which was destroyed during the Persian wars. The people were supposedly sent to Asia.
The peony also was once popular as a medicinal, only harvesting it was a problem. No man could touch it unless a woman's urine or menses was first placed on the ground near it. Some people would attach a rope to the plant and tie the rope to a dog, letting him pull it up. This plant was used for female complaints, along with other maladies.
During the seventeenth century it was thought that wearing an "anodyne necklace" made of old dried peony blossoms around the neck would prevent or cure illness.
SPECIES: There are four peony forms and many cultivars: *Singles:* One or more rows of petals surround a mass of showy golden stamens. *Japanese:* One or two rows of flowering carnationlike stamens, with petals the same color. *Anemone:* Similar to the Japanese except shaggier, with stamens transformed into petallike parts. *Doubles:* Fluffy and fragrant, with either inconspicuous or missing stamens.

PHLOX PANICULATA

(**flocks** pa-nik-ew-**lah**-ta)
SYNONYMS: Summer perennial phlox, border phlox
FAMILY: Polemoniaceae
HARDY TO ZONE: 3
HEIGHT: 3 feet
DESCRIPTION: Often found around old torn-down farmsteads, these plants are survivors under the worst of conditions. Long oval leaves. The original phlox is a mauve-purplish pink, but many hybrids have introduced pretty whites and pinks.

Phlox paniculata

BLOOM TIME: August
CULTIVATION: Full sun or partial shade in good rich soil. Space plantings for good air circulation to help prevent fungus diseases. Thin plants in spring; a few good ones are better than a mildewed clump. One complaint with phlox is that it reverts back to purple. This can be prevented by cutting seed heads off after blooming to prevent self-seeding, which often does produce the original color.
PROPAGATION: Seeds or division.
USES: Borders.
SPECIES: See chapter 12 for low creeping phlox.

PHYSOSTEGIA VIRGINIANA

(fie-sos-**tee**-gee-a vir-jin-ee-**ah**-na)
SYNONYMS: Obedient plant, false dragonhead, virginia's lionheart
FAMILY: Lamiaceae (formerly Labiatae)
HARDY TO ZONE: 2
HEIGHT: 3 to 4 feet
DESCRIPTION: Long, opposite, lance-shaped leaves. Many-branched, with

spike flowers of rose or white. The snapdragonlike head is hinged to the stalk and holds the new position if pushed to the right or left.

BLOOM TIME: August to frost

Physostegia virginiana

CULTIVATION: Sun to partial or filtered shade. It can be invasive in good to rich soil. Will grow in almost all soils.

PROPAGATION: Seeds or division of invasive roots.

USES: Makes good ground cover for unsightly areas. It is nice in fresh or dried arrangements.

SPECIES: *Bouquet rose* has green leaves. *Summer snow* has white flowers with green foliage. *Variegated* has green and cream leaves with rose flowers.

POLYGONATUM BIFLORUM

(po-li-go-**nah**-tum bi-**fl o**-rum)
SYNONYM: Solomon's seal
FAMILY: Liliaceae
HARDY TO ZONE: 3
HEIGHT: 3 feet
DESCRIPTION: Large, oval, lance-shaped, shiny leaves. The stems arch in a curve, with white bell-shaped flowers suspended under them followed by blue berries.
BLOOM TIME: June

CULTIVATION: Partial or filtered shade to shade; will tolerate full sun if very moist soil is provided. Once established, spreads quickly.

PROPAGATION: Division.

USES: Shade garden, wildflower garden, herb garden. Old-time medicinal known as a panacea for external wounds.

Polygonatum biflorum

HISTORY: The rhizome has a waxlike scar on it from the yearly withering of new stems. You can tell how old the perennial is by the number of scars. Called Solomon's seal because the scars are said to resemble the seal used by Solomon.

ROSA

(**roh**-za)
SYNONYM: Rose
FAMILY: Rosaceae
HARDY TO ZONE: 3
HEIGHT: 2 to 4 feet
DESCRIPTION: Shrubby woody perennials with terminal flowers. Thorns on stems. Flowers in red, pink, white, and yellow. Most have wonderful, well-known fragrance.
BLOOM TIME: Varies according to the species.
CULTIVATION: Full sun or small amount of shade in well-drained,

good to rich soil. Neutral to slightly acid soil (not less than 5.8 pH). It likes plenty of water, but not wet feet. Needs protection from high, dry winds. It is a heavy feeder; feed monthly with low-nitrogen fertilizer. Deadhead the flowers.

PROPAGATION: Buy through garden centers and farms. Division of old species.

USES: Fresh or dried. The oil is used in perfumes, bathwater, and lotions. Roses are edible—try a cream cheese sandwich with rose petals. And of course, they are beautiful growing in the garden.

Rosa

SPECIES: Check with your local greenhouse or mail-order catalog.

HISTORY: Roses have been used since ancient times. Romans strewed rose petals on their floors, and Roman women wore garlands and made the petals into perfumes and rose water. Both mythology and Christian tradition have symbolic meanings for the rose.

An old custom of hanging a rose over the dinner table meant that any conversation at that table was to be confidential. This may have been the beginning of the dinner table centerpiece. The rose is probably the best-known flower in history. Georgia, Iowa, New York, North Dakota, and Washington, D.C., honor the rose as their own flower (see the appendix for more state flower listings).

RUDBECKIA HIRTA

(rud-**bek**-ee-a **hir**-ta)

SYNONYMS: Black- or brown-eyed Susan

FAMILY: Asteraceae (formerly Compositae)

HARDY TO ZONE: 3

HEIGHT: 3 feet

DESCRIPTION: Dark-green, lance-shaped leaves on hairy stems. The flower disk center is black or brown, with ray flowers in yellow or orange, or bicolors of yellow and brown.

BLOOM TIME: July-August

Rudbeckia hirta

CULTIVATION: Sun to partial shade in lean to good soil. You can collect seed heads and sprinkle them beside roadways, adding beauty to the neighborhood.

PROPAGATION: Seeds or division. Self-seeds, often producing interesting hybrids.

USES: At the back of a border; also nice along highways or in wild areas.

SPECIES: **R. fulgida goldsturm** has large flowers on bushy stems. **R.** *subtomentosa* **"sweet cone,"** to zone 4, the rudbeckia with an anise fragrance. Yellow petals with a brown disk. **R. "goldilocks,"** a dwarf rudbeckia 12 inches high, self-seeds abundantly. **R. lacinata** var. **"hortensis,"** the old-fashioned golden glow. Grows to 12 feet in rich soil; average height is 8 feet. Wonderful in a background or a wild area.

TANACETUM VULGARE

(tan-ah-**see**-tum vul-**ga**-ray)

SYNONYM: Tansy

Tanacetum vulgare

FAMILY: Asteraceae (formerly Compositae)

HARDY TO ZONE: 3

HEIGHT: 3 to 4 feet

DESCRIPTION: Very aromatic fernlike leaves, with yellow button flowers on umbellike clusters. Invasive runners.

BLOOM TIME: August-September

CULTIVATION: Will grow almost anywhere; likes good drainage. Full sun to shade.

PROPAGATION: Division.

USES: Now banned by the FDA for internal use, tansy was once popular in tansy cakes, eaten at Easter time. It is a good plant for a wild area. Both fresh and dried flowers are used for arrangements. It is also used as an insect repellent against ants, fleas, and flies. Plant near fruit trees to repel insects.

Caution: Tansy taken in large amounts can be toxic.

VALERIANA OFFICINALIS

(va-le-ree-**ah**-na o-fis-i-**nal**-lis)

SYNONYMS: Valerian, garden heliotrope, phu, setwell

FAMILY: Valerianaceae

HARDY TO ZONE: 3

HEIGHT: 6 to 10 feet

DESCRIPTION: Large segmented leaves and sweet-scented white flowers with touches of pink and lavender.

BLOOM TIME: July-August

CULTIVATION: Full sun to partial shade. Not fussy about soil; will tolerate dry or moist conditions.

PROPAGATION: Seeds or division. Self-seeds.

Valeriana officinalis

USES: Areas where you need really tall plants. The roots are used medicinally for cleaning wounds and rashes. Internally, it works as a potent drug and should only be used under medical supervision.

Cichorium intybus

GORDON C. PINE

Dianthus barbatus

Digitalis purpurea

Lychnis coronaria

Myosotis sylvatica

MICHAEL H. DODGE, WHITE FLOWER FARM

Verbascum "Benary's Hybrids"

CHAPTER FIFTEEN

Biennials

*A tiny seed is planted. A year of hope and anticipation slowly passes
with a hint of green, followed by the second-year beauty of colorful flowers.
These are our biennials.*

—P.L.T.

I have heard people say, "I have an annual garden" or "I have a perennial garden."
But how often do you hear someone say, "I have a biennial garden"? Biennials are
usually interplanted with one of the other plant types. This is too bad, because
most biennials self-seed and can be planted two years in a row so that there will be
flowers every year once that two-year pattern is established.

It is difficult to find information on biennial plants because they are listed
with either annuals or, more often, perennials. Many people do not even realize
what a biennial plant is. So I have decided to honor these neglected, misplaced
biennials with a section of their own.

The biennials form a small exclusive club. If you remember from chapter 1, a
biennial is a plant that completes its life cycle in a two-year period. The first year
vegetation is formed, usually in a basal rosette. The second year the plant produces tall foliage and flowers. Seeds are formed, and the plant dies, completing its
two-year life cycle. The fallen seeds will develop into new plants. Very often when
purchasing biennials you will buy the second-year plant that flowers the year of
purchase and then wonder why it didn't come back the second year. Too often
biennials are not sold as biennials, but included in the perennial plant sections.

A good number of biennials self-seed to keep the species alive. With sweet
William (*Dianthus babatus*), the seeds drop and start new first-year seedlings before the winter comes. They then flower the following spring, making this plant

seem to act like a perennial. In the case of rose campion (*Lychnis coronaria*), the seeds overwinter and start new seedlings in the spring so that flowers are obtained every other year. In order to keep this biennial producing flowers every year, you must plant first-year seedlings two years in a row, so that each summer one set will be flowering and one set producing seedlings.

If you have extra space, you can start a biennial nursery and move the second-year plants that are ready to flower where you need them, but this can be a lot of extra work.

ALCEA

(**al**-kee-a)

(Also called *Althaea*)

SYNONYM: Hollyhock

FAMILY: Malvaceae

HARDY TO ZONE: 2

HEIGHT: 5 to 8 feet

DESCRIPTION: The hairy central stalk is covered with medium-green 7-lobed palmate leaves. Old-fashioned single flowers or hybrid double, full flowers come in a variety of colors.

BLOOM TIME: July to frost.

CULTIVATION: Full sun or partial shade in rich, well-drained soil. Fertilize with well-composted manures. Deadhead for continuous bloom, unless, of course, you want to save the seeds. Stake to keep upright.

PROPAGATION: Seeds.

USES: Back of a border. It is best grouped rather than used as a single plant.

HISTORY: Hollyhocks originated in China, where they were used as a pot herb. As a medicinal they are diuretic and emollient. Flowers can be dried for potpourri.

SPECIES: *A. rosea* "**nigra,**" black malva, is the closest to black I have seen; it is very nice.

CICHORIUM INTYBUS

(ki-**ko**-ree-um **i** n-tew-bus)

SYNONYMS: chicory, succory

FAMILY: Asteraceae (formerly Compositae)

HARDY TO ZONE: 3

HEIGHT: 2 to 3 feet

DESCRIPTION: Many-branched plant with a long taproot, which resists transplanting at maturity. A lazy plant that sort of lies down; if it stood upright it would be much taller. Its large hairy leaves emulate the dandelion leaf. Many light-blue flowers cluster on the entire plant. They open at daylight and then disappear in early afternoon.

BLOOM TIME: August-September

CULTIVATION: Full sun in almost any soil; likes average to rich soil. Chokes out weeds.

PROPAGATION: Seeds, small root cuttings.

USES: It has a good blue color that is difficult to find—too many advertised blues turn out to be purple or lavender. An excellent ground cover; once established will self-seed and spread quickly. Also used as a medicinal for pulmonary and rheumatic problems.

Caution: Continuous use or overuse of this plant may cause severe digestive or congestion problems. The root is used as a form of coffee.

HISTORY: This plant has not been very popular in the United States; it has been introduced as a field crop, herb, and vegetable, but just does not seem to catch on. Cows, horses, and rabbits enjoy eating it fresh. Roots are blanched by some people in the root cellar and eaten as a winter vegetable.

DIANTHUS BARBATUS

(dee-**anth**-us bar-**bah**-tus)

SYNONYM: Sweet William

FAMILY: Caryophyllaceae

HARDY TO ZONE: 3

HEIGHT: 6 to 12 inches

DESCRIPTION: Long lance-shaped leaves, dark green. The lovely little single to double flowers often are fringed on the edges and come in whites, pinks, reds, and some bicolors.

BLOOM TIME: June-July

CULTIVATION: Sun to partial or filtered shade. Sometimes they grow larger in sun, but some shade will provide longer-lasting blooms. They like a well-drained, average to good soil.

PROPAGATION: Seeds or root cuttings in the second year.

USES: Ground cover, rock gardens, edgings, or hanging baskets.

DIGITALIS PURPUREA

(di-gi-**tal**-is pur-**pewr**-ee-a)

SYNONYMS: Foxglove, witches' gloves, fairy caps, fairy thimbles, gloves of our Lady, folksglove

FAMILY: Scrophulariaceae

HARDY TO ZONE: 4

HEIGHT: 3 to 4 feet

DESCRIPTION: Deep green, large, lance-shaped leaves, becoming smaller in size as they go up the stalk. On the upper two-thirds it has two or more bell-shaped blooms hanging closely together on the stalk. Color of *purpurea* is lavender with brownish and white spots. Other varieties come in lavender, pink, yellow, and white.

BLOOM TIME: June-July

CULTIVATION: Enjoys good soil in full sun to partial shade.

PROPAGATION: Easy from seed, either by direct sowing or starting them inside six weeks before planting.

USES: Pretty in the garden, this biennial is a well-known medicinal. It should be used *only* by qualified medical persons. The incorrect dosage is fatal.

There are many stories about the various names: first, little woodland fairies can hide under these "fairy-caps." Gloves of our Lady, the Virgin Mary, is another meaning, making it a plant for the biblical garden. And then we have the bad witch who made little gloves from the plant for the foxes, so they could hunt in the farmer's chicken coop without him hearing them.

HESPERIS MATRONALIS

(hes-**per**-is mah-tro-**nah**-lis)

SYNONYMS: Sweet rocket, Dame's rocket, Mother of the evening, vesper flower

FAMILY: Cruciferae

HARDY TO ZONE: 2

HEIGHT: 2 to 3 feet

DESCRIPTION: Lance-shaped leaves with toothed edges on tall, erect stems. Four-petaled white or purple flowers on loose terminal racemes. June brings evening scented flowers.

BLOOM TIME: June

CULTIVATION: Sun, partial or filtered shade. Not fussy about soil conditions, but can become weedy with age.

PROPAGATION: Seeds; self-sows.

USES: Cut flowers. The bitter leaves are eaten in salads in other countries. For eating, harvest before bloom. It was once used medicinally as an antiemetic (to relieve vomiting and nausea).

HISTORY: Because of its night-blooming fragrance it was probably named for the Hesperides, the three daughters of the night in Greek mythology.

LUNARIA

(loon-**ah**-ree-a)

SYNONYMS: Honesty, money plant, moonwort, satin flower

FAMILY: Cruciferae

HARDY TO ZONE: 4

HEIGHT: 2 to 3 feet

DESCRIPTION: Medium-sized heart-shaped leaves, with purple or white flowers followed by interesting seed pods.

CULTIVATION: Full sun in moist, average to good soil that is well drained.

PROPAGATION: Seeds.

USES: Lunaria is usually grown for its pods for decorating wreaths and for dried arrangements. The pods are covered with a brown paperlike covering when they are ready to havest; when you remove this covering you will find a translucent silvery membrane. But don't overlook this biennial's beauty as a garden plant.

SPECIES: *L. annua* is the purple species; *L. annua alba* is the white form.

LYCHNIS CORONARIA

(**lik**-nis ko-ro-**nah**-ree-a)

SYNONYMS: Rose campion, mullein pink

FAMILY: Caryophyllaceae

HARDY TO ZONE: 4

HEIGHT: 2 to 3½ feet

DESCRIPTION: Rose campion never fails to receive a comment. Its woolly silver-gray foliage of medium lance-shaped leaves contrasts with the bright carmine-pink flowers on its many branches.

BLOOM TIME: July to frost

CULTIVATION: Full sun or partial shade. Lean to good soil.

PROPAGATION: Seeds. Will self-seed invasively, making it a good biennial for naturalizing.

USES: Borders, naturalizing.

SPECIES: *L. c. alba* is a white form for those who find the brilliant pink too harsh.

MYOSOTIS SYLVATICA

(mee-os-**o**-tis sil-**va**-ti-ka)

SYNONYM: Forget-me-not

FAMILY: Boraginaceae

HARDY TO ZONE: 3

HEIGHT: 8 to 12 inches

DESCRIPTION: Small oval-shaped leaves. It blooms in June and then off and on all season. Blue is the most common forget-me-not, with occasional pink and white species sprouting from the same seed strain. The flowers have tiny yellow centers.

BLOOM TIME: June

CULTIVATION: Full sun or partial shade. Likes good rich soil and blooms more in cool seasons, dying out in very hot, humid summers. In cold zones such as 3 and 4, some winter covering of evergreen boughs will aid winter survival.

PROPAGATION: Seeds.

USES: Good low groundcover, rock gardens, edging. Nice groundcover under taller perennials.

SPECIES: *M. alpestris* "**blue ball**" grows to 6 inches and flowers in spring. *M. s.* "**carmine king**" grows to 8 inches, with pink flowers.

OENOTHERA BIENNIS

(oy-no-**the**-ra bee-**en**-is)

SYNONYM: Evening primrose

FAMILY: Onagraceae

HARDY TO ZONE: 3

HEIGHT: 3 to 4 feet

DESCRIPTION: Flat basal growth, with gray-green, long lance-shaped leaves on long elegant spikes. The upper stalks support clear yellow primrose-type flowers in succession from June to frost. It has a slight fragrance in the evening, hence its name, which attracts night-flying insects for pollination. Unfortunately the Japanese beetles find the primrose a delicacy, too.

BLOOM TIME: June

CULTIVATION: Full sun in well-drained, lean to good soil.

PROPAGATION: Seeds. Self-seeds invasively.

USES: Borders, night gardens, naturalized areas. In other countries the roots are eaten in salads. As a medicinal, the bark and root is astringent and sedative. It has become popular and is available at health food stores in capsule form. Scientists have found it valuable in regulating the immune system; it functions by supplementing the diet with GLA (gammalinolenic acid), which is lost in the body because of an inadequate diet, alcoholism, or just from the natural process of aging.

VERBASCUM THAPSUS

(ver-**bas**-kum **thap**-sus)

SYNONYMS: Mullein, torches, velvet dock, candlewick, feltwort. And for those designing a biblical garden, Our Lady's flannel, Jacob's staff, Adam's flannel, and many others.

FAMILY: Scrophulariaceae

HARDY TO ZONE: 3

HEIGHT: 3 to 8 feet

DESCRIPTION: The first year's rosette is attractive in itself. The huge gray leaves are covered by minute hairs on both sides, giving the leaf a thick, soft, velvety feeling. It is often mistaken for large lamb's ears in its first season. The second year a large woolly stalk can grow to 8 feet, although 5 or 6 feet is more common. The top 1 to 2 feet are densely whorled, with small yellow flowers that are very attractive to small insects and bees.

BLOOM TIME: June

CULTIVATION: Full sun to partial or filtered shade, in any soil with good drainage. Very moist soil will rot the rosettes. You will notice that all gray-leaved plants throughout the profiles need good drainage. Otherwise very little is demanded by these majestic candles.

PROPAGATION: Seeds; self-seeds once established.

USES: Has been used since ancient times as a medicine for both internal and external use. Used for diarrhea, hemorrhoids, and respiratory problems, especially asthma. Fresh flowers steeped in olive oil act as a bactericide. Native Americans used the soft mullein leaves in their shoes for comfort.

HISTORY: Mullein has been an important plant since the beginning of written history, and probably well before. It was a favorite of the druids. In ancient times, just carrying a leaf with you would be a protector against evil and sickness.

Its name *candlewick* comes from its use as a candle: the top would be dipped into fats and burned. Gathered and dried, it was used as a tender to start fires. Its soft leaves will take even the slightest spark, which must have been important to people before the invention of matches.

Mullein grows in my garden wherever it happens to reseed itself. It never fails to receive compliments and when someone feels embarrassed when they discover it is just an "old roadside weed" I try to impress upon them its very important historical value and beauty in the modern garden.

SPECIES: I personally love the good old roadside plant; however, as so often happens, it has been hybridized into more colorful or better plants. **V. *blattaria*** is a 3- to 4-foot moth mullein hardy in zone 5 (I grow it in the greenhouse the first year to enjoy in the garden the second year in my lower zone 4). It also has a pink form. Those of you who live and garden in zone 6 can enjoy **V. *phoeniceum***, a many-branched yellow mullein of magnificent beauty.

Appendix

Perennial Specialists

Perennials for the Shady Garden
Ajuga
Aquilegia
Aruncus
Astilbe
Bergenia
Cimicifuga
Convalleria
Dicentra
Digitalis
Doronicum
Echinacea
Eupatorium
Ferns
Hemerocallis
Hostas
Lamiums
Polygonatum
Primula
Pulmonaria
Tradescantia
Trollius

Perennials for Acid Soil
Asclepias
Asperula odorata
Azalea
Iris kaempferi
Lilium tigrinum
Lupinus
Primula vulgaris

Perennials for Very Moist Soil
Arunucus dioicus
Aster novi-belgii
Astilbe
Eupatorium purpureum
Iris pseudocarus
Iris siberica
Lysimachia
Lythrum
Monarda
Royal fern
Trollius

Perennials for Drying and Crafts
Achillea
Agastache
Alchemilla
Alliums
Anaphalis
Artemisias
Astilbe
Baptisia (pod)
Catananche
Centaurea
Delphinium
Echinops
Gnaphalium
Gysophila
Heuchera
Lavendula
Monardas
Papaver (pods)
Physostegia
Rue (pods)
Stachys
Thyme

Plant Societies

If you are interested in one particular perennial, join one of the clubs for lovers of that species to learn more and get in touch with other plant lovers. Detailed information can be obtained through clubs and societies that is not always available from other sources. Send a self-addressed, stamped envelope for information.

In the United States:

The American Fern Society
Dr. Richard L. Hauke
456 McGill Place
Atlanta, GA 30312

The American Hemerocallis
Society
Elly Launius
1454 Rebel Drive
Jackson, MS 39211

The American Hosta Society
Dennis Paul Savory
5300 Whiting Avenue
Edina, MN 55435

The American Iris Society
Jeanne Stayer
7414 East 60th Street
Tulsa, OK 74145

American Peony Society
Greta M. Kessenich
250 Interlachen Road
Hopkins, MN 55343

American Primrose Society
Ann Lunn
6620 N.W. 271st Avenue
Hillsboro, OR 97124

American Rock Garden
Society
Jacques Mommens
P.O. Box 67
Millwood, NY 10546

The Herb Society of America
9019 Kirtland Chadon Road
Mentor, OH 44060

New England Wildflower
Society, Inc.
Gardens in the Woods
180 Hemenway Road
Framingham, MA 01701-2699

In Canada:

Alberta Horticultural
Association
Mrs. Muriel Conner
Box 223
Lacombe, Alberta
T0C 1S0

Canadian Horticultural
Council
3 Amberwood Crescent
Nepean, Ontario
K2E 7L1

Canadian Society for
Horticultural Science
Dr. J Cuteliffe
c/o Agriculture Canada
Box 1210
Charlottetown, Prince Edward
Island
C1A 7M8

Flowers Canada
155 Suffolk Street West
Guelph, Ontario
N1H 2J7

Horti-centre Du Quebec
Pavillion des Services
Local 2601, Universite de
Laval
2450 Boulevard Hochelaga
Sainte Foy, Quebec G1K 7P4

Saskatchewan Horticultural
Association
Mrs. K Robb
Box 152
Baclarres, Saskatchewan
S0G 0G0

Seed and Plant Catalogs

The following listing is but a wee sample of the many seed and plant catalogs that are available. I have personally had very good results with the following list, but keep in mind there are many other very good ones available.

Breck's Dutch Bulbs
6523 N. Galena Road
Peoria, IL 61632

Daystar
Rt. 2, Box 250
Litchfield, ME 04350
207-724-3369

Horticultural Products
P.O. Box 1
Graniteville, SC 29829
800-322-7288

Inter-State Nurseries
Catalog Division
Louisiana, MO 63353

Park's Seed Co.
Cokesbury Road
Greenwood, SC 29647-0001
803-223-7333

Pinetree Garden Seeds
Route 100
New Gloucester, ME 04260
207-926-3400

Schreiners (iris only)
3625 Quinaby Road
N.E. Salem, OR 97303

Siskiyou Rare Plant Nursery
2825 Cummings Road
Medford, OR 97501-1524
503-772-6846

Spring Hill Nurseries
110 West Elm Street
Tipp City, OH 45371
309-691-4616

Thompson & Morgan, Inc.
P.O. Box 1308
Jackson, NJ 08527
800-274-SEED

Van Bourgondien Bros.
245 Farmingdale Road
P.O. Box 1000
Babylon, NY 11702
800-622-9997

Wayside Gardens
1 Garden Lane
Hodges, SC 29695-0001
800-845-1124

White Flower Farm
Rt. 63
Litchfield, CT 06759-0050
203-567-4565

The Symbolism of Flowers

Flower language or symbolism has been practiced off and on since ancient times. This art was brought to a peak during the seventeenth and eighteenth centuries. The following list gives the meanings of some of our favorite perennials.

Carnation: adoration
Clove pink: resignation
Columbine: seven gifts of the Holy Spirit
Daisy: innocence of the Holy Child
Flax: appreciation
Foxglove: sincerity
Hyssop: cleanliness
Iris: majestic power
Jonquil: I desire a return of affection

Lavender: silence, bringing good luck
Lily: purity
Lily of the valley: return of happiness, humility
Mint: wisdom, virtue
Pennyroyal: flee
Poppy: oblivion
Primrose: melancholy
Rose: love
Rose, white: silent love
Rose, yellow: infidelity
Rosemary: remembrance

Rue: purification
Spiderwort: transient love
Stonecrop: tranquility
Tansy: hostile thoughts
Thyme: bravery
Tulip, red: declaration of love
Valerian: readiness
Veronica: fidelity
Violet, blue: loyalty
Violet, white: innocence
Yarrow: given to bride and groom to ensure seven years of love

State and Provincial Flowers

United States:

Alabama: Goldenrod (*Solidago*)

Alaska: Forget-me-not (*Mysotis*)

Arizona: Giant saguaro (*Carnegia giganteus*)

Arkansas: Apple blossom (*Malus*)

California: California poppy (*Eschscholtzia californica*)

Colorado: Colorado columbine (*Aquilegia caerulea*)

Connecticut: Mountain laurel (*Kalmia*)

Delaware: Peach blossom (*Prunus*)

Florida: Orange blossom (*Citrus sinensis*)

Georgia: Cherokee rose (*Rosa laevigata*)

Hawaii: Hibiscus (*Hibiscus*)

Idaho: Lewis mock orange (*Philadelphus lewisii*)

Illinois: Wood violet (*Viola*)

Indiana: Zinnia (*Zinna*)

Iowa: Wild rose (*Rosa*)

Kansas: Sunflower (*Helianthus annuus*)

Kentucky: Goldenrod (*Solidago*)

Louisiana: Magnolia (*Magnolia grandiflora*)

Maine: Pine cone and tassel (*Pinus strobus*)

Maryland: Black-eyed Susan (*Rudbeckia hirta*)

Massachusetts: Trailing arbutus (*Epigaea*)

Michigan: Apple blossom (*Malus*)

Minnesota: Showy lady slipper (*Cypripedium reginae*)

Mississippi: Magnolia (*Magnolia grandiflora*)

Missouri: Downy hawthorn (*Crataegus mollis*)

Montana: Bitteroot (*Lewisia rediviva*)

Nebraska: Goldenrod (*Solidago*)

Nevada: Sagebrush (*Artemisia tridentata*)

New Hampshire: Lilac (*Syringa*)

New Jersey: Violet (*Viola*)

New Mexico: Yucca (*Yucca*)

New York: Rose (*Rosa carolina*)

North Carolina: Ox-eye daisy (*Chrysanthemum*)

North Dakota: Wild prairie rose (*Rosa arkansana*)

Ohio: Red carnation (*Dianthus*)

Oklahoma: Mistletoe (*Phoradendron serotinum*)

Oregon: Oregon holly grape (*Mahonia nervosa*)

Pennsylvania: Mountain laurel (*Kalmia*)

Rhode Island: Violet (*Viola*)

South Carolina: Carolina jessamine (*Gelsemium sempervivens*)

Tennessee: Iris (*Iris*)

Utah: Sego lily (*Calochortus nuttallii*)

Vermont: Red clover (*Trifolium pratense*)

Virginia: Dogwood (*Cornus florida*)

Washington: Rhododendron (*R. macrophyllum*)

Washington, D.C.: American beauty rose (*Rosa*)

West Virginia: Rhododendron (*R. maximum*)

Wisconsin: Violet (*Viola*)

Wyoming: Indian paintbrush (*Castilleja coccinea*)

Canada:

Alberta: Wild rose (*Rosa acicularis*)

British Columbia: Dogwood (*Cornus nuttallii* "audubon")

Manitoba: Pasque flower (*Anemone patens*)

New Brunswick: Purple violet (*Viola cuculata*)

Newfoundland: Pitcher plant (*Sarracenia purpurea*)

Northwest Territories: Mountain avens (*Dryas integrifolia*)

Nova Scotia: Trailing arbutus (*Epigaea repens*)

Ontario: White trillium (*Trillium grandiflorum*)

Prince Edward Island: Lady's slipper (*Cypripedium acaule*)

Quebec: White garden (Madonna) lily (*Lilium candidum*)

Saskatchewan: Western red lily (*Lilum philadelphicum andinum*)

Yukon Territory: Fireweed (*Epilobium angustifolium*)

Perennial Families

In this book I have presented the current family names as well as the old names because many catalogs and old books still use the old family names. Probably by the time this book is published there will be other changes.

Knowing your family groups can be helpful in your gardening adventures. Even though family affiliation is based primarily on foliage and flower characteristics, members of the same family usually need the same or similar cultural needs.

Only those families of interest to the perennials in this book are included here.

AGAVACEAE
(ah-gah-**vay**-see-ee), the agave family.
These plants like warm weather and a lean soil. Usually have fleshy leaves, often with spines.
Example: Yucca.

AMARYLLIDACEAE
(ah-mah-ri-li-**day**-see-ee), the amaryllis family.
Predominantly bulb-type plants with strap and onionlike leaves and flowers. Flowers are small, mostly in globe form, and petalless, and grow on scapes.
Example: Narcissus.

APIACEAE
(ay-pee-**ay**-see-ee), the carrot or parsley family. Formerly *Umbelliferae*.
Hollow-stemmed herbaceous plants, with flat clusters or umbels; some have compound umbels.

Example: Bishopweed (*Aegopodium*).

ASCLEPIADACEAE
(as-**klee**-pee-ah-**day**-see-ee), the milkweed family.
Usually drought-resistant plants. Most have some kind of milky sap. Pollen grains are carried on waxy masses. Many are valuable medicinal plants.
Examples: Butterfly weed (*Asclepias*).

ASTERACEAE
(a-ster-**a**-see-ee), the aster family (formerly Compositae). One of the largest family groups, with over 1,000 species. They are mostly sun-loving, usually with a daisy-type flower.
Examples: Yarrow (*Achillea*), leopard's-bane (*Doronicum*), chrysanthemums.

BORAGINACEAE
(boh-**raj**-in-**aye**-see-ee), the borage family.

Usually rough or hairy leaves and stems; predominantly blue flowers.
Examples: Navelwort (*Omphalodes*), lungwort (*Pulmonaria*).

BRASSICACEAE
(**bra**-si-ka-see-ee), the mustard family. Cruciferae (krew-**s i f**-er-ay) is used interchangeably with Brassicaeae.
Four-petaled flowers resemble a cross.
Examples: Candytuft (*Iberis*), rock cress (*Arabis*).

CAMPANULACEAE
(kam-**pan**-yoo-**lay**-see-ee), the bellflower family.
Mostly herbaceous perennials with five-lobed, bell-shaped flowers. Good number of bluish-purple flowers on spike stems.
Examples: Bellflower (*Campanula*), sheep's bit (*Jasione*).

CARYOPHYLLACEAE

(kar-ee-**oh**-fil-ay-see-ee), the pink family.
Short-lived plants that like full sun with alkaline soil. Often very fragrant. Narrow leaves with swollen joints.
Examples: Clove pink (*Dianthus*), baby's breath (*Gypsophila*).

COMMELINACEAE

(koh-mel-in-**ay**-see-ee), the spiderwort family.
Prefers rich moist soil. Has three petals and three sepals per flower.
Example: Spiderwort (*Tradescantia*).

CRASSULACEAE

(**kras**-yoo-**lay**-see-ee), the orpine family.
Many tropical-type plants, with fleshy succulent foliage often in rosette form. They like sun and dry soil.
Examples: Sedums, hens and chickens (*Sempervivum*).

CRUCIFERAE

(krew-**s i f**-er-a). *See Brassicaeae.*

DIPSACACEAE

(**dip**-sa-kay-ee-ee), the teasel family.
These plants have dense, stiff spike heads.
Example: Teasel (*Dipsacus*).

EUPHORBIACEAE

(yoo-**for**-bee-**ay**-see-ee), the spurge family.
Cactuslike; may or may not have some sort of spine. Usually have an acrid sap, sometimes toxic. May have showy flowers; some have colorful bracts instead of flowers.
Example: Spurge (Euphorbia Epithymoides).

FABACEAE

(fah-**bay**-see-ee), the bean and pea family (formerly *Leguminosae*).
Pealike flowers and foliage. These family members live in mutual cooperation with a nitrogen-fixing bacteria that collects nitrogen from the air and fixes it in the soil for its own use. Most *Fabaceae* members have an interesting pod.
Examples: Baptisia, lupines.

FUMARIACEAE

(fyoo-**may**-ree-**ay**-see-ee), the fumitory family.
Deeply cut leaves, flowers irregular in form.
Example: Bleeding hearts (*Dicentra*).

GERANIACEAE

(jur-ay-nee-**ay**-see-ee), the geranium family.
Several good scented plants.
Examples: Cranesbill geranium.

IRIDACEAE

(i-ri-**day**-see-ee), the iris family.
Fleshy root stalks, and long narrow leaves with three stamens.
Examples: Iris, crocus.

LAMIACEAE

(lam-ee-**ay**-see-ee), the mint family (formerly *Labiatae*).
Square stems; most have scents.
Examples: Hyssop (*Hyssopus*), lavender (*Lavendula*)

LILIACEAE

(lil-ee-**ay**-see-ee), the lily family.
Large showy flowers and sword-shaped or large oval leaves.
Examples: Hosta, hemerocallis.

LINACEAE

(lee-**ah**-see-ee), the flax family.
Five petaled flowers, with narrow leaves.
Example: Blue flax (*Linum*).

LOBELIACEAE

(loh-**bee**-lee-**ah**-see-ee), the lobelia family.
Five-lobed, two-lipped flowers.
Example: Lobelia.

LYTHRACEAE

(lith-**ray**-see-ee), the loose-strife family.
Ornamentals with long tubular flowers.
Example: Purple loosestrife (*Lythrum*).

MALVACEAE

(mal-**vay**-see-ee), the mallow family.

Simple palamate-lobed leaves and five-petaled flowers.
Example: Muskmallow (*Malva*).

ONAGRACEAE
(oh-nah-**gray**-see-ee), the evening primrose family. Usually scented, with clawlike petals around a long calyx.
Example: Evening primrose (*Oenothera biennis*).

PAEONIACEAE
(pee-oh-nee-**ah**-see-ee), the peony family (formerly *Fanunculaceae*).
Example: Peony.

PAPAVERACEAE
(pah-**pay**-vur-**ay**-see-ee), the poppy family. Showy flowers with a milky or colored sap.
Example: Poppy (*Papaver*).

PLUMBAGINACEAE
(plum-**baj**-in-**ay**-see-ee), the leadwort family. Tolerant of seashore salt air.
Example: Sea thrift (*Armeria*).

POLEMONIACEAE
(poh-le-moh-nee-**ay**-see-ee), the phlox family. Loose multiple flowers.
Example: Jacob's ladder (*Polemonia*), phlox.

POLYPODIACEAE
(pah-li-**poh**-dee-**ay**-see-ee), the fern family.

Over three-quarters of the ferns belong to this family. Spore-bearing on underside of leaves.
Example: Common polypody fern (*Polypodium vulgare*).

PRIMULACEAE
(prim-yoo-**lay**-see-ee), the primrose family. Five-petaled flowers, like partial shade.
Example: Yellow loosestrife (*Lysimachia*)

RANUNCULACEAE
(rah-nun-kyoo-**lay**-see-ee), the buttercup family. Petals, sepals, stamen, and pistils are separate from each other. Like good soil.
Example: Anemone, columbine (*aquilegia*), trollius.

ROSACEAE
(roh-**zay**-see-ee), the rose family. Slightly to very scented
Example: Rose (*Rosa* sp.), lady's mantle (*Alchemilla vulgaris*).

RUBIACEAE
(roo-bee-**ay**-see-ee), the madder family. Mostly tropicals, with some important useful plants, used for coffee, dye, and medicinals.
Example: Sweet woodruff (*Asperula odorata*).

RUTACEAE
(**roo**-tay-see-ee), the rue family. Usually compounded leaves, aromatic plants.
Example: Rue (*Ruta*).

SAXIFRAGACEAE
(sak-si-frah-**gay**-see-ee), the saxifraga family. Basal rosettes. Like partial shade.
Examples: Astilbe, bergenia.

SCROPHULARIACEAE
(skrahf-you-**lair**-ee-**ay**-see-ee), the figwort family. Usually irregular, lipped or hooded flowers.
Example: Foxglove (*Digitalis*).

VALERIANACEAE
(vul-lee-ree-**ay**-nay-see-ee), the valerian family. Aromatic (but not always pleasant).
Example: Patrinia (*Scabiosifolia*).

VIOLACEAE
(**vi**-o-lah-see-ee), the viola family. Low-growing, usually grouped in bunches, with both sterile and fertile flowers.
Example: Violet (*Viola*).

Cooperative Extension Services

The cooperative extension service provides agricultural research and garden information to members of its state. There are also local extension organizations in some towns and cities that will welcome your questions. Contact the cooperative extension in your state or consult the Yellow Pages for more information.

In the United States:

Alabama
Alabama A & M University
Normal, AL 35762

Alaska
University of Alaska
Fairbanks, AK 99775

Arizona
University of Arizona
Tucson, AZ 85721

Arkansas
Extension Administration
P.O. Box 391
Little Rock, AR 72203

California
University of California
College of Agriculture and
   Environmental Sciences
Davis, CA 95616

Colorado
Colorado State University
College of Agricultural
   Sciences
Fort Collins, CO 80523

Connecticut
Connecticut Agricultural
   Experiment Station
P.O. Box 1106
New Haven, CT 06504

Delaware
University of Delaware
College of Agricultural
   Sciences
Newark, DE 19711

Florida
University of Florida
College of Agriculture
Gainesville, FL 32611

Georgia
University of Georgia
College of Agriculture
Athens, GA 30602

Hawaii
University of Hawaii
Honolulu, HI 96822

Idaho
University of Idaho
College of Agriculture
Moscow, ID 83843

Illinois
University of Illinois
College of Agriculture
Urbana, IL 61801

Indiana
Purdue University
School of Agriculture
West Lafayette, IN 47904

Iowa
Iowa State University
College of Agriculture
Ames, IA 50011

Kansas
Kansas State University
College of Agriculture
Manhattan, KS 66506

Kentucky
University of Kentucky
College of Agriculture
Lexington, KY 40506

Louisiana
Southern University and
   A & M College
Baton Rouge, LA 70813

Maine
University of Maine
College of Agriculture
Orono, ME 04469

Maryland
University of Maryland
College of Agriculture
College Park, MD 20742

Massachusetts
University of Massachusetts
College of Agriculture
Amherst, MA 01003

Michigan
Michigan State University
College of Agriculture
East Lansing, MI 48824

Minnesota
University of Minnesota
College of Agriculture and
    Natural Resources
St. Paul, MN 55108

Mississippi
Mississippi State University
College of Agriculture
Mississippi State, MS 39762

Missouri
University of Missouri
College of Agriculture
Columbia, MO 65211

Montana
Montana State University
College of Agriculture
Bozeman, MT 59717

Nebraska
University of Nebraska
Institute of Agriculture and
    Natural Resources
Lincoln, NE 68583

Nevada
University of Nevada
College of Agriculture
Reno, NV 89557

New Hampshire
University of New Hampshire
College of Agriculture
Duham, NH 03824

New Jersey
Rutgers State University
College of Agriculture
New Brunswick, NJ 08903

New Mexico
New Mexico State University
College of Agriculture
Las Cruces, NM 88003

New York
Cornell University
College of Agriculture
Ithaca, NY 14853

North Carolina
North Carolina State
    University
College of Agriculture
Raleigh, NC 27695

North Dakota
State University
Agriculture and Applied
    Science
State University Station
Fargo, ND 58105

Ohio
Ohio State University
College of Agriculture
Columbus, OH 43210

Oklahoma
Langston University
Agriculture Research
P.O. Box 730
Langston, OK 73050

Oregon
Oregon State University
College of Agriculture
Corvallis, OR 97331

Pennsylvania
Pennsylvania State University
College of Agriculture
University Park, PA 16802

Rhode Island
University of Rhode Island
Kingston, RI 02881

South Carolina
Clemson University
College of Agriculture
    Sciences
Clemson, SC 29631

South Dakota
South Dakota University
College of Agriculture
Brookings, SD 57007

Tennessee
University of Tennessee
Institute of Agriculture
Knoxville, TN 37901

Texas
Texas A & M University
College of Agriculture
College Station, TX 77843

Utah
Utah State University
College of Agriculture
Logan, UT 84322

Vermont
University of Vermont
College of Agriculture
Burlington, VT 05405

Virginia
Virginia State University
College of Agriculture
Blacksburg, VA 24061

Washington
Washington State University
College of Agriculture
Pullman, WA 99164

West Virginia
West Virginia University
College of Agriculture
Morgantown, WV 26506

Wisconsin
University of Wisconsin
College of Agriculture
Madison, WI 53706

Wyoming
University of Wyoming
College of Agriculture
Laramie, WY 82071

In Canada:

Alberta
Department of Agriculture
Information Services
7000 113 Street
Edmonton, Alberta T6H 5T6

British Columbia
Ministry of Agriculture,
Fisheries, & Food, Public
Affairs Branch
Parliament Buildings
Victoria, British Columbia
V8W 2Z7

Manitoba
Manitoba Agriculture
Administration
401 York Avenue
Winnipeg, Manitoba
R3C 0P8

New Brunswick
Communications and
Education Branch,
Department of Agriculture
P.O. Box 6000
Fredricton, New Brunswick
E3B 5H1

Newfoundland
Department of Forestry and
Agriculture
P.O. Box 8700
St. John's, Newfoundland
A1B 4J6

Nova Scotia
Administration Division,
Department of Agriculture
and Marketing
P.O. Box 190
Halifax, Nova Scotia
B3J 2M4

Ontario
Agriculture Canada
Plant Research Library
Ottawa, Ontario
K1A 0C6

Information Centre
Ministry of Agriculture &
Food
801 Bay Street
1st Floor
Toronto, Ontario M7A 2B2

Prince Edward Island
Information Division
Department of Agriculture
P.O. Box 2000
Charlottetown, Prince Edward
Island
C1A 7N8

Québec
Ministère de l'Agricultre
des Pecheries et de
l'Alimentation
Communications
200A ch. Sainte-Foy, 7e étage,
Québec, PQ
G1R 4X6

Saskatchewan
Communications Branch
Saskatchewan Agriculture &
Food
Walter Scott Building
3085 Albert Street
Regina, Saskatchewan
S4S 0B1

Yukon
Agriculture Branch
P.O. Box 2703
Whitehorse, Yukon
Y1A 2C6

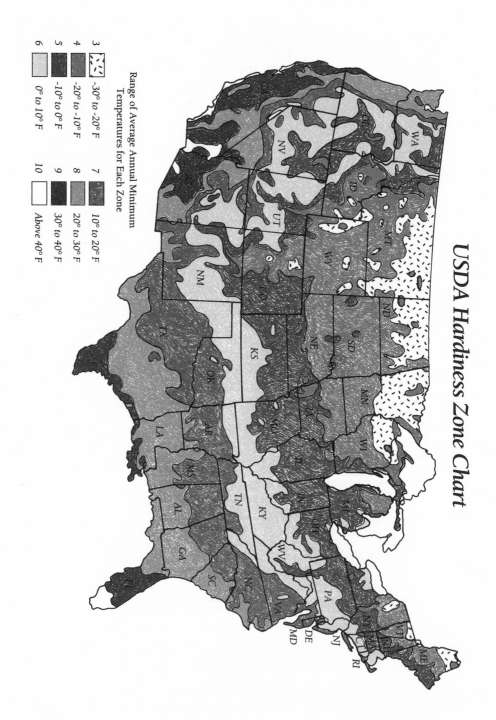

USDA Hardiness Zone Chart

Range of Average Annual Minimum
Temperatures for Each Zone

3 -30° to -20°F   7 10° to 20°F
4 -20° to -10°F   8 20° to 30°F
5 -10° to 0°F   9 30° to 40°F
6 0° to 10°F   10 Above 40°F

Bibliography

Art, Pamela B., ed. *The Wise Garden Encyclopedia* (revised). New York: Harper Collins Pub., 1990.

Bown, Deni. *Alba: The Book of White Flowers*. Portland, Or.: Timber Press, 1989.

Brookes, John. *The Garden Book*. New York: Crown, 1984.

Calkins, Carroll. *Gardening with Water, Plantings, and Stone*. New York: Walker, 1974.

Carter, Brian, ed. *The Garden Palette*. Garden City, N.Y.: Doubleday, 1986.

Clarkson, Rosetta E. *Green Enchantment*. New York: Macmillan, 1940.

Clauson and Ekstron. *Perennials for American Gardens*. New York: Random House, 1989.

Clute, Willard N. *Our Ferns in Their Haunts*. New York: Frederick A. Stokes, 1921.

Dana, Mrs. William Starr. *How to Know the Wildflowers*. New York: Dover, 1963.

Durant, Mary. *Who Named the Daisy, Who Named the Rose*. Congdon & Weed, 1976.

Ely, Helena Rutherford. *The Practical Flower Garden*. New York: Macmillan, 1916.

Erichsen-Brown, Charlotte. *Use of Plants for the Past 500 Years*. Breezy Creek Press, 1979.

Ferguson, Nicole. *Right Plant, Right Place*. New York: Summit Books, 1984.

Fleming, Laurene, and Alan Gore. *The English Garden*. London: Michael Joseph, 1979.

Foster, Catherine Osgood. *Organic Flower Gardening*. Emmaus, Pa.: Rodale Press, 1975.

Foster, H. Lincoln. *Rock Gardening*. Portland, Or.: Timber Press, 1968.

Fox, Helen Morgenthau. *Gardening with Herbs*. New York: Macmillan, 1943.

Friend, Hilderic. *Flower Lore*. Rockport, Mass.: Para Research, 1981.

Grieve, Mrs. M. *A Modern Herbal*. New York: Dover, 1971.

Highstone, John. *Victorian Gardens*. San Francisco: Harper & Row, 1982.

Hobhouse, Penelope. *Color for Your Garden*. Boston: Little, Brown & Co., 1984.

Hollingsworth, Buckner. *Flower Chronicles*. New Brunswick, N.J.: Rutgers University Press, 1958.

Hylander, C. J. *The World of Plant Life*. New York: Macmillan, 1944.

King, Eleanor Anthony. *Bible Plants for American Gardens*. New York: Dover, 1975.

Kloss, Jethro. *Back to Eden*. Santa Barbara, Ca.: Woodbridge Press Publishing Co., 1975.

Lees-Milne, Alvilde, and Rosemary Verey. *The Englishwoman's Garden*. London: Chatto & Windus, 1982.

Leighton, Ann. *Early American Gardens*. Amherst, Mass.: University of Massachusetts Press, 1985.

Massingham, Betty. *A Century of Gardeners*. London: Faber & Faber, 1982.

Reilly, Ann. *Park's Success with Seeds*. Greenwood, S.C.: Geo. Park Seed Co., 1978.

Riotte, Louise. *Astrological Gardening*. Pownal, Vt.: Storey

Rohde, Eleanour Sinclair. *Gardens of Delight*. Boston and New York: Hale, Cushman & Flint, 1936.

Scott, Temple. *In Praise of Gardens* (poetry). Baker & Taylor, 1911.

Stearn, William T. *Botanical Latin*. London: David Charles Inc., 1983.

Stein, Deni W. *Ortho's Complete Guide to Successful Gardening*. San Francisco, Ca.: Ortho Books, 1983.

Tekulsky, Matthew. *The Butterfly Garden*. Boston: Harvard Common Press, 1985.

Turcotte, Patricia. *The New England Herb Gardener*. Woodstock, Vt.: Countryman Press, 1990.

Webster, Nancy Noyes. *Herbs*. Lexington, Mass.: Adams Press, 1939.

Wilson, Ernest H. *If I Were to Make a Garden*. Boston: The Stratford Co., 1931.

Wilson, Helen VanPelt. *The New Perennials Preferred*. New York: M. Barrows & Co., 1961.

Wyman, Donald. *Wyman's Gardening Encyclopedia*. New York: Macmillan, 1971.

Yepsen, Roger B., Jr., ed. *Organic Plant Protection*. Emmaus, Pa.: Rodale Press, 1965.

General Index

Boldface page numbers indicate illustrations or photographs.

Index of Plant Names

Boldface page numbers indicate illustrations or photographs.

Also from The Countryman Press

The Countryman Press, long known for fine books on nature and manuals for healthful living, offer a range of practical and readable books for those interested in herbs, gardening, and nature.

Herbs, Gardening, and Wild Plants

The Earth Shall Blossom: Shaker Herbs and Gardening, by Galen Beale and Mary Rose Bosewell, $18.95

Earthmagic: Finding and Using Medicinal Herbs, by Corinne Martin, $15.00

The New England Herb Gardener: Yankee Wisdom for North American Herb Growers and Users, by Patricia Turcotte, $14.95

Nature and Country Living

Backyard Bird Habitat, by Will and Jane Curtis, $9.95

Backyard Livestock: Raising Good Natured Food for Your Family, by Steven Thomas and George Looby, DVM, $14.95

Backyard Sugarin', by Rink Mann, $8.00

Earth Ponds: The Country Pond Maker's Guide to Building, Maintenance and Restoration, by Tim Matson, $17.00

Surveying Your Land, by Charles Lawson, $10.00

Cookbooks for Healthful and Tasty Living

The Best from Libby Hillman's Kitchen: Treasured Recipes from 50 Years of Cooking and Teaching, by Libby Hillman, $25.00

The King Arthur Flour 200th Anniversary Cookbook, by Brinna Sands, $21.00

Seasoned With Grace: My Generation of Shaker Cooking, by Eldress Bertha Lindsay, $12.95

Our books are available through bookstores and specialty shops, or they may be ordered directly from the publisher. Shipping and handling costs are $2.50 for 1-2 books, $3 for 3-6 books, and $3.50 for 7 or more books. To order, or for a free catalog, please write to Countryman Press, Inc., P.O. Box 175, Dept. APC, Woodstock, VT 05091, or call our toll-free number, (800) 245-4151. Prices and availability are subject to change.